A Handbook on Drug
and Alcohol Abuse

A Handbook on Drug and Alcohol Abuse

THE BIOMEDICAL ASPECTS   THIRD EDITION

Gail Winger

Frederick G. Hofmann

James H. Woods

New York   Oxford
OXFORD UNIVERSITY PRESS
1992

Oxford University Press

Oxford   New York   Toronto
Delhi   Bombay   Calcutta   Madras   Karachi
Kuala Lumpur   Singapore   Hong Kong   Tokyo
Nairobi   Dar es Salaam   Cape Town
Melbourne   Auckland

and associated companies in
Berlin   Ibadan

Published by Oxford University Press, Inc.,
200 Madison Avenue, New York, New York 10016

Oxford is a registered trademark of Oxford University Press

Library of Congress Cataloging-in-Publication Data
Winger, Gail.
A handbook on drug and alcohol abuse : the biomedical aspects
Gail Winger, Frederick G. Hofmann, James H. Woods. — 3rd ed.   p. cm.
Rev. ed. of: A handbook on drug and alcohol abuse
Frederick G. Hofmann. 2nd ed. 1983.
Includes bibliographical references and index.
ISBN 0-19-506396-1
ISBN 0-19-506397-X (pbk.)
1. Drug abuse — Handbooks, manuals, etc.
2. Alcoholism — Handbooks, manuals, etc.
I. Hofmann, Frederick G.   Handbook on drug and alcohol abuse.
II. Hofmann, Frederick G.   III. Woods, James H.   IV. Title.
[DNLM: 1. Alcoholism. 2. Substance Abuse.   WM 270 H713h]
RC564.W56   1992   616.86—dc20   DNLM/DLC
for Library of Congress   91-32040

9 8 7 6 5 4 3 2 1

Printed in the United States of America
on acid-free paper

To Vernon

Preface to the Third Edition

Fred Hofmann's handbook on drug and alcohol abuse stands out among the many similarly titled books because of its authoritative approach to the issues and because of its very readable style. We were thus distressed to learn that Fred was not physically able to produce a third edition. We were, however, very pleased to accept this task in his stead.

The impact of drug abuse on America has changed dramatically over the past 10 years. As the number of people using illicit drugs skyrocketed throughout the 1970s, attitudes towards drug abuse began to change from general disinterest to intense concern. At the same time, medical and public health research turned more of their attention to how drugs affect our bodies and our behavior so that our knowledge about drugs and drug abuse has also increased dramatically. This is, therefore, an appropriate time to update this Handbook, and we have done so extensively.

Two completely new chapters have been added, one on cocaine and one on tobacco and nicotine. Updated epidemiological data have been incorporated into virtually every chapter; information about caffeine, khat, and MDMA (ecstasy) has been added to the chapter on stimulants. Our further understanding of the mechanism of action and toxicity of most drugs of abuse, including marijuana, LSD, PCP, barbiturates, opioids, and cocaine is reflected in this edition. The contributions that animal research has made to understanding drugs and drug abuse are touched on in several places. At the same time, Dr. Hofmann's clinical perspectives, particularly on the diagnosis of drug abuse, have been retained.

The book as it now stands will be useful to a range of students and practitioners. Those who teach courses on the pharmacology and behavioral aspects of drugs of abuse at either the undergraduate or graduate level should find it to be an informative and straightforward text. Counselors and therapists may find that the information on the basic pharmacology of drugs enhances their understanding of the problem of drug abuse. The chapters on diagnosis and pharmacological treatment of drug abuse will be particularly relevant to medical students and physicians.

The process of updating this handbook was fascinating, educational, and time-consuming. We came to appreciate the patience of Jeffrey House as this edition came together, just as had Fred with the two earlier editions. We also acknowledge with thanks the assistance of Eric Hoenicke with some of the figures and Rebecca McLaughlin with the indexing. Public Health Service grants through the National Institute on Drug Abuse (DA00254, DA04403, and DA05951) provided partial support for the updating of this text.

Ann Arbor, Mich.   G.W.
June 1991   J.H.W.

Contents

1. Introduction   3

The Problem of Drug Abuse   3
Why People Abuse Drugs   4

Theories of Drug Abuse   4
Dopamine Theory of Reward   8
Factors that Affect Reinforcing Effects of Drugs   9

Patterns and Development of Drug Use   10
Polydrug Abuse   12
Non-Drug Related Medical Problems   12

Infectious Diseases   13

Terminology   16

Terms to Be Used in This Book   18

References   20

2. Tobacco and Nicotine   22

Tobacco Culture   22
Epidemiology and Patterns of Use   24
Pharmacokinetics and Pharmacodynamics   27
Effects of Nicotine   28

Subjective Effects   28
Physiologic Dependence and Tolerance   29
Physiologic Effects   30

Mechanism of Action   31
Morbidity and Mortality   32

Coronary Heart Disease   33
Cancer   33
Morbidity   34
Smoking and Fetal Development   34

Passive Smoking   35
Contribution of Nicotine to Cigarette Smoking Toxicity   36

References   37

3. Opioid Drugs   39

Sources of Opioid Drugs   40
Patterns of Use   44
Effects of Opioid Drugs   46

Subjective Effects   46
Analgesia   47
Gastrointestinal System   48
Respiration   48
Physiologic Dependence   48
Tolerance   49

Mechanism of Action   50
Absorption and Fate   52
Toxicity   53
References   54

4. Depressants of the Central Nervous System: Alcohol, Barbiturates, and Benzodiazepines   56

Alcohol   57

Diagnosis and Epidemiology of Use   58
Genetics and Alcoholism   60
Pattern of Use   60
Central Nervous System Effects of Alcohol   61
Alcohol and the Digestive System   66
In Utero Effects of Alcohol   68
Beneficial Effects of Alcohol   69
Morbidity   69
Mortality   73

Barbiturate and Nonbarbiturate Sedative-Hypnotics   73

Patterns of Use   74
Effects of Sedative-Hypnotics   75
Absorption, Distribution, and Metabolism   76
Tolerance   77
Physiologic Dependence and the Withdrawal Syndrome   78

Benzodiazepines and Other Minor Tranquilizers   78

Effects of Benzodiazepines   79
Patterns of Use   79

Tolerance and Physiologic Dependence 80
Other Minor Tranquilizers 81

References 82

5. Depressants of the Central Nervous System: Volatile Solvent and Aerosol Inhalation 85

Preparations Used 87
Patterns of Use 88
Effects of Volatile Solvents 90
Habitual Use of Volatile Solvents 91

Psychologic Dependence 91
Tolerance 91
Physiologic Dependence 91

Toxic Effects of Volatile Solvents: Morbidity and Mortality 92

Aliphatic Hydrocarbons 92
Aromatic Hydrocarbons 92
Halogenated Hydrocarbons 93
Ketones 94
Esters 94
Alcohols 94
Glycols 94
Nitrites 95

References 95

6. Hallucinogens: Phencyclidine, LSD, and Agents Having Similar Effects 98

Phencyclidine 98

Patterns of Use 100
Effects 100
Tolerance and Physiologic Dependence 101
PCP Toxicity; Overdose 101
Mechanism of Action 102

LSD 103

Patterns of Use 104
Effects of LSD 105
Mechanism 106
Absorption, Fate, and Excretion 107
Tolerance and Physiologic Dependence 107
Mortality and Morbidity 108

Peyote and Mescaline 110
DOM (STP) 111

Psilocybin   113
DMT   114

References   115

7. **Marihuana and Hashish**   117

Chemistry   118
Absorption, Biotransformation, and Excretion   120
Patterns of Use   122
Physiologic Effects   122
Psychologic (Subjective) Effects   123
Mechanism of Action   125
Physiologic Dependence and Tolerance   126
Adverse Effects   127

  Acute Adverse Effects   127
  Persistent Adverse Effects   128
  Potential Therapeutic Uses of THC   130

References   130

8. **Central Nervous System Stimulants: Amphetamines,
   Caffeine, and Related Drugs**   132

The Amphetamines   134

  Patterns of Use   134
  Effects of Stimulants   136
  Mechanism of Action   139
  Absorption and Fate   139
  Stimulant Toxicity   140

Khat Chewing and Cathinone   141
Caffeine and Theophylline   142

  Patterns of Use   142
  Effects   143

Methylenedioxymethamphetamine (MDMA)   145
Drugs Used to Treat Hyperactivity and Obesity   147

References   148

9. **Central Nervous System Stimulants: Cocaine**   150

Cocaine Production   151
Pharmacology and Behavior   154

  Patterns of Use   154
  Effects of Cocaine   155
  Mechanism of Action   159

Absorption and Fate 160
Legalization of Cocaine? 160

References 162

10. The Medical Diagnosis of Drug Abuse 164

History 165
Physical Examination 166

Appearance 166
Sensorium 166

Vital and Other Signs 167

Blood Pressure 168
Pulmonary Ventilation 168
Pulse Rate 168
Temperature 169
Integument 169
Lymph Nodes 171
Eyes 171
Nose 172
Mouth and Throat 172
Chest 173
Heart 173
Abdomen 174
Kidney 175
Endocrine System 175
Nervous System 176
Summary 176

Laboratory Detection 177
References 177

**11. Management of Selected Clinical Problems:
Pharmacologic Aspects** 179

Overdose 179

Opioids 179
*Barbiturate and Other Central Nervous
   System Depressants* 181
Stimulants 182

Drug Withdrawal 182

Opioids 182
Central Nervous System Depressants 184
Stimulants 184

Treating Infants Born of Drug-Abusing Mothers 185

Opioids 185

Alcohol   186
Stimulants   186

Pharmacologic Management of Drug Abuse   187

Opioids   187
Alcohol   189
Stimulants   190
Nicotine   191

References   192

12. Drug Abuse and the Law   194

Drug Abuse and the American Federal Law   194
The English "System"   204
References   207

Index   209

A Handbook on Drug
and Alcohol Abuse

CHAPTER 1

Introduction

Drug abuse refers to the nonmedical use of drugs, both drugs that have and those that do not have generally accepted medical value. Almost all drugs that are subject to abuse have central nervous system (CNS) effects, producing changes in mood, levels of awareness or perceptions and sensations. Most of these drugs also produce marked alterations in systems other than the CNS. Not all centrally acting drugs are subject to abuse, suggesting that simply altering consciousness is not sufficient for a drug to have abuse potential. Among drugs that are abused, some appear to be more likely to lead to uncontrolled use than others, suggesting a possible hierarchy of drug-induced effects relative to abuse potential.

THE PROBLEM OF DRUG ABUSE

There has been a dramatic increase in the prevalence of drug abuse in the United States during the last 30 years. Although the use of illicit drugs in this country follows a cyclic pattern, it reached an all-time peak during the late 1970s and early 1980s. Estimates indicate that in the early 1960s less than 5 percent of the population of this country had ever tried an illicit drug. By the early 1970s, evidence suggested that 10 percent of Americans, primarily those less than 25 years of age, had used such drugs (Gfroerer, 1991). In 1982 an estimated 66 percent of American youth had used an illicit drug before they graduated from high school (*Drug Abuse*, 1984).

Fortunately, more recent measures of population use of illicit drugs indicate that the current trend is downward. There was a significant decrease in lifetime use of marijuana, hallucinogens, cocaine, cigarettes, and alcohol among the young between 1979 and 1990. According to the 1990 National Household Survey on Drug Abuse, between 1985 and 1990 there was a 44 percent decrease in the number of current users (those reporting use in the past 30 days) of any illicit drug; this number declined from 23 million people to 13 million people. The 72 percent decrease in cocaine use during this time is particularly striking (National Household Survey, 1990). Since this decrease has occurred in the face of an increased supply of drugs, it is most likely due to increasing awareness of the dangers of using drugs such as cocaine (Gfroerer, 1991).

As indicated in each of the surveys, the most commonly used illicit drug in America is marihuana. In 1990, one-third of the population over the age of 12 had tried marihuana at least once in their lives, 5.7 percent had used marihuana in the past month, and 2.7 percent reported using the drug once or more each week. In comparison, 11.3 percent of the population (23 million people) had tried cocaine at least once, and 0.8 percent had used the drug in the past month.

Although data in 1990 and 1988 indicated that overall use of cocaine was declining, there had been an increase in the frequent (weekly or more) use of cocaine, suggesting that the heavy use of cocaine and crack is not showing the same pattern of decline as is less frequent use. It is estimated that there are nearly 500,000 current users of crack cocaine and 1.6 million current users of cocaine in any form in the United States (National Household Survey, 1990; Gfroerer, 1991).

Heroin use is more difficult to assess accurately, but data indicate that at least 1 percent of the population (1.9 million Americans) have tried heroin at least once and about 500,000 people are current users of heroin. Hallucinogens and inhalants are estimated to be used by approximately 2 percent of the population under 25 years of age, the age group where the prevalence is the highest (Gfroerer, 1991).

Not surprisingly, the legal drugs alcohol and nicotine are by far the most frequently used. In 1990, a total of 167 million Americans over the age of 12 (83.2 percent) reported using alcohol at least once, and 103 million (51.2 percent) indicated they had used alcohol in the past month. One hundred forty-seven million (73.2 percent) people had smoked cigarettes at least once, and 53.6 million (26.7 percent) had smoked cigarettes in the past month.

WHY PEOPLE ABUSE DRUGS

Theories of Drug Abuse

The question why people abuse drugs has been with us a long time but remains incompletely answered. Typically, two approaches are taken to the question of why some people start using drugs and persist in doing so. One is to look at the drugs and suggest that those that are abused have some underlying biochemical effect in common that results in their capacity to induce abuse. The second is to look at the person and suggest personality factors and/or genetic factors as critical elements in the development of drug abuse. These factors yield differences in the probability that drug abuse will develop if an individual is exposed to the drug. The popular "disease concept" of alcohol abuse, for example, considers the drug as a vector that can result in abuse if susceptible people are exposed to it.

The question of why people abuse drugs has been directed more often at alcohol than at other drugs of abuse. The most likely reason for this is that a vast majority of people in Western cultures are exposed to alcohol, yet a relatively small percentage of those so exposed develop problems related to drinking alcohol. Thus, it is natural to question why some individuals develop alcoholism and others do not. With other drugs of abuse, particularly opioids and cocaine, a much smaller segment of the population is exposed and probably a larger fraction goes on to use these drugs frequently. It is easier to attribute abuse of these drugs to the effects of the drugs themselves, to factors related to drug availability, or to socioeconomic issues than to genetic vulnerability or personality differences. Nevertheless, there is no clear reason to separate alcohol use from the use of other drugs in developing theories about the underlying causes of drug abuse.

Several of the currently popular theories of drug abuse were originally developed to explain behavior in general; they consider drug abuse as behavior that is a variant of normal behavior and subject to the same rules. These theories subscribe to the notion that the problem of drug abuse has its nexus primarily within the drugs themselves rather than in aberrant personality or genetics, since drug-taking behavior is subject to the same influences that control behavior in all of us.

Conditioning theories, both classical and operant conditioning, have been among the most useful of the theories applied to drug abuse. Classical conditioning theory generally deals with changes in the autonomic nervous system that occur when a stimulus is presented, and the association of these autonomic changes with other stimuli in the environment. The autonomic nervous system is responsible for aspects of bodily function that we usually do not consider to be under our direct control, such as blood pressure, heart rate, perspiration, salivation, pupil size, and sexual responses. In the case of drug taking, the autonomic effects of the drug, such as vasoconstriction, gastrointestinal changes, or pupil dilation, become associated with the external stimuli present in the environment in which the drug is taken. These associated stimuli become conditioned to the effects of the drug and thereby take on attributes that can modify responses to drugs or elicit drug-related responses in the absence of drugs.

Classical conditioning theories have been brought to bear most often in studies of drug tolerance and drug withdrawal (see the end of this chapter for a definition of these terms), which have strong autonomic components. For example, experiments have demonstrated that certain types of tolerance (e.g., drug-induced body temperature changes) occur only if measurements are taken when the animal is in the environment where it is accustomed to receiving the drug. Much less tolerance develops if evaluation is done in a novel environment. Environmental cues also become classically conditioned to drug withdrawal experiences so that some of the autonomic symptoms of drug withdrawal develop in environments where they were experienced previously even if the individual has been drug-free for months or years. To the extent that withdrawal symptoms contribute to drug taking, it can be expected that conditioned withdrawal will also increase the likelihood of drug taking and could contribute to the relapse that often occurs when former drug users return to the neighborhoods where they previously experienced both the pleasurable effects of drug taking and the aversive effects of drug withdrawal (Wikler, 1980).

Operant conditioning principles deal with motivated behavior that people generally believe is under their direct control, such as going to the refrigerator to get something to eat. According to operant conditioning theory, behavior in general is controlled by its consequences and everything we do moves us either toward pleasurable consequences (i.e., increases the likelihood of positive reinforcement) or away from painful consequences (i.e., decreases the likelihood of negative reinforcement). Operant conditioning theory accounts for drug abuse by suggesting that drugs can function as reinforcing stimuli, just as food, water, physical intimacy, and social interaction function as reinforcing stimuli. The reinforcing nature of drugs is indicated by the increased frequency of drug-taking behavior following initial exposure. Some stimuli may be better reinforcers than others, and some drugs appear to be among the most powerful reinforcers available. As such, they may come to control a great deal of behavior, in which case the individual demonstrates the characteristics of a drug "addict." The ability of drugs to serve as reinforcers (i.e., to maintain behavior such as lever pressing when that behavior results in delivery of the drug) has been studied extensively in research animals and, to a lesser extent, in human experimental subjects. The results of some of this research will be discussed in the following chapters. Classical and operant conditioning theories, which coexist quite comfortably by accounting for different aspects of drug abuse, are generally accepted as relevant to drug abuse.

Social learning theory has embellished conditioning theory to account for the complexity and cognitive aspects of human behavior. It has added cognitive attributes to drug abuse theory, such as vicarious learning (e.g., a child can learn about drug abuse by observing his parents abusing drugs), coping skills (e.g., individuals can gain more control over their drug-taking behavior if they are taught to view slips as caused by external, controllable factors rather than by internal factors such as lack of will power), self-regulatory processes (e.g., people develop internal standards of behavior and may resort to drug use when they fail to meet these standards), and learned expectations (e.g., having experienced the intoxicating effects of drugs, the individual comes to expect these effects when he takes drugs) (Wilson, 1988).

Whereas conditioning theories of drug abuse focus primarily on individual behavior, there are several social theories of behavior that stress cultural and sociological aspects of drug use. Systems theory, for example, emphasizes organized human groups, such as family units, working groups, or religious groups, where hierarchy, interdependence, stability, and predictable patterns of behavior are found. A person's behavior is explained primarily by group dynamics, which vary from individual to individual, rather than by psychological attributes of the person. Each person's behavior feeds back to modify the behavior of those in social contact with him or her. Thus, drug and alcohol abuse may be responses to a group that includes drug abusers, or it may serve some function in maintaining the group, although it is destructive to the individual (Pearlman, 1988).

Anthropological theories of alcoholism are concerned with the drinking practices of populations and how these are influenced by that population's beliefs, attitudes, and values with respect to the political, economic, social, and psychological consequences of alcohol consumption (Heath, 1988). Drug-related problems develop when an individual deviates from the population's norms with respect to drug use, and this deviant behavior may be influenced by the amount of stress generated by that population's demands and by its accepted ways of dealing with stress.

In addition to social and psychological theories, there are biological theories that attempt to explain alcoholism or drug abuse. These theories consider drug abuse as an abnormal form of behavior and attempt to explain why it develops in some people and not in others. Genetic theory suggests that susceptibility to alcohol abuse is an inherited trait, passing from one generation to another. It may be a consequence of genetically determined neural dysfunctions that manifest themselves as behavioral disturbances, including alcoholism (Tarter et al., 1988). Population studies that attempt to demonstrate the inherited nature of alcoholism using data in identical and fraternal twins and in adopted-out offspring of alcoholic parents are widely accepted as establishing that genetically controlled factors are responsible for much of the variance of the risk of alcoholism (Anthenelli and Schuckit, 1990–1991). These studies, however, are not without major flaws (Lester, 1988).

A search for potential mediators of the genetic influence on alcoholism has resulted in some interesting findings. A greater percentage of young men with a family history of alcoholism have unusual electroencephalographic patterns than men with negative family histories (Anthenelli and Schuckit, 1990–1991). Inherited differences in alcohol-metabolizing enzymes, in enzymes that degrade certain neurotransmitters, and in certain blood proteins are also being considered as potential "trait markers" of predisposition to alcoholism (Anthenelli and Schuckit, 1990–1991).

Some genetic theories of alcoholism suggest that inherited differences in personality traits may be important in the development of this condition. Personality theories have traditionally looked for individual differences in needs, drives, and motives that might be related to alcoholism in some. An array of personality evaluation tests has been given to alcoholic and prealcoholic individuals in attempts to identify factors that may contribute to overindulgence in alcohol. In general, factors of impulsiveness, unconventionality, and social adroitness are currently thought to contribute to the development of alcoholism (Cox, 1988). A genetic connection between personality and drug abuse is indicated by the finding that young people with antisocial personality disorder (ASPD), which may be genetically influenced, are more likely to develop alcoholism and drug abuse and are much more difficult to treat for these problems. This provides support for genetic influences on the development of alcoholism through personality type, although there is little overlap in the factors that influence heritability of ASPD and heritability of alcoholism (Anthenelli and Schuckit, 1990–1991). Another line of investigation has postulated that inherited neurochemical changes may be responsible for personality disorders that may in turn increase the likelihood of alcoholism (Anthenelli and Schuckit, 1990–1991).

Dopamine Theory of Reward

If there prove to be individual differences in susceptibility to drug abuse and these are related to inherited differences in neurochemical function, the chemical that might very well be involved is dopamine. Within the past decade or so, a theory of dopamine-mediated reward has become an important driving force in research on experimental models of drug abuse. This theory, in recent formulations, holds that it is the release of dopamine within certain regions of the brain, particularly the mesolimbic areas, that is responsible for the motivating properties of virtually all positively reinforcing stimuli. Among the positively reinforcing stimuli that have been studied most extensively for their ability to increase dopamine release are the various drugs of abuse.

Modern technology permits direct measurements of extracellular levels of dopamine in awake, behaving animals. Using this technology, research has demonstrated that many drugs increase extracellular dopamine levels. Cocaine, phencyclidine, ethanol, nicotine, and various opioid drugs lead to localized increases in dopamine levels, whereas drugs that have no clear reinforcing effects, such as imipramine and atropine, do not have this effect (e.g., Di Chiara and Imperato, 1988). Among the most interesting of these experiments are those that have measured dopamine levels under conditions in which the animal is self-administering the drug. Although several of these studies have shown similar increases under these conditions as when the animals receive drug passively, Hurd and associates (1989) noted that this effect may be limited to initial experience with drug self-administration. Rats with a history of cocaine self-administration did not show the increased dopamine levels that were observed in rats who self-administered cocaine for the first time. It is not yet known whether this represents neurochemical tolerance to the effects of cocaine or whether it is accompanied by any changes in the behavioral effects of cocaine. Clearly, a great deal more work needs to be done in this area before a causal role can be assigned to dopamine in mediating drug-taking or other positively reinforced behavior.

Factors that Affect Reinforcing Effects of Drugs

It is commonly thought that some drugs are more likely to be abused than others. Cocaine, for example, is thought by many scientists and lay people alike to be particularly dangerous because of its potential for abuse, whereas caffeine is not thought to present a particularly serious abuse risk. An empirical way to formulate this notion is to suggest that if a group of people were exposed to both drugs, most would indicate a preference for cocaine over caffeine. Despite this widespread opinion, the question of relative abuse potential of various drugs has not been clearly answered because it is hard to pose in experimental terms. Equating doses of various psychoactive drugs is difficult, because they often have very different effects. The ability of a range of doses of different drugs to maintain self-administration behavior in animals can be compared, but at larger doses virtually all drugs produce side effects that are probably not related to their reinforcing effects and act to decrease behavior. Thus, drugs with different ratios of side effects to reinforcing effects are difficult to compare. Eventually, it may be possible to compare the ability of a number of drugs to produce the biochemical event that is determined to be closely related to abuse potential (perhaps dopamine release, for example), but even this measure will undoubtedly be complicated by dose comparisons and side effect limitations.

The rapidity with which a drug reaches the appropriate CNS receptors and exerts its effects appears to be related to the likelihood that the drug will be subject to abuse, given that it has positive reinforcing effects. All other things being equal, the most rapid method of delivering drug to the brain is through the lungs, via inhalation. The second most rapid route is intravenous administration, followed by absorption through mucous membranes, absorption from subcutaneous sites, and finally oral administration and absorption from the gastrointestinal system.

The importance of rapid onset of action probably explains why intravenous delivery of drug is more popular among hard-core drug users than is subcutaneous or oral administration. It may also help explain the widespread use of nicotine, which produces only subtle changes in mood, sensations, or level of awareness, but does have an extremely rapid onset of action when inhaled in cigarette smoke. Similarly, cocaine absorbed through the mucous membranes of the nose has a slower onset of action than cocaine absorbed through the membranes of the lungs. When smoked cocaine (crack) became available, there was an explosive increase in the number of people who abused this substance, and the control that crack had over users' behavior seemed more profound than that of snorted cocaine.

One other important difference between cocaine available for snorting and cocaine available for smoking is that the latter form, when it hit the street, was much cheaper and much more readily available than the former preparation. The availability of a drug obviously has a major influence on patterns of drug use. When high-quality heroin is difficult to find or unusually costly, hospitals and treatment centers quickly see an increase in patients who are abusing other drugs that are more readily available. Alcohol, which is available in nearly unlimited amounts most adults in Western cultures, is the most widely used and abused drug in these cultures. In Eastern cultures, where alcohol is forbidden, alcoholism is virtually unknown.

Although these points may seem so obvious as to be hardly worth mentioning, the issues of availability, price, dose, and speed of action may be as important in determining patterns of drug use as are the more often discussed variables of socioeconomic conditions, genetics, and personality.

PATTERNS AND DEVELOPMENT OF DRUG USE

Epidemiologic research indicates that there may be a typical sequence of drug use in adolescence: the licit drugs, cigarettes and alcohol, are used before marihuana, and marihuana is used before other illicit drugs (Kandel and Yamaguchi, 1985). The latter association is particularly strong; in the United States it is extremely unlikely for adolescents to use other illicit drugs if they have not previously used marihuana. Abuse of prescribed psychoactive drugs comes last in the progression. Some research, however, has suggested that if problem drinking develops in adolescence, it is most likely to occur between the use of marihuana and the use of other illicit drugs (Donovan and Jessor, 1983).

Women may differ from men in their developmental sequence of drug use. Women are more likely than men to progress from cigarette smoking to smoking marihuana without overusing alcohol. Men, on the other hand, typically abuse alcohol before progressing to marihuana, even if they do not initially smoke cigarettes (Kandel and Yamaguchi, 1985).

Although this sequence seems especially well established, it does not mean that the use of a particular drug at a particular stage will lead to use of the next drug in the progression. Many young people proceed to a certain drug and go no further; some do not use drugs at all.

There are certain ages at which use of a particular drug is most likely to start. A graphic representation of the pattern of initiation of first use (indicated as "hazard rate") of several drugs is shown in Figure 1–1. First use of alcohol

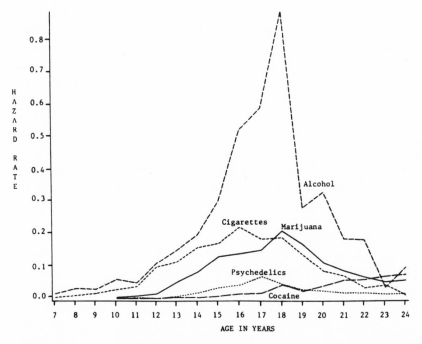

FIGURE 1-1. Age at which various psychoactive compounds are first used (hazard rate). (Source: Kandel and Logan, 1984. Copyright 1984, American Public Health Association.)

begins early, with 20 percent of those sampled indicating that they had drunk alcohol by age 10; 50 percent had used alcohol by age 14. Once individuals reach 18 years of age, if they have not tried alcohol, they become less and less likely to start. The pattern for starting cigarette use is similar to that for alcohol, reaching a peak at age 16. If cigarette smoking has not been tried by that age, it is less likely to begin later. First use of marihuana begins at age 13 for 5 percent of those studied, and the initiation rate increases to a peak at age 18, falling off more slowly than with alcohol or cigarettes. Individuals over 22 years of age are much less likely to start using marihuana than those less than 20 years of age. The pattern of initiation of cocaine use is unique among the drugs surveyed in that it increased throughout the age range studied, 10 to 24 (Kandel and Yamaguchi, 1985).

There is a decline in the most intense use of alcohol and illicit drugs at age 22 and after. This decline is not typically seen with cigarettes. The decline in drug use may occur when a young person assumes roles, such as husband or wife, employee, or parent, that are less compatible with drug use than the roles of child and student (Kandel and Yamaguchi, 1985).

The value of these data in focusing efforts to prevent drug abuse is clear. If initiation of cigarette smoking can be prevented, the risk of marihuana use may be decreased and so the risk of beginning to take other illicit drugs is reduced as well. The finding that use of illicit drugs is virtually nonexistent among those who have not used marihuana suggests that drug abuse education might be most profitably aimed at preventing marihuana use. Unfortunately, adolescents seem to respond most strongly to demonstrations of potentially severe consequences, particularly death, of using what they consider more powerful drugs, such as cocaine. Marihuana is an extremely safe drug in that it lacks acute toxicity; its greatest risk seems to be that it can lead to the use of more dangerous drugs. This may be difficult to impress on young people who resist accepting the fact that drugs can reduce much of the control they think they have over their own behavior.

POLYDRUG ABUSE

The length of this unfortunately short section on abuse of several different substances by the same person reflects our lack of knowledge about this type of drug abuse; it does not reflect its prevalence or its importance. Indeed, virtually all people who abuse an illicit drug probably take more than one drug and may often use several different drugs in close temporal approximation. Some combinations are especially popular at a given time (tripelennamine and pentazocine in the 1970s, for example, and glutethimide and codeine currently). Some drug classes, such as the CNS depressants, are usually taken in combination with other drugs. Combinations of CNS depressants and CNS stimulants are favored by some individuals. Concurrent administration of cocaine and opioids (termed "speedball") has been popular for decades. Recent data indicate that many cocaine users drink alcohol after a cocaine binge. It thus appears that multiple drug use is very common among drug-abusing populations. Yet this book, and books like it, is carefully divided into distinct chapters dealing with each drug individually. This is because we have a fairly extensive understanding of the pharmacology of individual drugs and much less understanding of the pharmacology of drugs in combination. Even more unfortunate than our lack of knowledge is the fact that very little progress is being made in this important area. For example, research in animals using drug combinations is slow, tedious, and difficult compared to studies with individual drugs.

NON-DRUG RELATED MEDICAL PROBLEMS

Drug abusers may be at risk of developing a wide variety of medical problems as a result of their drug-taking behavior. Some of these result from the irritant properties of the substances injected; others result from unsterile injection procedures. Examples of the former are abscesses caused by the subcutaneous injection of heroin diluted with quinine or other irritant adulterants. Multiple abscesses and scars are found also on the skin of intravenous barbiturate abusers, because of the low pH of the drug or the high molecular weight of the alcohols in which the drug is dissolved (Eiseman et al., 1964). When such scars occur in muscle, permanent muscular contractions can result, so that fingers, or even an arm (depending on the site of the scar), become "frozen" in one position.

Irritation can occur in other organ systems. Talc, an ingredient in the formulation of some drug tablets, may be injected intravenously if the tablet is ground up, dissolved in water, filtered through cotton, and injected. Talc causes serious pulmonary complications when it lodges in lung tissue.

Infectious Diseases

Although the irritant properties of drug diluents can put the drug user's health at risk, it is the infectious diseases associated with intravenous use of drugs that puts public health at risk. Infectious diseases can be spread when blood of an infected person comes in contact with blood from a noninfected person. When people inject drugs intravenously using the same needle and syringe used by others, the situation is ripe for the spread of infectious diseases. Group sharing of needles, with each person drawing his or her blood into the syringe and slowing injecting the drug, is probably related to the scarcity of needles. Unfortunately, this procedure greatly enhances the possibility of spread of infectious disease.

AIDS

Acquired immunodeficiency syndrome is an invariably fatal disease that is most often transmitted through blood-to-blood and semen-to-blood contact. Sexual intercourse is the most common way in which AIDS is spread, particularly when other venereal diseases have caused genital lesions, or when harsh intercourse produces lesions. In the United States the highest prevalence of AIDS is among male homosexuals. Once the causes of AIDS and the means of its transmission were understood and publicized in the homosexual community, many people changed their behavior and the spread of AIDS declined among this group. Concurrently, the spread of AIDS has been rising among intravenous drug abusers, 70 to 100 percent of whom are thought to share needles and syringes. According to the Centers for Disease Control, over 25 percent of all AIDS cases reported in adults and adolescents as of 1988 in the United States could be attributed to intravenous drug abuse. Fifty-one percent of heterosexual African-Americans with AIDS and 30 percent of Hispanic-Americans with AIDS are intravenous drug abusers. Among adult and adolescent women, 52 percent of all AIDS cases can be attributed to intravenous drug abuse (Amsel, 1990). The presence of AIDS in female drug abusers may pose the greatest risk to the non-drug-using heterosexual community, since women who use drugs often earn money for drugs through prostitution, thus exposing their customers and their customers' other sexual partners to the disease.

Providing intravenous drug users with information to help them protect themselves from AIDS has proven to be difficult. This population is not easily reached or affected by factual information on the disease transmitted over radio or television, in seminars, or in magazines. They may not be searching for answers to questions about AIDS with an intent to protect themselves once they have the necessary information. Even if the information is conveyed, intravenous drug abusers are less likely than many others to alter their behavior to reduce their chances of getting the disease.

HEPATITIS

There are several viruses that can cause hepatitis. Hepatitis A virus causes an acute disease and is transmitted primarily by the fecal-oral route. There has been an increase in the number of hepatitis A cases among intravenous drug abusers and marihuana smokers in the United States and Scandinavia in recent years (Mutchnick et al., 1991). The reasons for this are not clear, since this disease is not directly linked to use of contaminated needles.

Hepatitis B, on the other hand, is usually transmitted by blood-to-blood contact or by intimate personal contact; it is not transmitted via the nasal, oral, or respiratory routes. Ten to 15 percent of the reported cases of acute hepatitis B in the United States are intravenous drug abusers, and from 50 to 94 percent of intravenous drug abusers in the United States have been found to have present or past hepatitis B infection (Mutchnick et al., 1991). Intravenous drug abusers are no more likely than the rest of the population to develop chronic hepatitis B or to become carriers of the disease.

The hepatitis D virus was discovered relatively recently. It requires coinfection with hepatitis B in order to replicate, which means that intravenous drug abusers are more likely than the rest of the population to be infected with this virus. Hepatitis D is particularly dangerous because the virus itself damages the liver, which is not the case with either hepatitis A or B. Coinfection with hepatitis B and D viruses appears responsible for the increased rate of development of fulminant, severe hepatitis in drug addicts (Perillo and Regenstein, 1989). Similarly, the superinfection of the D virus in a person who is a carrier for the B virus can result in fulminant acute hepatitis or severe chronic liver disease (Mutchnick et al., 1991).

Hepatitis that can not be attributed to either of the above viruses is, by exclusion, Non-A, Non-B (NANB) hepatitis. This disease is difficult to screen for, so it is not known whether its prevalence is greater among intravenous drug abusers. Intravenous drug abuse is thought to be the most common risk factor in the development of NANB hepatitis, however (Mutchnick et al., 1991). NANB hepatitis is not usually a serious disease in drug addicts, but when fulminant hepatitis does result from this infection, survival is less likely than with fulminant hepatitis A or B alone.

ENDOCARDITIS

Endocarditis is characterized by colonization of infectious agents (typically gram positive bacteria, less commonly gram negative bacteria or fungi) on the valves of the heart. Endocarditis presents quite a different picture in the intravenous drug abuser than in the general population. The intravenous drug abuser is more likely to have tricuspid valve (right side) involvement, and to be infected with *Staphylococcus aureus*. Autopsy reports on intravenous drug abusers with endocarditis indicate that, although all of the cusps on the tricuspid valve are usually involved in the disease, the remainder of the heart is usually spared. Thus, the clinical picture may not suggest heart disease as much as pulmonary disease (Levine, 1991).

The etiology of right-side endocarditis appears to be the frequent intravenous injection of particulate impurities. The longer the history of intravenous drug injection, the more likely right-side endocarditis is to develop (Levine, 1991).

More serious endocarditis, that involving the aortic and mitral (left-side) valves, occurs with equal frequency among the general population and intravenous drug abusers. It is associated with predisposing heart disease, and develops when this disease produces abnormal blood flow in the heart. The infecting organism is more likely to be streptococcus, and left-side endocarditis is more likely to be associated with infection and abscess formation throughout the heart (Levine, 1991).

PULMONARY COMPLICATIONS

Emboli, some of them infected, may form as a consequence of endocarditis; these may lodge in the lungs and there give rise to embolic pneumonia. This disease may also be caused by emboli originating in infected injection sites (Louria et al., 1967). It is commonly severe and sometimes fatal.

Bacterial pneumonia also occurs among drug users. As yet, it has not been demonstrated clearly that any causal relationship exists between heroin addiction and this type of pneumonia. The available evidence has been interpreted to indicate that addicts are unusually susceptible and that susceptibility increases with the duration of addiction (Louria et al., 1967; Louria, 1969).

Some reduction in the ability of gases to diffuse across the alveolar surface of the lungs has been measured in individuals who have been intravenous drug users for many years but had not recently suffered the effects of an "overdose," which produces pulmonary congestion. The etiology of this mild form of chronic lung disease has no easy explanation, though a mechanism involving deposits of heroin diluents within the lungs has been considered (Karliner et al., 1969).

Although this section specifically excluded conditions not caused by drugs, it is important to point out that there may be a specific interaction between pulmonary complications and use of opioid drugs. These drugs compromise the ability of the lungs to protect themselves by depressing the muscles and reflexes of the oropharynx. Thus, opioid-induced depression of the cough reflex and reduction of ciliar movement decrease the removal of aspirated or foreign material from the respiratory tract. Furthermore, persons under the influence of opioid drugs are relatively immobile, and a lack of physical activity reduces the ability of physical mechanisms to protect the respiratory system. Opioids reduce rate of respiration and this allows secretions to be retained, and any bacteria they contain are given more time to adhere to mucous membranes and cause pneumonia (Greville, 1991).

TERMINOLOGY

The various terms that refer to the illicit use of drugs were originally coined and defined by physicians and pharmacologists who have managed subsequently to use them in most confusing ways. In the early decades of this century, the term *drug addiction* was felt to denote satisfactorily the illicit use of drugs, and the term *drug addict* reflected the immoral and possibly criminal nature of the user of illicit drugs. As the characteristics of drug abuse became better understood, differing patterns of illicit use became more clearly delineated. Not only were the effects produced by heroin and cocaine, for example, different, but the problems faced by the users of these two drugs were, in certain respects, dissimilar. It became possible to classify differing patterns of illicit drug use on the basis of their pharmacologic characteristics, thus, the process of terminological proliferation began.

An early and notable attempt to use pharmacologic criteria to designate differing patterns of drug misuse was made in 1931 by Tatum and Seevers, with their definitions of the terms *drug addiction* and *drug habituation*. An addicting drug was distinguished from a habituating drug principally on the basis that, in drug addiction, physiologic dependence on the effects of the drug developed. This meant that involuntary physiologic illness (the withdrawal or abstinence syndrome) would be precipitated if the intake of the drug was markedly reduced or stopped altogether. By way of contrast, withdrawal from a habituating drug might provoke emotional distress, but no physiologic upset.

In the years following 1931, the distinction between addicting and habituating drugs proposed by Tatum and Seevers was respected by some and disregarded by many. The Expert Committees of the World Health Organization attempted to clarify matters frequently during the period 1950 through 1964. The Expert Committee on Drugs Liable to Produce Addiction offered the following definition of *drug addiction* in 1950:

Drug addiction is a state of periodic or chronic intoxication, detrimental to the individual and society, produced by the repeated consumption of a drug (natural or synthetic). Its characteristics include: 1. An overpowering desire or need (compulsion) to continue taking the drug and to obtain it by any means; 2. A tendency to increase the dose; 3. A psychic (psychological) and sometimes a physical dependence on the effects of the drug.

Drug habituation was considered to be fairly innocuous drug taking that did not harm the individual or society. These definitions appeared to classify all the medically and socially significant patterns of drug abuse under the heading of addiction; habit-forming drugs did not seem worthy of concern, as their use, according to the definition, harmed no one.

In 1957, the Expert Committee on Addiction-Producing Drugs modified slightly its definition of *drug habituation,* but perhaps in part because of semantic difficulties with this term, it has disappeared from general use. Prescriptions still indicate that some drugs may be "habit forming," a term that is rarely defined, but the word *habituation* is rarely used today to refer to any type or pattern of drug use.

The Expert Committee on Addiction-Producing Drugs recommended in 1964 that the term *drug dependence* be used in place of *addiction.* The new term was preliminarily defined in the most general way: "a state arising from repeated administration of a drug on a periodic or continuous basis." Recognizing some of the shortcomings of previous definitions, the committee then went on to say, "Its characteristics will vary with the agent involved and this must be made clear by designating the particular type of drug dependence in each specific case—for example, drug dependence of morphine type, of cocaine type, of cannabis type, of barbiturate type," and so on.

Although the new term *drug dependence* seemed largely free of the connotative liabilities of its predecessors, it seemed too benign a term to some for so grave a problem. In the mid-1960s, particularly in the United States, one increasingly encountered the term *drug abuse.* Usually used without being defined, abuse is a more comprehensive, a more graphic, and in the view of some, a more censorious word than *dependence.* For perhaps just these reasons, an American reader may expect to meet the term *drug abuse* considerably more often than *drug dependence.*

Since drug abuse has become more of a medical concern, medical definitions have been developed to permit easier diagnosis of this condition. The most recent Diagnostic and Statistical Manual of the American Psychiatric Association (DSM III-R) defines *psychoactive substance dependence* as a "cluster of cognitive, behavioral, and physiological symptoms that indicate that the person has impaired control of psychoactive substance use and continues use of the substance despite adverse consequences" (DSM III-R, 1987, p. 166). This dependence can occur in the absence of either tolerance or withdrawal signs. The nine symptoms, three of which must be present for a diagnosis of substance dependence to be made, are (1) the individual takes the substance in larger amounts or over a longer time period than originally intended; (2) he or she has not been able to or is not willing to reduce use of the substance; (3) the individual spends a great deal of time obtaining, using, and recovering from use of the substance; (4) the individual may be intoxicated at inappropriate times (e.g., when job or child care responsibilities must be met); (5) other activities are given up so that substance use can continue; (6) use of the substance results in social, psychological, and physical problems; (7) tolerance develops if the substance is one that produces tolerance; (8) withdrawal develops on discontinuation of use if the substance produces physiologic dependence; (9) if withdrawal signs have occurred in the past, the individual takes the substance to prevent withdrawal signs (DSM III-R, 1987).

The essential elements of drug abuse are more succinctly included in Jaffe's definition of the term *addiction:* "a behavioral pattern of drug use, characterized by overwhelming involvement with the use of a drug (compulsive use), the securing of its supply, and a high tendency to relapse after withdrawal" (Jaffe, 1990).

Terms to Be Used in This Book

Four terms are used in this book to indicate drug seeking and/or drug taking: *drug use, drug abuse, drug addiction,* and *psychologic dependence. Drug use* is the most general term, incorporating all the others, and means to us any instance of nonmedical use of drugs, including infrequent consumption of legal drugs such as alcohol. *Drug abuse* is slightly more restrictive, indicating any use of illicit drugs or use of drugs to the point where some harm may be done to the individual or to society. An adolescent's initial use of marihuana is an example of drug abuse, as is consumption of intoxicating amounts of alcohol. *Psychologic dependence* and *addiction* are synonymous, indicating more compulsive and frequent use, and meet the definition of addiction given by Jaffe. These terms are used less often in this text than is *drug abuse,* even though much of what we discuss is compulsive drug use. *Addiction,* as indicated earlier, has taken on additional pejorative meaning that is inappropriate in a scientific text; it is used infrequently, except in Chapter 12, where it seemed unavoidable. *Psychologic dependence* is a more precise and useful term but has the disadvantage of incorporating the word *dependence,* which, when used alone or when modified by *physiologic,* has an entirely different meaning.

The term *dependence,* when it is used without a modifier, is used in the same way that *physiologic dependence* has been used previously. In contrast to the way this word is defined in DSM III-R and in previous editions of this book, where it is synonymous with addiction and abuse, in this volume *dependence* is strictly limited to the development of a withdrawal syndrome when chronic administration of a drug is discontinued. For such a syndrome to meet the definition of dependence, it must become less severe as time since last drug administration passes and it must be relieved by readministration of the drug. Here, more clearly than elsewhere, the suggestion of the Expert Committee on Addiction-Producing Drugs applies: Each drug class has its own characteristic withdrawal syndrome and dependence can therefore be labeled as morphine type, barbiturate type, and so on. The relation between physiologic dependence (the appearance of withdrawal signs on discontinuation of drug administration) and psychologic dependence (compulsive use of drugs) is an important but poorly understood aspect of drug abuse. In the early years of drug abuse research, it was assumed that if the capacity of a drug to produce physiologic dependence could be removed, it would no longer be subject to abuse. This is clearly not the case. For some drugs, such as the opioids, the onset of withdrawal signs in drug users appears to increase their motivation to seek and take the drug. For other drugs, such as the stimulants, the onset of withdrawal signs appears to decrease drug seeking.

Tolerance is a word that is frequently used in the literature on drug abuse. It is considered by some to be, along with dependence, a defining characteristic of drug abuse. Actually, tolerance and dependence simply indicate that a drug has been taken in relatively large doses on a chronic basis; this may or may not reflect abuse of that drug. Pharmacologic tolerance refers to a decrease in a drug's effect as a consequence of chronic administration or, alternatively, a requirement to increase the amount of drug taken to produce the same effect that smaller doses once produced. Since both tolerance and dependence are functions of duration and amount of drug administered, they have been considered by some to be different manifestations of the same phenomenon. Research to demonstrate this to be the case is still continuing and a final determination at a biochemical level has not yet been made.

As will be discussed in the following chapters, tolerance does not develop equally to all of a given drug's effects. It is commonly thought that tolerance develops to a drug's reinforcing effects and that this accounts for the tendency of drug abusers to increase the amount of drug they take. This has not been clearly demonstrated and remains an interesting research question.

Cross-tolerance—the ability of chronic administration of one drug to confer tolerance to another drug—develops if the two drugs are of the same pharmacologic class. Thus, cross-tolerance is clearly demonstrable among the various opioid drugs, but no tolerance develops between opioids and barbiturates or between opioids and cocaine.

Tolerance and *dependence* have precise definitions in part because they can be accurately measured and are clear pharmacologic phenomena. The term *po-*

tency, which is used occasionally in this text, is also a precisely defined pharmacologic construct, but the word is still frequently misunderstood by nonpharmacologists. *Potency* refers to the dose of drug required to produce a given effect and is often used as a relative term to compare different drugs. The drug alfentanil, for example, is more potent than morphine, although both drugs have precisely the same actions by acting through the same receptors. It simply takes much less alfentanil in milligrams per kilogram to produce a given effect than it takes of morphine. Potency does not reflect the *ability* of a drug to produce an effect; it simply indicates, usually in relative terms, the *amount* of drug required to produce that effect.

REFERENCES

Amsel, Z. Introducing the concept "community prevention." In: Leukefeld, C. G., R. J. Battjes, and Z. Amsel, eds., *AIDS and Intravenous Drug Use: Future Directions for Community Based Prevention Research.* NIDA Research Monograph 93, Department of Health and Human Services. Washington, D.C.: U.S. Government Printing Office, 1990, p. vii

Anthenelli, R. M., and M. A. Schuckit. Genetic studies of alcoholism. *Int J Addict* 25:81, 1990–1991

Cherubin, C. E. The medical sequelae of narcotic addiction. *Ann Int Med* 67:23, 1967

Cox, W. M. Personality theory. In: Chaudron, C. D., and D. A. Wilkinson, eds., *Theories on Alcoholism.* Toronto: Addiction Research Foundation, 1988, p. 143

Diagnostic and Statistical Manual of Mental Disorders, 3rd ed., revised (DSM III-R). Washington, D.C.: American Psychiatric Association, 1987

Di Chiara, G., and A. Imperato. Drugs abused by humans preferentially increase synaptic dopamine concentrations in the mesolimbic system of freely moving rats. *Proc Natl Acad Sci* 85:5274, 1988

Donovan, J. E., and R. Jessor. Problem drinking and the dimension of involvement with drugs: A Guttman Scalogram Analysis of adolescent drug use. *Amer J Pub Health* 73:543, 1983

Drug Abuse and Drug Abuse Research. First in a series of triennial reports to Congress from the Secretary, Department of Health and Human Services. Washington, D.C.: U.S. Government Printing Office, 1984

Eiseman, B., R. C. Lam, and B. Rush. Surgery on the narcotic addict. *Ann Surg* 159:748, 1964

Gfroerer, J. Nature and extent of drug abuse in the United States. In: *Drug Abuse and Drug Abuse Research: The Third Triennial Report to Congress.* National Institute on Drug Abuse, DHHS. Washington, D.C.: U.S. Government Printing Office, 1991

Greville, H. W. Pulmonary infections in intravenous drug abuse. In: Levine, D. P. and Sobel, J. D., eds., *Infections in Intravenous Drug Abusers.* New York: Oxford University Press, 1991, p. 208

Heath, D. B. Emerging anthropological theory and models of alcohol use and alcoholism. In: Chaudron, C. D., and D. A. Wilkinson, eds., *Theories on Alcoholism.* Toronto: Addiction Research Foundation, 1988, p. 353

Hurd, Y. L., F. Weiss, G. F. Koob, N. E. And, and U. Ungerstedt. Cocaine reinforcement and extracellular dopamine overflow in rat nucleus accumbens: An in vivo microdialysis study. *Brain Res* 498:199, 1989

Jaffe, J. H. Drug addiction and drug abuse. In: Gilman, A. G., T. W. Rall, A. S. Nies, and P. Taylor, eds., *Goodman and Gilman's The Pharmacological Basis of Therapeutics,* 8th ed. Elmsford, N.Y.: Pergamon, 1990, p. 522

Kandel, D. B., and K. Yamaguchi. Developmental patterns of the use of legal, illegal and medically prescribed psychotropic drugs from adolescence to young adulthood. In: LaRue Jones, C., and R. J. Battjes, eds., *Etiology of Drug Abuse: Implications for Prevention.* NIDA Research Monograph 56, Department of Health and Human Services. Washington, D.C.: U.S. Government Printing Office, 1985, p. 193

Karliner, J. S., A. D. Steinberg, and M. H. Williams, Jr. Lung function after pulmonary edema associated with heroin overdose. *Arch Int Med* 124:349, 1969

Lester, D. Genetic theory—an assessment of the heritability of alcoholism. In: Chaudron, C. D., and D. A. Wilkinson, eds., *Theories on Alcoholism.* Toronto: Addiction Research Foundation, 1988, p. 1

Levine, D. P. Infectious endocarditis in intravenous drug abusers. In: Levine, D. P. and J. D. Sobel, eds. *Infections in Intravenous Drug Abusers.* New York: Oxford University Press, 1991, p. 251.

Louria, D. B., T. Hensle, and J. Rose. The major medical complications of heroin addiction. *Ann Int Med* 67:1, 1967

Louria, D. B. Medical complications of pleasure-giving drugs. *Arch Int Med* 123:82, 1969

Mutchnick, M. G., H. H. Lee, and R. R. Peleman. Liver disease associated with intravenous drug abuse. In: Levine, D. P. and J. D. Sobel, eds. *Infections in Intravenous Drug Abusers.* New York: Oxford University Press, 1991, p. 13

National Household Survey on Drug Abuse, National Institute on Drug Abuse DHHS. Washington, D.C.: U.S. Government Printing Office, 1990

Pearlman, S. Systems theory and alcoholism. In: Chaudron, C. D. and D. A. Wilkinson, eds., *Theories on Alcoholism.* Toronto: Addiction Research Foundation, 1988, p. 289

Perillo, R. P. and R. G. Regenstein. Viral and immune hepatitis. In: Kelley, W. N., editor-in-chief, *Textbook of Internal Medicine.* Philadelphia: J. B. Lippincott, 1989, p. 603

Tarter, R. E., A. I. Alterman, and K. L. Edwards. Neurobiological theory of alcoholism etiology. In: Chaudron, C. D., and D. A. Wilkinson, eds., *Theories on Alcoholism.* Toronto: Addiction Research Foundation, 1988, p. 73

Tatum, A. L., and M. H. Seevers. Theories of drug addiction. *Physiol Rev* 11:107, 1931

Wikler, A. Conditioning factors in opiate addiction and relapse. In: Wikler, A., ed., *Opioid Dependence: Mechanisms and Treatment.* New York: Plenum, 1980

Wilson, G. T. Alcohol use and abuse: A social learning analysis. In: Chaudron, C. D., and D. A. Wilkinson, eds., *Theories on Alcoholism.* Toronto: Addiction Research Foundation, 1988, p. 239

Tobacco and Nicotine

The tobacco plant *Nicotiana tabacum* is native to America. Christopher Columbus, in his first voyage in 1492, found the Arawak Indians of the West Indies smoking crude cigars of tobacco leaf. These Indians had probably learned about the cultivation and use of tobacco from Mayan Indians, who inhaled the smoke of burning, dried tobacco leaves over 2000 years ago. The purpose of smoking tobacco was primarily medicinal for the Indians and for that reason the seeds were taken or sent to Europe for cultivation. Nicotine and the plant genus are named for Jean Nicot, the French ambassador to Portugal who sent tobacco seeds to France in 1556. Sir Walter Raleigh was in part responsible for the popularity of tobacco smoking in Great Britain in the sixteenth century. James I, however, condemned the practice and prohibited tobacco production in his country.

Until the late 1880s, tobacco was smoked as cigars or in pipes, or inhaled as snuff. A cigarette-making machine was invented in the United States in 1881 and cigarettes quickly became the overwhelmingly favorite method of using tobacco. Cigarette smoke, in contrast to cigar or pipe smoke, is sufficiently mild that it can be inhaled, a fact that increased both the abuse liability of tobacco and the health hazards of smoking.

TOBACCO CULTURE

Tobacco is grown initially as protected seedlings that are transplanted at appropriate times into carefully prepared fields located in warm, frequently moist climates. The plant is an annual, growing 2 to 9 feet tall, with alternate sessile, oval, or lanceolate leaves. The flowers appear at the top of the stalk and are self-pollinating if they are left in place. Typically, the plants are topped and the flowers removed to increase the size of the topmost leaves.

Harvesting is done either by removing the individual leaves as they ripen or by cutting the entire stalk. Several leaves are bound together or the stalk and its leaves are kept intact for drying. The process of drying or curing changes the protein, carbohydrate, acid, alkaloid, and enzyme level of the tobacco and is accomplished by one of several methods. Most tobacco that appears in cigarettes has been flue cured. During the process of flue curing, the leaves are hung in an enclosed building with a ventilation and exhaust system (flues) and a heat source. After six to eight days, the green leaves become lemon, orange (leading to the term *bright* tobacco), or deep brown in color and have a high sugar content and a medium to high nicotine content.

Cigar tobacco, consisting of filler (the primary content of the cigar), binder (the initial wrapping of the filler), and wrapper (the outside wrapping of the cigar) tobacco, is air cured. This tobacco is hung on a weather-protected, open framework for one to two months, where it slowly dries and turns yellow. Air-cured tobacco, also mixed with flue-cured tobacco for use in cigarettes, is low in sugar and has a variable nicotine content.

Fire-cured tobacco is principally used in pipe tobacco mixtures and as snuff and chewing tobacco. The green leaves are placed in an enclosed barn and small wood fires on the floor of the barn produce a creosote-flavored product. Fire curing takes up to four weeks and results in a low-sugar, low-nicotine tobacco.

In the more arid regions of Turkey, Greece, Yugoslavia, and other European and Asian countries, sun curing is popular. The resulting tobacco, used principally in cigarette mixtures, has a characteristic aroma and low sugar and nicotine content.

An important difference between flue-cured and air-cured tobacco is in the resulting pH. Flue-cured tobacco is acidic and becomes more acidic as a cigarette is burned and smoke is inhaled. At the resulting pH values (5.5–6.0), nicotine is nearly completely ionized, with the result that little is absorbed through the mucous membranes of the mouth, but continues to the lungs. Air-cured tobacco is alkaline and becomes more alkaline with progressive puffs. Nicotine at higher pH values (6.5–7.5) is primarily un-ionized; as such, it is well absorbed in the mouth.

Once cured, the leaves are fermented by storing them in a moisture-controlled (15 percent), warm (80–110°F) environment for six weeks to two years. In addition to altering the flavor of the tobacco, fermenting rehydrates the leaves to a certain extent so that they are no longer brittle but can be baled for sale with little damage.

The tobacco leaf is processed by removing the leaf material from the stalk and ribs, which have little nicotine content. Various flavoring and brand-specific "secret" ingredients may be added to the selected mixture of leaves, and this is then chopped to a consistency appropriate to the product being manufactured.

The nicotine content of tobacco is 1.5 percent on average and represents the major alkaloid in cigarettes. Cigarettes contain about 1 mg of nicotine. Nicotine is far from the only alkaloid found in tobacco, however, and the pharmacologic properties of such other tobacco-containing alkaloids as nornicotine, cotinine, anabasine, antabine, and myosmine are largely unstudied. Additional alkaloids are generated when the tobacco is burned and these appear in cigarette smoke. Even though many of these alkaloids are found in tobacco smoke, they represent only a small fraction of the more than 4000 detected constituents of such smoke. The particulate matter of cigarette smoke other than the nicotine is known as "tar." The relation of tar to smoking behavior is controversial, but the general opinion is that it affects the taste and aroma of cigarettes and as such may affect smokers' choice of brands (Surgeon General's Report, 1988). Aroma and taste are also modified by the presence of various waxes, lipids, phenolics, acids, nitrogenous and sulfur constituents, which in turn are determined by the quality of the tobacco leaf, its position on the plant, the type of tobacco used, the method of drying it, and the duration of the fermentation process.

The vapor phase of cigarette smoke has substantial amounts of highly toxic carbon monoxide. Carbon monoxide combines with blood hemoglobin to form carboxyhemoglobin, which can no longer carry life-sustaining oxygen. Levels of carboxyhemoglobin increase as a cigarette is smoked and decrease once smoking stops. The median level of carboxyhemoglobin has been reported to be from 3.2 to 14 percent (Surgeon General's Report, 1988). Rate of removal of carbon monoxide through expired air is variable, depending on pulmonary blood flow and ventilation, which in turn depend on other cardiovascular parameters. The gas phase of cigarette smoke also contains volatile aldehydes, such as acetaldehyde, which is the major metabolite of ethanol, and acrolein. Aldehyde condensation products have been identified in tobacco smoke as well, and whereas all these constituents have biological and toxic effects, their contribution to the toxic effects of cigarette smoking remains undetermined (Surgeon General's Report, 1988).

EPIDEMIOLOGY AND PATTERNS OF USE

Cigarette smoking is a complex behavior that has been observed and measured from the level of single inspirations to the frequency of number of smoking events during a single day. Observations at the first level of analysis reveal that, by drawing on a lighted cigarette, smokers pull a volume of smoke (called a puff) into their mouths. The puff is usually held in the mouth for a short period of time before it is mixed with ambient air drawn through the mouth, nose, or both and inhaled into the lungs. The size of this inhalation is usually longer and larger in volume than other nonpuff inhalations. The smoker usually holds his breath for a variable length of time and then exhales, usually through the mouth (Surgeon General's Report, 1988).

There is a tendency for the duration of each puff to decrease and the time between each puff to increase over the course of smoking each cigarette. This may be because the nicotine concentration of smoke increases as the cigarette becomes shorter, indicating that feedback mechanisms may control smoking to some extent. The puff intensity over time, the latency to peak puff pressure, and the inhalation volume and duration apparently do not change much during the smoking of a single cigarette (Surgeon General's Report, 1988).

This smoking behavior becomes fairly stereotyped in long-term smokers. It maximizes the exposure of the lung alveoli to the nicotine contained in tobacco smoke and serves to increase and maintain blood nicotine levels. Measures of blood nicotine levels in groups of smokers indicate that these levels are stable from day to day within individuals, although they vary dramatically across individuals. Two basic patterns of plasma nicotine levels have been measured in different smokers. In individuals who smoke and inhale smoke from one cigarette per hour, plasma nicotine levels rise quickly and dramatically at the time each cigarette is smoked and fall to relatively low levels between cigarettes. The overall daily pattern is thus one of peaks and valleys of blood nicotine (see Figure 2–1).

In chain smokers, where smoking frequency is higher, the peaks are less pronounced, even with the first cigarette of the day, but the valleys are less pronounced as well. The overall pattern is one of a gradual increase in nicotine blood levels, reaching a peak about midday and being maintained during the remainder of the day (see Figure 2–2). The suggestion has been made that the first pattern reflects smoking for the positive attributes of blood nicotine levels, whereas the second pattern reflects avoidance of the negative aspects of nicotine withdrawal (Russell, 1987).

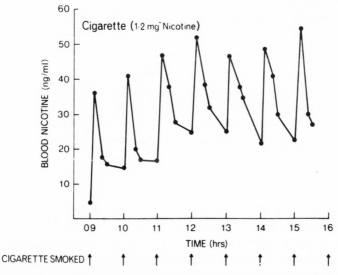

FIGURE 2–1. Blood nicotine levels of an inhaling smoker, smoking one cigarette an hour. (From Russell, 1987.)

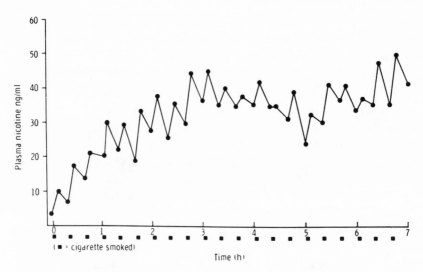

FIGURE 2–2. Blood nicotine levels of a heavy smoker, smoking three cigarettes an hour. (From Russell, 1987.)

Patterns of cigarette, cigar, and pipe smoking and smokeless tobacco use vary widely among individuals. Some smokers are content with an infrequent after-dinner cigar; others, "chain smokers," are only without a cigarette in their mouths when they are eating or sleeping. Among those whose use of tobacco is intermediate, the pattern of smoking is usually one of regular, spaced use. The preferred tobacco product is taken or smoked within 30 minutes of awakening and at regular intervals thereafter. These intervals can vary from every 15 minutes to every 2 or 3 hours or more, depending on the individual, and sometimes they show an increase (or less often, a decrease) in rate over the course of months or years.

Smoking rates may change temporarily under some conditions. Students have been found to increase their rate of cigarette smoking during examination periods (Warburton, 1987). Cigarette smoking may decrease in frequency when an individual has a cold or other illness and sometimes decreases in women during pregnancy.

Several surveys have been conducted over the years to determine the number of people in the United States who smoke cigarettes. In general, these surveys indicate that smoking behavior in men peaked in the mid-1950s at approximately 54 percent of males over the age of 18 and has been declining steadily since then to a prevalence of about 30 percent in 1985 (Surgeon General's Report, 1988). Cigarette smoking in women has been declining over a longer period, showing the highest prevalence (36 percent) in 1944, the first year it was measured, and declining to 28 percent by 1985. Per capita cigarette consumption in persons 18 years of age and over has declined from estimates of 4148 cigarettes per person in 1973 to 3196 per person in 1987.

Smoking prevalence is inversely correlated with years of education and is greater among the unemployed than among the employed. Also, white-collar workers are less likely to smoke than blue-collar or service workers. Smoking is more prevalent among people who are divorced or separated than among the married, single, or widowed, and it is more common among lower-income people than among higher-income people.

A survey taken of high school seniors indicates that students who plan to graduate from college smoke at a rate half that of those who do not have such plans. Daily use among high school seniors has declined 35 percent since 1976, with the greatest decline occurring between 1977 and 1981. Interestingly, smoking rates for female high school seniors are consistently greater than rates for males (Surgeon General's Report, 1988).

PHARMACOKINETICS AND PHARMACODYNAMICS

When tobacco is burned, nicotine is released into the smoke and is carried in the vapor and on small droplets of tar into the smoker's mouth, from which it is inhaled into his lungs. It is rapidly absorbed through the lungs because of the very large surface of the alveoli available for such absorption and because nicotine dissolves rapidly in fluids at physiologic pH. Nicotine is carried rapidly from the lungs to the brain; this time course of about seven seconds is much faster than even an intravenous injection into a vessel in the arm (14 seconds) (Russell, 1987).

Measures of plasma nicotine levels in smokers indicate that these levels rise very quickly when cigarette smoking is initiated and peak as the cigarette is finished. The amount of nicotine absorbed depends on the topography of the smoking behavior as described in the previous section and on the experience of the smoker. Experienced smokers will absorb as much as 90 percent of the available nicotine; nonsmokers will absorb much less even when they are instructed to inhale deeply. Those who do not inhale will absorb relatively little.

At physiologic pH, nicotine is approximately 69 percent ionized and is poorly bound to plasma proteins, making its passage across biological membranes relatively rapid. Nicotine distributes throughout the body, where it is most quickly absorbed by tissues with greater blood supply, such as the brain, liver, spleen, and lungs.

As is typical for a drug with this pattern of initial distribution, movement away from these tissues to less-well-perfused tissues such as fat and muscle is the first mechanism by which the drug is removed from the brain. The distribution half-life is approximately nine minutes; the elimination half-life, since it is about two hours, is less important with respect to the time course of central nervous system effects of inhaled nicotine.

Nicotine is metabolized almost exclusively by the liver; about 70 percent of the nicotine in the blood is extracted with each pass through the liver. The primary metabolite of nicotine is cotinine, which, because of its greater stability in the blood, is frequently used in experimental studies as an indicator of nicotine ingestion. Cotinine is further metabolized to a number of substances whose activity is presumed to be slight.

EFFECTS OF NICOTINE

Subjective Effects

In many descriptions of drugs' effects in this book, an attempt is made to relate the "feelings" and mood changes that are produced by the ingested drugs. It is difficult to do this with nicotine; the subjective effects of this drug appear to be extremely subtle. Cigarette smoking, for example, is not reported by high school seniors to be behavior that results in getting "high." Therefore, it is important to determine whether nicotine has effects that are critical to the maintenance of cigarette smoking, or whether, as appears to be the case with caffeine (see Chapter 8), the drug is incidental to the ingestional behavior, which is maintained for other reasons.

Observations of the fact that people maintain fairly constant blood nicotine levels over the course of weeks or years suggest that nicotine is controlling smoking behavior. Research to support this indication has usually involved attempts to determine the contribution that nicotine makes to smoking behavior. Typically, such research has evaluated changes in smoking behavior that occur when blood levels of nicotine are artificially altered by giving intravenous injections of nicotine, by altering the amount of nicotine in the smoked cigarettes, or by having subjects chew nicotine-laced gum. The object is to determine whether smokers regulate the amount of nicotine in their blood and adjust their smoking behavior to maintain "customary" nicotine blood levels. If they do, this is good evidence that nicotine is the principal stimulus that is maintaining smoking behavior.

In studies reviewed by Russell (1987) slow infusions of nicotine led to a 27 percent reduction in the number of cigarettes smoked in a session; subjects took fewer puffs and discarded their cigarettes earlier on sessions in which nicotine was infused. When the amount of nicotine in cigarettes was altered, investigators found that the subjects compensated by adjusting the number of cigarettes they smoked. Studies of the effects of switching to a low-nicotine cigarette brand demonstrated that smokers compensated for reduced nicotine intake by changing their smoking behavior. The size and frequency of the puffs were altered so that the amount of nicotine taken in remained nearly the same. Studies suggest a weak relationship between the nicotine content of cigarettes and nicotine blood levels in smokers. This points to the importance of smoking behavior itself, rather than the nicotine content of cigarettes, in determining the amount of nicotine inhaled and the amount of resulting nicotine in the blood and brain.

Individual smokers tend to show little day-to-day variation in their blood nicotine levels, although this level varies a great deal from individual to individual. This suggests that each person smokes to a blood nicotine level that is satisfactory for him or her. In contrast to many other drugs of abuse, levels of nicotine above those customary for an individual appear to be aversive. Thus, when blood nicotine levels are artificially increased, by, for example, chewing nicotine-containing gum, adjustments are made in smoking behavior to maintain a constant blood nicotine level rather than simply adding additional nicotine from smoking to the nicotine blood levels resulting from chewing the gum.

The most dramatic demonstration of the reinforcing effect of nicotine is to observe it directly. Human volunteers who were smokers were given the opportunity to respond on a lever and receive intravenous injections of nicotine. Each of the subjects learned the necessary behavior and learned as well to choose injections of nicotine rather than injections of placebo when a choice was presented (Henningfield et al., 1987). Similar studies in animals have also demonstrated a reinforcing function for nicotine and have indicated that nicotine does not appear to maintain behavior under as wide a set of conditions as do such drugs as morphine or cocaine. For example, nicotine does not maintain behavior as well under simple ratio schedules as other drugs and may not maintain behavior as well over time; moreover, nicotine-maintained responding may be acquired less rapidly than behavior maintained by some other stimulant drugs (Henningfield and Goldberg, 1983).

Physiologic Dependence and Tolerance

Although the development of physiologic dependence on nicotine has long been suspected and, in fact, has been thought to be related to the difficulty chronic cigarette smokers have in abstaining from drug use, its signs and symptoms are apparently mild. Thus, it has not been carefully described until fairly recently. Studies done at the University of Minnesota in subjects who were chronic cigarette smokers demonstrated that, when subjects were asked to abstain from cigarette use, a variety of physiologic changes could be observed. Heart rate decreased, sleep was disrupted, food intake increased, the desire to smoke cigarettes increased, and confusion increased. Administration of nicotine in the form of nicotine-containing chewing gum was able to attenuate some of the behavioral deficits that occurred during nicotine withdrawal (Henningfield et al., 1987).

Tolerance to nicotine has also been suggested, and as has been shown with most other drugs, it does not develop equally to all actions of nicotine. Thus, the nausea produced by nicotine in human studies continues to occur with only a slight increase in the amount of nicotine administered (Surgeon General's Report, 1988). In animal studies, chronic administration of nicotine has been shown to produce tolerance to the ability of the drug to decrease ongoing rates of behavior. The biphasic nature of nicotine's effects on behavior (depression followed by stimulation) is modified by chronic nicotine administration so that the stimulation phase begins sooner after nicotine administration. This indicates tolerance to the depressive aspect of nicotine's actions and less tolerance to the ability of the drug to stimulate behavior. This pattern of tolerance development is also observed in drugs that more characteristically produce increases in rates of behavior.

Physiologic Effects

Nicotine acts on both the central and the peripheral nervous systems to produce a variety of physiologic changes. These effects are complex and dose related, and the net effect on any one organ system is the result of a combination of nicotine effects on this and other organs. Nicotine can modify heart rate through opposing actions on the peripheral sympathetic and parasympathetic cardiac ganglia, through a direct effect on the medullary centers that control heart rate, by altering firing of the chemoreceptors on the aortic and carotid bodies, through compensatory mechanisms resulting from nicotine's effects on blood pressure, and by releasing epinephrine from the adrenal medulla (Taylor, 1990). The net result is usually an increase in heart rate as well as blood pressure. A similarly complicated interaction of nicotine on autonomic ganglia results in increased gastrointestinal secretions and a short-lived decrease in gastrointestinal motility (Surgeon General's Report, 1988).

Nicotine has marked neuroendocrine effects. It releases acetylcholine and norepinephrine from peripheral autonomic sites as well as from central sites. Levels of serotonin, endogenous opioid peptides, pituitary hormones, vasopressin, and various catecholamines are increased in both the blood and brain following nicotine administration (Surgeon General's Report, 1988). The pituitary hormones that have been found to be released following smoking of high-nicotine cigarettes include prolactin, occasionally ACTH, beta-endorphin/beta-lipotropin, growth hormone, and vasopressin (Surgeon General's Report, 1988). Increased levels of adrenal cortex hormones have also been noted and the mechanism has been postulated to be through central release of ACTH or via adrenal release of catecholamines (Surgeon General's Report, 1988). Plasma levels of both androgens in males and estrogens in females are decreased by nicotine. The effect of nicotine-induced changes in levels of these hormones is not known. It should be noted, however, that many of these hormones are released normally in response to stressful stimuli. Although smokers often report that smoking reduces stress, the physiologic result of smoking appears to be more like increasing stress.

Smoking produces decreases in weight. Comparisons between smokers, nonsmokers, and ex-smokers in body weights have been made in cross sections of the population and in certain subjects over time. Smokers weigh approximately 7 pounds less than nonsmokers of the same age and sex. Smokers who quit smoking gain weight and come to weigh more than nonsmokers. People who initiate smoking lose weight in relation to those who do not start smoking. Nicotine itself appears to be responsible for the decrease in body weight caused by smoking since nicotine produces weight loss in experimental animals, and smokers who stop smoking cigarettes but chew nicotine polacrilex gum gain less weight than those who stop using nicotine altogether (Surgeon General's Report, 1988). The mechanism of this effect of nicotine is not known, although the weight gain seen in those who stop smoking seems to occur through increases in food intake rather than through decreases in metabolic rate. Some studies suggest that nicotine produces a decrease in consumption of sweet foods, and cessation of smoking results in an increase in consumption of these types of food (Surgeon General's Report, 1988).

MECHANISM OF ACTION

Nicotine has classically described effects on nicotinic receptors in all (sympathetic and parasympathetic) autonomic ganglia. In small doses, nicotine mimics the effects of the natural neurotransmitter, acetylcholine, at these ganglia. In larger doses, nicotine produces a short-lasting stimulation followed by a long-lasting block of transmission through these ganglia. Presumably, these peripheral nicotinic receptors are not involved in any substantial way in the behavioral effects of nicotine. They can, however, serve in a limited way as a model of central nicotinic receptors.

Central nicotine receptors have been characterized as very high, high, or low affinity and the location of these various receptors has been described in the brain (Clarke and Pert, 1987). Evidence obtained from studies of local cerebral glucose utilization indicates that receptors in the medial habenula, the superior colliculus, and the anteroventral thalamic and interpeduncular nuclei may have particular functional relevance to nicotine binding (Surgeon General's Report, 1988).

The large number of changes in hormone and neurotransmitter levels produced by nicotine through its action on central nicotinic receptors was noted in the preceding section. It is not known which, if any, of these measured changes is relevant to the reinforcing effects of nicotine. Since reinforcing effects of drugs in general have often been related to increased dopamine levels in certain areas of the brain (see Chapter 1), the ability of nicotine to produce such changes has been evaluated. Accumulated evidence indicates that nicotine acts presynaptically to release catecholamines (norepinephrine, dopamine, and serotonin) from the hypothalamus and the striatum. Release from the mesolimbic system, the area most frequently linked to mediation of reinforcing stimuli, has unfortunately been measured to a very limited extent. Available evidence suggests that such release does occur (Powell, 1987).

Nicotine-induced release of neurotransmitters is generally found to be calcium dependent, suggesting that the action is via a normal physiologic process. In several studies, nicotine antagonists such as hexamethonium and mecamylamine have been shown to block this release. There is, therefore, no evidence to contradict the postulation that nicotine acts via release of dopamine in the mesolimbic system to produce its reinforcing effects. Caution should be exercised in using this lack of contradictory evidence as support for the notion that this is the critical aspect of nicotine's widely varied effects. Much more research remains to be done before any conclusions can be made.

MORBIDITY AND MORTALITY

Prior to 1964, the health risks of smoking were not of great concern to the several million cigarette smokers in the United States. Cigarette smoking had been frowned on as a health risk by some prominent individuals since the sixteenth century, but without carefully obtained scientific evidence to support the danger, it was not taken particularly seriously by those who enjoyed their cigarettes. In 1964, the Advisory Committee to the Surgeon General reported, on the basis of 6000 published articles, that smoking, particularly cigarette smoking, was causally related to increased incidence of lung cancer, bronchitis, and probably coronary artery disease.

In 1979, studies of the health consequences of smoking were again thoroughly reviewed in a report of the Surgeon General. Several thousand additional studies were evaluated, including eight large prospective studies that were specifically designed to determine the interaction between cigarette smoking and increased mortality and morbidity. The conclusions of the report were based on overpowering evidence of the dangers of cigarette smoking, supporting those of the earlier study: Mortality ratios of smokers are 70 percent greater than those for non-smokers; mortality ratios increase as the number of cigarettes smoked per day increases; they increase with the duration of smoking and are higher for those who start smoking at a younger age; mortality ratios decrease among smokers who stop smoking. It is fairly easy for a smoker to distance himself from "mortality ratios"; it may be more difficult to ignore the fact that a man between 30 and 35 years of age who smokes two packs of cigarettes a day will die eight to nine years earlier than a nonsmoker. The introductory sentence of the 1979 report states the fact emphatically: "Cigarette smoking is the single most important environmental factor contributing to premature mortality in the United States" (Surgeon General's Report, 1979, p. 2).

Coronary Heart Disease

The chief cause of increased mortality rates among smokers is coronary heart disease. This includes arteriosclerotic disease, which is usually related retrospectively to smoking by correlating identification of the disease at autopsy with reports of friends and relatives of the smoking behavior of the decedent. Although this is not the most satisfactory method of establishing a causal relationship, some of the statistics are impressive. In a Veterans Administration study, microscopic thickening of the arterioles of the myocardium, unrelated to arteriosclerosis, was found in 90.7 percent of those smoking two or more packs a day, in 48.4 percent of those smoking less than one pack a day, and in none of those who never smoked (Surgeon General's Report, 1979). The consequence of this specific thickening may be difficult to ascertain but it may enhance the vascular restriction that accompanies arteriosclerosis.

Myocardial infarction, the classic "heart attack," is a coronary heart disease closely related to arteriosclerosis. Since it is easier to relate myocardial infarction to smoking behavior than it is to relate arteriosclerosis to smoking behavior, myocardial infarction has become a more widely recognized smoking-related problem. Smoking, high blood pressure, and high serum cholesterol levels appear to be equally and independently related to likelihood of coronary heart disease, with each producing "dose"-related increases in susceptibility (Surgeon General's Report, 1979). Clearly, a combination of smoking, high blood pressure, and high serum cholesterol levels yields a greatly increased risk of myocardial infarction.

Cancer

After coronary heart disease, lung cancer and chronic obstructive lung disease (emphysema and chronic bronchitis) are the most frequent causes of increased mortality and morbidity among smokers. The number of cases of lung cancer increased from 18,313 in 1964 to an estimated 92,400 in 1978. These cancers, killing approximately 280 people daily in the United States, are largely due to cigarette smoking. As in the case of coronary heart disease, the causal relation between smoking and lung cancer can be inferred from the fact that the risk of getting lung cancer is related to the cigarette "dose" as measured by the daily number of cigarettes smoked, the length of time the individual has smoked, the amount he or she inhales, the total number of cigarettes smoked in patient's lifetime, the age at which he or she started smoking, the brand of cigarettes smoked (tar and nicotine content), and the number of puffs taken per cigarette. Furthermore, the risk of lung cancer declines over years since a person stopped smoking cigarettes. .

The risk of lung cancer among women, traditionally less than that among men, is increasing. Lung cancer moved from the fifth leading cause of death by cancer in women to the third leading cause of death by cancer in women in the five-year period from 1964 to 1969 (Surgeon General's Report, 1979). By 1986, the rate of lung cancer in women was equal to that of breast cancer, the leading cause of cancer in women. The risk of lung cancer in women is currently equal to that in men (Surgeon General's Report, 1989), reflecting the fact that women now start smoking at the same time, or even earlier, than men.

Cancers of the upper respiratory tract, such as mouth, larynx, and esophageal cancers, account for increased mortality among pipe and cigar smokers as well as cigarette smokers, and cancer of the urinary bladder and of the pancreas is also associated with smoking. Cancer of the kidney and stomach may be related to smoking, but the data are insufficient to be certain of this. Cancer of the intestine and of the rectum is not associated with smoking.

Morbidity

In addition to suffering increased mortality rates, chronic cigarette smokers suffer from increased morbidity as well. Chronic conditions of bronchitis, sinusitis, arteriosclerotic heart disease, and peptic ulcers are more common among smokers than among nonsmokers. Acute conditions such as influenza and pneumonia are also more frequent among smokers, suggesting a possible impairment in the immune systems of smokers.

Smoking and Fetal Development

A large amount of evidence suggests that women who smoke while they are pregnant give birth to infants that are smaller (on average, 200 g smaller) than infants of mothers who do not smoke. The more cigarettes the mother smokes during pregnancy, the lighter her baby is likely to be, and if she quits smoking during her pregnancy, her baby probably will be of the same birth weight as that of nonsmoking mothers. Lower birth weight in these infants is correlated with decreased body length and head and shoulder circumference. This effect is not due to a shorter gestational period, indicating that smoking may actually retard fetal growth. This appears to be a direct effect, not related to maternal dietary habits or weight gain during pregnancy (Surgeon General's Report, 1979).

It is not clear whether prenatal exposure to increased nicotine and carbon monoxide levels is responsible for the decrease in birth weight in these infants, nor has it been determined whether these differences at birth continue to be manifested during later growth and development. There is some evidence that children born of mothers who smoke have slightly retarded physical and mental development, but the effect is small and may be related to postnatal exposure as opposed to prenatal exposure to smoke.

Passive Smoking

Since smoking cigarettes is clearly very dangerous, nonsmokers who breathe the cigarette smoke from parents, spouses, co-workers, or others in their environment should be concerned about the possible toxic effects this secondary smoke may have on them. Passive smoking involves inhaling the contents of sidestream smoke—the smoke that comes from the burning end of a cigarette, cigar, or pipe—as well as breathing the smoke that the smoker has exhaled. This environmental smoke has been found to be no less carcinogenic than the mainstream smoke that the smoker actively inhales. When sampled with a probe close to the burning end of a cigarette, sidestream smoke was found to have a higher pH, smaller particle size, and greater amounts of toxic substances, such as carbon monoxide, benzene, toluene, ammonia, and nicotine. In a concentrated form, sidestream smoke has 20 to 100 times more volatile N-nitrosamines than mainstream smoke (Surgeon General's Report, 1986).

The toxic material in sidestream smoke is diluted and aged before it is inhaled by the passive smoker, losing considerable toxicity. The primary difference between passive smokers and active smokers is therefore the concentration of the inhaled smoke, the "dose" of smoke, to which they are exposed. Estimates indicate that nonsmokers, on average, smoke the equivalent of 0.1 to 1 cigarette per day, absorbing 0.5 to 1 percent of the nicotine absorbed by active smokers (Surgeon General's Report, 1986).

To demonstrate that passive smoking is dangerous to health, it is important to show that people exposed to different amounts of passive smoke are differentially at risk for health problems. It is difficult, however, to establish clear differences in exposure among this group of nonsmokers. Measures usually include use of questionnaires that ask about smoking habits of spouses and parents and about exposure outside of the house. These questionnaires are able to separate those with low exposure to cigarette smoke from those with high exposure to cigarette smoke; levels of cotinine in body fluids have been found to correlate with questionnaires on smoke exposure (Surgeon General's Report, 1986).

Infants and young children are among the most vulnerable victims of passive smoke inhalation. They are less able to remove themselves from parents who smoke and less able to understand the dangers they are inadvertently being exposed to. In one study, the infants of mothers that smoked had a 27.5 percent greater hospital admission rate for bronchitis and pneumonia (Surgeon General's Report, 1986). Other studies have found that symptoms of chronic respiratory problems such as coughing and wheezing are greater in the offspring of parents who smoke; the problems were greater if both parents smoked (Surgeon General's Report, 1986). Children of parents who smoke were found overall to have a 30 to 80 percent excess prevalence of chronic respiratory problems compared to the children of nonsmokers. Children of smokers have decreased lung function and more risk of chronic middle ear infections as well.

Adult passive smokers are also at risk of impaired health. Epidemiologic studies have compared the development of lung cancer in women whose husbands smoke with lung cancer development in wives of nonsmoking husbands. Most of the studies of this sort (11 of 13) demonstrated a small increase (10 to 300 percent) in risk of lung cancer development in this group of passive smokers. Six of these studies showed statistically significant differences in the risk of developing lung cancer in these two groups (Surgeon General's Report, 1986). Although there are technical difficulties of assessing differences in exposure level, the evidence suggests that people who are chronically exposed to the cigarette smoke of other individuals are at risk of developing lung cancer. Only a very few studies have attempted to evaluate the effects of passive smoke on risk of cardiovascular disease, and thus far the results are negative.

Contribution of Nicotine to Cigarette Smoking Toxicity

Although most of the toxic effects of cigarette smoking are attributed to the irritation of the smoke itself and to the carcinogenic material found in the tar constituent of cigarette smoke, it must be recognized that nicotine itself is an extremely potent poison that, when taken chronically in small doses, may have serious effects. Nicotine poisoning results in nausea, vomiting, abdominal pain, weakness, confusion, convulsions, hypotension, and coma. The vomiting caused by nicotine serves to protect individuals (children, for example) from death due to ingestion of nicotine-containing products. Paralysis of respiratory muscles or suppression of central nervous control of respiration is the usual cause of death.

Contact with tobacco leaves, particularly wet, green leaves, by harvesters can result in nicotine poisoning. This happens less often in those workers who use tobacco products themselves, indicating the effects of tolerance to the toxic effects of this drug (Surgeon General's Report, 1988).

Nicotine increases serum levels of low-density lipoproteins, causes more rapid clotting of blood, and increases heart rate and blood pressure, which may increase flow turbulence and may directly damage endothelial cells. Each of these factors could contribute to the atherosclerotic problems that are associated with cigarette smoking. Carbon monoxide is probably the most responsible agent in cardiac disease, since those who use tobacco products other than cigarettes also have increased blood levels of nicotine but are at less risk of developing the diseases related to cigarette smoking. It is likely, however, that the combination of nicotine and carbon monoxide is more toxic than either would be alone. Specifically, nicotine increases myocardial oxygen consumption by increasing heart rate and blood pressure and may also decrease cardiac blood flow through its actions on sympathetic nerves or release of epinephrine. Carbon monoxide reduces the oxygen-carrying capacity of the blood, decreasing the amount of oxygen available to the heart muscle. In susceptible individuals, this combination could prove to be lethal (Surgeon General's Report, 1988).

Nicotine could also be related directly to pulmonary disease through one or more of several properties of this alkaloid. Nicotine stimulates elastase, an enzyme that destroys alveolar function. It produces edema when applied directly to airways. It has little carcinogenic properties on its own, but when tobacco is burned, nicotine can be chemically modified to produce a very carcinogenic nitrosamine.

Although it is unlikely that nicotine is responsible for the morbidity and mortality produced by cigarette smoking, and treatment of smokers with nicotine-containing products should certainly be encouraged as a safer alternative to smoking, evidence suggests that the toxicity of nicotine itself is substantial. When it is combined with other toxic constituents of tobacco smoke, this toxicity undoubtedly enhances the risk of development of smoking-related diseases.

REFERENCES

Clarke, P. B. S., and A. Pert. Autoradiographical evidence of nicotinic receptors in rat brain. In: Martin, W. D., G. R. Van Loon, E. T. Iwamoto, and L. Davis, eds., *Tobacco Smoking and Nicotine*. New York: Plenum, 1987, p. 151

The Health Consequences of Involuntary Smoking. A Report of the Surgeon General. U.S. Department of Health and Human Services. Washington, D.C.: U.S. Government Printing Office, 1986

The Health Consequences of Smoking: Nicotine Addiction. A Report of the Surgeon General. U.S. Department of Health and Human Services. Washington, D.C.: U.S. Government Printing Office, 1988

Henningfield, J. E., and S. R. Goldberg. Nicotine as a reinforcer in human subjects and laboratory animals. *Pharmacol Biochem Behav* 19:989, 1983

Henningfield, J. E., S. R. Goldberg, and D. R. Jasinski. Nicotine: Abuse liability, dependence potential and pharmacologic treatment of dependence. In: Martin, W. D., G. R. Van Loon, E. T. Iwamoto, and L. Davis, eds., *Tobacco Smoking and Nicotine*. New York: Plenum, 1987, p. 81

Powell, P. Current concepts on the effect of nicotine on neurotransmitter release in the central nervous system. In: Martin, W. D., G. R. Van Loon, E. T. Iwamoto, and L. Davis, eds., *Tobacco Smoking and Nicotine*. New York: Plenum, 1987, p. 191

Reducing the Health Consequence of Smoking: 25 Years of Progress. A Report of the Surgeon General. U.S. Department of Health and Human Services. Washington, D.C.: U.S. Government Printing Office, 1989

Russell, M. A. H. Nicotine intake and its regulation by smokers. In: Martin, W. D., G. R. Van Loon, E. T. Iwamoto, and L. Davis, eds., *Tobacco Smoking and Nicotine*. New York: Plenum, 1987, p. 25

Smoking and Health. A Report of the Surgeon General. U.S. Department of Health, Education, and Welfare. Washington, D.C.: U.S. Government Printing Office, 1979

Taylor, P. Agents acting at the neuromuscular junction and autonomic ganglia. In: Gilman, A. G., T. W. Rall, A. S. Nies, and P. Taylor. *Goodman and Gilman's The Pharmacological Basis of Therapeutics,* 8th ed. Elmsford, N.Y.: Pergamon, 1990, p. 166

Warburton, D. M. The functions of smoking. In: Martin, W. D., G. R. Van Loon, E. T. Iwamoto, and L. Davis, eds., *Tobacco Smoking and Nicotine*. New York: Plenum, 1987, p. 51

CHAPTER 3

Opioid Drugs

In 1971, President Richard Nixon declared a War on Drugs. By now this call to arms has become very familiar, but in the 20 years since the battle was enjoined, the enemy has apparently changed. The drug that Nixon was at war against was heroin, a true narcotic, the abuse of which was reported to be a serious menace to American society. Today, of course, that role and the campaigns that accompany it belong to cocaine; heroin no longer heads the list as the drug most to be feared in America.

Nixon's declaration of war followed a period of increased heroin use in this country. There has been a dramatic rise in the number of individuals who started using heroin, from approximately 30,000 per year in 1965 to approximately 180,000 new users per year from 1968 to 1972. This increase, which occurred throughout the country among young people from 12 to 25 years of age, has been attributed to greater availability and purity of heroin in the early 1970s. There was a second "epidemic" of heroin use in the mid-1970s, followed by a dramatic decrease in the number of individuals who initiated heroin use in the late 1970s and early 1980s (Crider, 1985). The drop corresponded to a decrease in imports from Turkey and Mexico, which were the primary suppliers of heroin at that time (Gardiner and Shreckengost, 1985). Recent data on the incidence and prevalence of heroin abuse are incomplete, but imported heroin appears to have become purer and more plentiful by 1983 and 1984, which could portend another increase in heroin abuse in this country.

Nixon's war on drugs, which consisted largely of increased law enforcement and interdiction measures, apparently had the temporary effect of slowing the flow of heroin into the country. It also had much wider, more lasting ramifications. Part of the war effort involved support of basic research on the pharmacology of opioid drugs. The increased funding in this area brought some of the best scientific minds to focus on these fascinating drugs, and this, plus the fact that opioids were unusually willing to yield their secrets to researchers, means that they currently stand among our best understood behaviorally active drugs. It should be pointed out that the enhancement of our knowledge about the basic aspects of this class of drugs has done very little to explain the nature of heroin abuse, to reduce the incidence or prevalence of this problem, to increase the number of individuals in treatment programs, or to increase the number, variety, and success of treatment programs. This is not to say that the knowledge has proven useless, nor is it to suggest that continued basic science research as well as application of what has been learned about opioids will not prove eventually to be beneficial to those who abuse this class of drugs. Rather, it is an indication of the enormous challenges involved in attempting to change some types of human behavior and an indication that understanding more about the drugs themselves does not always help to change behavior controlled by the drugs.

SOURCES OF OPIOID DRUGS

In earlier editions of the *Handbook,* this chapter was entitled "Narcotic Drugs." However, the word *narcotic* has been applied loosely to any drug of abuse, in part because some legislation, such as the Harrison Narcotic Act of 1914, covered a much broader class of abused drugs than simply opioidlike narcotics. Two replacement terms have emerged: *Opiate* refers to any drug that is derived from the opium poppy, including the natural products, morphine and codeine, and the semisynthetic drugs such as heroin; *opioid* is more general, referring to any drug that acts on the opioid receptor, including the totally synthetic opioids, such as meperidine, as well as endogenous peptides, such as the endorphins and the enkephalins, found in many animal brains.

Opium is obtained from the poppy, *Papaver somniferum,* an annual plant, 3 to 5 feet in height, that appears to have originated in Asia Minor. It grows in many parts of the world, but Turkey and the countries of the Far East remain the primary sources of both legal and illegal opiates. In the Near East, certain strains of poppy, known to yield opium with a high opiate content, are cultivated. As with many plants that produce drugs, the time of harvest is critical. Several days after the poppy's petals fall, a greenish seed pod (2 inches long and 2 inches wide) forms on the plant. While it is still unripe, and at a time dictated by experience, a shallow cut is made on, but not into, the pod. A milky juice is exuded through the cut and coagulates upon exposure to air. The coagulated exudate (opium) is brownish in color and has a musty odor. In samples of good quality, its content of morphine can range from 9 to 20 percent; its content of codeine can range from 0.5 to 2.5 percent.

In addition to morphine and codeine (Figure 3–1), opium contains approximately 20 other alkaloids, only a few of which (papaverine, for example) have ever been regarded as having medicinal value. Thebaine is one of the alkaloids of opium that has been used as a starting material for synthesis of other opiates, such as oxycodone, naloxone, and the extremely potent opiate etorphine (Jaffe and Martin, 1980). Opium of United States Pharmacopia standards consists of

Naturally occurring and semisynthetic opioids

Synthetic opioids

Opioid Contaminant

Opioid antagonists

FIGURE 3–1. Chemical structures of a variety of opioid drugs. Morphine and codeine both occur naturally in the opium poppy. Heroin is synthesized readily using morphine as starting material. Methadone and meperidine are completely synthetic and have quite different chemical structures. Nevertheless, these drugs have much pharmacology in common with the naturally occurring opioids, particularly the ability to produce analgesia. Fentanyl is an extremely potent synthetic opioid, and MPTP is a contaminant of some opioid preparations and can produce Parkinson-like motor effects. The three compounds on the bottom are chemically similar to naturally occurring and semisynthetic opioids, but each has the capacity to reverse or prevent the effects of other opioids. Nalorphine has some opioid effects of its own, but naloxone and naltrexone have no effects except to antagonize opioid actions.

thoroughly dried and subsequently ground material whose relative content of morphine has been adjusted to 10 percent.

Heroin, the most widely abused semisynthetic opiate (see Figure 3–1), was first synthesized from morphine in 1874. The chemical transformation is a simple one, entailing only acetylation of the two hydroxyl groups on morphine. Because it is a relatively simple and fairly rapid reaction that provides a high yield of the desired product, it is well suited to the conditions obtaining in the illicit drug trade. Little laboratory equipment is required, and if police activities result in a rapid turnover of personnel, new "chemists" can be readily trained.

The opium trade routes in the 1960s and early 1970s took morphine from its source in the East to clandestine laboratories—in reality, simply kitchens—in southern France, where morphine was converted to heroin. There was nothing special about the south of France, at least as far as the materials and skills necessary to convert morphine to heroin were concerned, and such kitchens are now located in a variety of different countries.

For several reasons, morphine is converted to heroin before it is shipped to the United States or used by opioid abusers. Heroin is 10 times more potent than morphine, so that a given weight of heroin contains 10 times more doses than does the same weight of morphine. Thus, heroin takes less space and is cheaper and easier to hide. More important is the difference in lipid solubility of the two drugs. Heroin, as the more lipid-soluble compound, enters the brain much more rapidly than does morphine after intravenous administration. Drugs that gain rapid access to the brain are more likely to be abused than drugs with slower onsets of action. Once in the blood and brain, heroin is converted to morphine, and both heroin and morphine can act on central opioid receptors.

A number of other derivatives of morphine and codeine have also been prepared in the clandestine kitchens. Many of them—including dihydromorphinone (hydromorphine, Dilaudid), oxymorphone (dihydromorphinone, Numorphan), and metopon (methyldihydromorphone)—are effective analgesics and presumably subject to abuse by those who use heroin. Heroin's reputation, however, has made it the apparent drug of choice among opiate abusers. Although opiate users substitute a variety of drugs for heroin when heroin is not available, the other semisynthetic opioids are likely to be in short supply whenever there is a reduced supply of heroin. Thus, the substituted drugs are often nonopioid compounds, such as alcohol, sedatives, or amphetamines.

One of the most interesting and useful facts about opioids is that they can have a wide variety of structural conformations. Opioid effects are not limited to the naturally occurring plant alkaloids or endogenous peptides. Many synthetic chemicals also possess opioidlike activity (see Figure 3–1). The first wholly synthetic opioid drug, meperidine (pethidine, Demerol, etc.), was introduced in 1939, and the second, methadone, was discovered in 1945 to have been synthesized by German chemists during World War II. Since that period, chemists have synthesized thousands of opioid drugs. In the past, pharmaceutical companies were primarily responsible for producing opioids with novel structures, usually in an attempt to develop analgesics with reduced potential for abuse. There is currently much less interest on the part of United States pharmaceutical companies in developing new opioid analgesics. This is in part because past efforts have failed to produce a product that is superior to morphine in its analgesic efficacy and in part because hope has dimmed for synthesizing an opioid that has analgesic properties but little or no abuse potential. Synthesis of novel opioids continues nevertheless. The major contributors are academic, chemical, and medicinal chemical laboratories within the United States, and foreign pharmaceutical companies and academic laboratories. Although the search for better analgesics remains one goal of this research, attempts to make interestingly different drugs for basic science propel a great deal of the academic research as well.

Chemists in clandestine laboratories, interested in reaping profits in the market for abusable opioids, have taken advantage of the fact that a wide range of chemical compounds can have opioid activity. In fact, given the tremendous amount of public information on the synthesis of opioid drugs, it is surprising that many more "designer" opioids are not on the illicit market. One of the most interesting examples of abuse of synthetic opioids is that of China White, an extremely potent opioid that was in vogue on the West Coast in the early 1980s. Evidence of abuse of China White first appeared with the deaths of a number of individuals who were heroin users, who died in circumstances highly suggestive of overdose but in whom no heroin or other drugs could be detected at autopsy. Some of these individuals had a small amount of white powder in their possession, but it was apparently not a drug. It took a great deal of chemical and investigative research to determine that an opioid was, in fact, causing the deaths and to identify that opioid. It was a very potent fentanyl analog, alpha-methylfentanyl. Fentanyl (see Figure 3–1) is a commercially available, potent opioid used with nitrous oxide for anesthesia. The contaminants that accompanied alpha-methylfentanyl indicated that the drug was not made from diverted sources of fentanyl, but more likely was synthesized de novo by trained organic chemists, using published information on the procedure. The difficulty in identifying alpha-methylfentanyl in body tissue, or even in the ingested powder, resulted from the fact that it is even more potent than fentanyl, as much as 6000 times more potent than morphine. The amount required to kill a person was so small that it was not detected by the procedures used to identify drugs at that time. Furthermore, fentanyl and its analogs are chemically quite different from other opioids, and the detection procedures, designed to reveal the presence of specific known chemical structures, could not deal with this unknown entity (Henderson, 1988).

Incidents of overdose from China White and a series of related fentanyl analogs increased until the mid-1980s. Then the drugs suddenly disappeared from the streets and overdose cases decreased dramatically. The reasons for this sudden turnaround in opioid abuse are not readily available. This is most unfortunate; the more we know about why a drug of abuse is no longer being abused, the more clues we have about ways to reduce the use of the drugs that remain. Although one might assume that the drugs become unpopular when they get a reputation for being dangerous, the most recent outbreak of deaths from fentanyl contamination of heroin supplies indicates that heroin users are more interested in a good high from these drugs than they are in their safety. Although police drive through drug-infested neighborhoods with loudspeakers announcing the dangers of "Tango and Cash," the street name for this potent opioid analog in 1991, the addicts themselves are actively seeking the drug as an opportunity to experience a better drug effect. Thus, although many abused drugs (e.g., PCP and LSD) are popular for a brief time and then appear to lose their appeal, in part through bad publicity, it seems unlikely that this would be the reason for the decline in abuse of a drug that substitutes for heroin, has a very rapid onset of action, and produces the same subjective effects as opioids that have been abused for centuries.

An extremely curious, unfortunate, but fascinating result of the use of "designer" drugs was observed in a localized area in northern California in the early 1980s. A number of relatively young people, known to be heroin abusers, very rapidly developed a disease that closely resembled Parkinson's disease. Investigators, with considerable good luck, quickly found that the cause of this serious motor disturbance was ingestion of the chemical MPTP (1-methyl-4-phenyl-1,2,3,6-tetrahydropyridine) (see Figure 3–1). This product forms when attempts are hurried to synthesize the opioid MPPP (4-propyloxy-4-phenyl-N-methylpiperidine), which is an analog of two controlled analgesics meperidine and alphaprodine. Once administered, MPTP is converted to MPP+ (methylphenylpyridine). This toxic compound accumulates in dopamine-rich parts of the brain, where it inhibits some of the biochemical processes of nerve cells, causing them to die (Weingarten, 1988). The result is a disease with symptoms very much like those of Parkinson's disease and signs of destruction of the substantia nigra area of the brain, similar to those seen in Parkinson's patients. This disease is a very sad result of illegal chemists' attempts to cash in on drug abusers' willingness to buy and self-administer almost anything that is offered to them.

PATTERNS OF USE

Morphine and heroin are effective by a number of routes, including oral, intramuscular, transmucosal (snorting), subcutaneous, and intravenous, and they are effective when inhaled as smoke. It is very unusual for drug users to administer their opioid orally. Both heroin and morphine are metabolized more rapidly after oral than other routes of administration, so that relatively large amounts are necessary to perceive an effect. Not only is this a waste of precious drug, but the onset of action of orally administered heroin is gradual and delayed; the "rush" that results from a rapid onset of action does not occur, and one of the more intense aspects of drug taking is bypassed. Those who use the drug on an intermittent basis may prefer to snort it or administer it subcutaneously. Regular (i.e., daily or several times daily) users may be more likely to move to intravenous use. This yields a rapid onset of action, the maximum "rush," and is the most efficient use of the drug. Long-term intravenous heroin users may find it difficult to locate veins to inject. Frequent injections with unsterile needles and with contaminated and adulterated drug lead to infection and vein scarring. Although users may be ingenious in locating injectable veins, at some point they may have to resort to subcutaneous injections once again. Interestingly, although smoking heroin is fairly popular in the Middle East and Far East and was a popular route of heroin administration by American soldiers in Vietnam (Rosenbaum, 1971), it is not a common route of heroin administration in this country.

The procedure for "mainlining" (i.e., intravenously injecting) heroin may be performed in a fairly ritualized manner with a common group of fellow addicts. The ritual often involves sharing scarce needles, which is one reason AIDS and other infections have spread so widely among intravenous drug users. The white powder, which is typically adulterated with compounds such as lactose, mannitol, and quinine so that it may contain less than 2 to 3 percent heroin, is dissolved in water in a spoon or bottle cap. A match is placed under the container to heat the combination to speed its dissolution. The solution is drawn through a needle into a syringe or eyedropper, often through a small ball of cotton that serves to filter out the larger contaminates. A tourniquet is usually applied to a limb to raise a vein and facilitate injection. The needle is inserted and blood is drawn back before the solution is injected. Injection may be in an intermittent pattern, with the addict waiting to feel the rush of a small amount of drug before he proceeds to administer a bit more. Thus, the process of administering the drug is prolonged as much as possible.

The daily pattern of drug administration in the regular user begins with an early-morning injection. Drug users may reserve drug expressly for the purpose of providing an early-morning "hit." The user will then "go on the nod" for several hours, during which time he is lethargic and does very little. As the drug begins to wear off, the time comes to "take care of business," the process of obtaining more drug. Money must be located to buy the drug, a process that depends on the means, sex, and occupation of the user. Typically, a supplier is located, the drug is purchased, the group assembles, and the ritual drug injection procedure is repeated.

For those who use the drug only intermittently, it is snorted or injected in the late afternoon or evening, most likely on weekends with a group of like-minded friends. Those who proceed from infrequent to frequent use of heroin usually do so within one to three years. It is unusual for people to remain intermittent users for long periods of time; typically, they either quit using the drug altogether or become frequent users.

When high-quality heroin is difficult to come by, there may be a general switch of the abusing population to a substitute drug. This was thought to be the reason for the large-scale abuse of the combination of tripelennamine, an antihistamine, and pentazocine, a synthetic opioid analgesic. Known as *Ts and Blues* (pentazocine is sold under the trade name Talwin and tripelennamine is a blue tablet), this combination was popular in the Midwest, particularly in Chicago and St. Louis. The pills were crushed and dissolved, much as heroin is, and injected intravenously. The effect was reported to be much like that of heroin. In studies of experienced drug abusers, both pentazocine and tripelennamine produced an effect that the subjects described as opioidlike. When given in combination, tripelennamine appeared to block some of the unpleasant side effects of large doses of pentazocine and intensified the pleasant effects (Jasinski et al., 1984).

EFFECTS OF OPIOID DRUGS

Subjective Effects

For people who abuse opioid drugs, one of the first sensations experienced after intravenous injection of heroin is in the abdomen. The feeling has been likened to a sexual orgasm and has been referred to variously as a thrill, kick, or flash. It has been characterized as a "turning in the stomach," accompanied by a tingling sensation and a pervasive sense of warmth, which may be felt most intensely in the epigastric region. Nausea and vomiting may occur but are of little concern to the opioid abuser. Release of histamine occurs promptly too and is manifested in several ways: a sense of itching, which may be bodywide, a reddening of the eyes, and a fall in blood pressure. The fall in blood pressure probably cannot be attributed wholly to histamine; it is only partially prevented or reversed by antihistamine drugs. The central nervous system depressant effects of heroin also appear rapidly after intravenous injection. Until tolerance to this effect develops, users of heroin become heavily sedated. Mental clouding develops, visual acuity is decreased, the extremities feel "heavy," and there is little inclination toward physical activity. During this period, the user may experience frequent periods of light sleep, during which vivid dreams may be prominent. There may also be a feeling of sublime contentment during which anxiety and worry are absent, the whole body is suffused with a feeling of warmth, and sweating may be profuse.

It is very important to point out that although opioids produce similar effects in most people, not everyone responds to them with the same positive feelings of warmth and contentment. The nausea and vomiting are unpleasant to normal, nonabusing individuals and the mental clouding that the addict finds appealing may be viewed as an undesirable inability to concentrate by most people. Those who receive opioids for the treatment of pain have a different response from that of either the normal, pain-free individual or the opioid abuser. They are less likely than the normal individual to be bothered by the nausea and may welcome the drowsiness. In these respects, their response is like that of the drug abuser. The effect they appreciate the most, however, is the relief of pain that accompanies drug administration. Although there has been considerable concern in the past that individuals in chronic pain who receive opioids to treat that pain may develop into opioid abusers, a developing body of data indicates that this is not often the case. Even patients who have the opportunity to self-administer their opioid analgesic appear to take the drug solely to reduce the pain, do not increase the dose greatly over time, and stop administration if and when the pain goes away. Their overall daily dose is often less than that in patients who receive continuous infusions of morphine for pain relief, their level of analgesia is often much better, and less tolerance develops to the analgesic effects (Hill et al., 1990). In these patients, physiologic dependence to opioids may develop if treatment is long enough and the doses administered are large enough. The withdrawal syndrome, described later, is the same as that observed in withdrawn heroin abusers except that it generally lacks the motivational component that leads the abuser to seek additional drug.

Analgesia

Opioids are used therapeutically to treat pain; they are the most popular and the most effective agents in dealing with moderate to severe pain. Morphine is the opioid used most often to treat patients with pain and is the standard against which other analgesics, including other opioid analgesics, are usually compared. Morphine reduces not only the perception of pain, but also the emotional component of pain, and it accomplishes this without greatly impairing consciousness. Some mental clouding accompanies administration of analgesic doses of morphine, particularly at first, but this is not nearly as great as the impairment of consciousness that occurs when analgesic doses of nitrous oxide or ethanol are administered.

Morphine is particularly effective in reducing dull, chronic pain. Larger doses are required to reduce sharp, intermittent pain. Opioids have been considered to have little effect on deafferentation pain, which results when afferent (sensory) nerves are cut or damaged. Deafferentation pain includes phantom limb pain, or pain resulting from spinal cord or nerve injuries (Arner and Meyerson, 1988). Some clinicians, however, find morphine reduces this type of pain as well, although larger doses may be necessary. Physicians resist prescribing large doses of opioids even to people in pain who could get relief from larger doses. Their concern, largely unfounded, about making a patient into a drug abuser prevents them from doing everything they can to help the patient.

Gastrointestinal System

The other primary clinical use of opioids is in the treatment of diarrhea. In this capacity, diphenoxylate and loperamide are particularly useful, since they have selective gastrointestinal action. Their solubility characteristics are such that they are not well absorbed from the gastrointestinal tract, so they have few side effects while remaining at the site where their effects are most needed. The primary action of opioids in the gastrointestinal tract is to decrease propulsive contractions of the stomach and of the small and large intestine and to increase the tone of the sphincters and of the smooth muscle of the tract. There is more time for water to be removed from the contents and movement of material is greatly reduced (Jaffe and Martin, 1990). This results in constipation in normal individuals but produces an attenuation of diarrhea in those so afflicted.

Respiration

One of the first effects of morphine, even in fairly low doses, is to decrease the rate of respiration. This is the primary toxic effect of many opioids, as discussed later. Decreased respiration is due primarily to an opioid-induced reduction in the responsiveness of the centers in the brain that control rate of respiration to the presence of CO_2 in the blood. Some opioids have limited capacity to suppress respiration. As the dose of these drugs is increased, the rate of breathing decreases until a certain maximum is reached, beyond which further increases in dose do not decrease the rate of respiration further. Among these drugs are opioid partial agonists such as buprenorphine and nalbuphine. They have less efficacy than other agonists and cannot fully suppress respiration even in large doses. These drugs are also more limited than full opioid agonists in the amount of pain relief they can provide, although this limitation may not be of great importance in the treatment of acute postoperative pain.

Physiologic Dependence

Dependence to opioids develops as a function of the dose of drug administered and the duration of administration. As with tolerance, dependence develops most rapidly and to the greatest extent when the opioid receptor sites are in uninterrupted contact with the drug. Dependence cannot be observed until drug administration is terminated. At that time, a withdrawal syndrome appears that is characteristic of opioid dependence. The time after the last dose of opioid at which withdrawal signs begin to appear depends on the duration of action of the opioid being taken. A long-acting opioid such as methadone has a "self-tapering" effect that results in a mild but protracted abstinence syndrome with a delayed onset. If a shorter-acting opioid such as heroin is the abused opioid, withdrawal signs may begin to appear four to eight hours after the last dose. The signs increase in intensity over the next 36 to 72 hours and subside until there is little sign of withdrawal after five to 10 days. Some studies have demonstrated a "protracted withdrawal" syndrome that takes the form of weeks- to months-long altered sensitivity to the respiratory effects of CO_2 (Jaffe, 1990). There is also a very-long-lasting conditioned-abstinence syndrome, in which the individual experiences a mild form of withdrawal when he returns to places where he has experienced withdrawal in the past. Forms of conditioned abstinence have been demonstrated in experimental animals and have been used to explain, in part, relapse to the use of opioids when a past abuser returns to his drug-abusing environment (Wikler, 1980; Chapter 1).

The first symptoms of withdrawal are likely to be rhinorrhea, lacrimation, yawning, and sometimes perspiration. The abuser may sleep briefly some 10 to 15 hours after the last dose, but the sleep is not refreshing. He has no appetite, nausea usually is present, and vomiting and diarrhea commonly follow. The abuser is restless and irritable; he feels chilly and has "gooseflesh," and these symptoms are succeeded periodically by episodes of flushing and profuse perspiration. His pupils are dilated, his heart rate and blood pressure are increased, and he may experience involuntary twitching and kicking movements. Spontaneous orgasm may occur in both men and women. Tremors may be evident and muscle spasms in the back and extremities are common. If vomiting, diarrhea, and profuse sweating occur, the withdrawn abuser may become severely dehydrated and suffer from acid–base imbalance. Although death from opioid withdrawal is rare, when it occurs, it is probably due to cardiovascular collapse secondary to dehydration and disruption of acid–base balance (Jaffe, 1990).

During withdrawal, the opioid abuser typically has a much stronger inclination to obtain and administer heroin. For a great many years it was thought that the desire to attenuate withdrawal signs was the fundamental reason for opioid abuse. Although it is clear now that this is not the case, it is also clear that the reinforcing effects of opioids are increased in the face of withdrawal symptoms. Certainly, administration of sufficient dose of an opioid will quickly and completely attenuate all the withdrawal signs the user is suffering.

Tolerance

One of the most impressive effects of opioid drugs is the large amount of tolerance that develops to some of their effects. Fourfold increases in the dose of opioid necessary to suppress operant behavior has been reported in rats (Adams and Holtzman, 1990). There is considerable development of tolerance to the lethal effects of opioids, because of use-induced decreases in their ability to suppress respiration. Chronic administration of opioids appears to lead to a shortened duration of their analgesic effects.

Tolerance does not develop equally to all the effects of opioids. The constipating effects and the ability of opioids to change pupil size are retained to a considerable extent in people who take opioids on a chronic basis. It is not clear that tolerance develops to the reinforcing effects of opioids. Although an increase in opioid self-administration has been shown over time in both human and animal experiments, it has not been clearly determined whether this reflects a decrease in the reinforcing effects of the drug or tolerance to the ability of the drugs to suppress behavior in general.

MECHANISM OF ACTION

A great many drugs, particularly those with behavioral activity, are postulated to act by binding to specific sites in the brain, which in turn produce biochemical or structural changes that are the basis of the drug's action. Specific opioid receptors in the brain were suggested early in the pharmacologic study of morphine and its congeners, but real evidence for an opioid receptor was first provided with the synthesis and evaluation, in the 1940s and 1950s, of a drug called nalorphine (see Figure 3–1). Nalorphine was found to antagonize the acute effects of administered morphine, including the ability of morphine to produce respiratory depression and analgesia. This suggested that both morphine and nalorphine bound to the same site, morphine with the ability to produce an effect, nalorphine without this ability. The presence of nalorphine reduced the opportunity for morphine to bind, resulting in a reversal of morphine's effects. Nalorphine had effects of its own that differed from those of morphine, but its discovery spurred the synthesis of a wide variety of other opioid drugs, among them naloxone (see Figure 3–1), a "pure" and potent opioid antagonist. Naloxone and morphine provide a classical example of the interaction, also seen in other classes of drugs, between agonists and antagonists at single receptors. A competitive antagonism, by which larger and larger doses of naloxone produced a requirement for larger and larger doses of morphine to generate the same effect, occurred with these two drugs. All that was needed to demonstrate directly that opioid drugs were binding to a specific site was an appropriate biochemical procedure.

This was found in 1973, when three different laboratories identified a binding site for opioid drugs. The basic procedure was to combine rat brain tissue with a small amount of a radioactive opioid and allow the drug to bind to the site on the tissue. The tissue was washed free of all the drug that was not bound to the receptor. Then various other opioids were added to the tissue; if they bound to the same receptor as the radioactive drug, they would force some of the radio-activity off the binding site. Thus, increased amounts of radioactivity in solution around the tissue indicated that the other opioids were in fact binding to the same site where the radioactive drug had bound.

It was somewhat more difficult to demonstrate to everyone's satisfaction that this binding site was relevant to the observed action of the drugs. Among the criteria that can be used to demonstrate that a binding site is in fact a receptor and not simply a binding site is that binding is stereoselective. The l-isomer of most opioids is the active isomer; the d-isomer is "unnatural," having little, if any, opioid activity. Therefore, the l-isomer should bind to the near exclusion of the d-isomer. This was found to be the case. It is also important to demonstrate a good correlation between the binding potency of a group of opioids and their potency in producing an opioid agonist or antagonist effect. Several drugs do not show this correlation well, but often there are obvious reasons for this. Co-deine, for example, is a well-known opioid, but it does not bind well to the opioid receptor. This may be explained by the fact that codeine is fairly inactive biologically until it is converted to morphine. Most of the tested opioids, how-ever, met these criteria in a satisfactory manner. The existence of an opioid receptor is well accepted by pharmacologists today; it is a concept that has gen-erated a great deal of interesting basic research on the pharmacology of these drugs.

With the discovery of central nervous system binding sites for opioids came the question of why they were there. The possibility that morphinelike drugs existed naturally in the human body, perhaps to modulate sensations of pain, was an intriguing one that sent a number of scientists hunting. The first compounds isolated from tissue and found to bind to opioid receptors and to have opioidlike effects were the enkephalins. Further research uncovered the existence of beta-endorphin and, more recently, dynorphin. These compounds are all peptides and therefore do not readily cross the blood–brain barrier, and they are rapidly de-graded following systemic administration. Thus, the behavioral effects of these endogenous opioids have not been well evaluated. However, they have been thoroughly studied using neurochemical and neuroanatomic procedures. They exist in three distinct anatomic systems in the brain and there are separate pre-cursor proteins for each system. The procedures whereby these proteins are made and subsequently cleaved to result in the active products have been described in detail (Watson et al., 1989).

The role of these opioid peptides in the normal nervous system is not well understood. Since opioid alkaloids are effective analgesics, it has been postu-lated that the endogenous peptides may modulate the response of the brain to painful stimuli, and some of the endogenous peptide systems are located in areas of the brain that are involved in pain transmission and perception. The relation between endogenous opioid peptides and opioid abuse is less clear. Opioid peptides are located in areas of the brain that some regard as critical for mediating the reinforcing effects of stimuli in general and those of drugs in particular. This neural interconnection, involving the nucleus accumbens and ventral tegmental area, has dopamine as a primary neurotransmitter and receives innervation from and sends output to areas of the limbic system (see Chapter 1). Direct administration of opioids to the nucleus accumbens and the ventral tegmental area is reinforcing in rats. The nucleus accumbens is especially rich in opioid–peptide-containing fibers. Thus, it is possible that the reinforcing effects of drugs are related in some fashion to opioid peptide systems (Watson et al., 1989).

ABSORPTION AND FATE

The fact that heroin and morphine are effective by virtually any route of administration indicates that they are absorbed from gastrointestinal, intramuscular, mucosal, lung, and subcutaneous sites. After oral administration, morphine and heroin in particular are metabolized to less active products on their first pass through the liver. The duration of action of orally administered morphine is slightly longer than that of intramuscularly administered morphine, but eight times more drug must be given to produce the same degree of analgesic effect (Jaffe and Martin, 1980).

Codeine and methadone, in contrast, are much more effective when given orally than are morphine and heroin. These drugs are not as completely metabolized by the liver on the first pass. Ten percent of ingested codeine is converted to morphine, and the analgesic property of codeine may be due largely to this conversion (Jaffe and Martin, 1990). The abuse liability of codeine may also be related to its metabolism to morphine, since it is one tenth as potent as morphine as a reinforcer in monkeys.

Although heroin is very lipophilic and therefore passes the blood–brain barrier readily, morphine enters the brain with difficulty. The rapid entrance of heroin into the central nervous system is the main reason it is the opioid of choice among drug abusers. Once in the brain, heroin is quickly hydrolyzed to monoacetylmorphine and morphine, which are thought by some to be the active component of heroin (Jaffe and Martin, 1990). Some synthetic opioids, such as etorphine and etonitazine, are extremely lipophilic and bind to CNS opioid receptors without conversion. They are also extremely potent; 1000 times less etorphine is necessary to produce analgesia as compared to morphine.

Morphine is conjugated in the liver to morphine glucuoronide, which is excreted in the urine. The half-life for morphine after intravenous administration is between 2.5 and 3 hours in young adult humans (Jaffe and Martin, 1990). Heroin, insofar as it is hydrolyzed to morphine, is metabolized and excreted in a similar fashion. Some free heroin is also excreted in the urine. The variety of other opioid drugs is so vast that it would be difficult to catalog the method of elimination of each one.

TOXICITY

Opioids such as morphine and heroin are fairly nontoxic compounds, particularly in comparison to stimulant and sedative drugs. Addicts with a stable supply of drug, or those taking methadone regularly, or patients taking opioids on a chronic basis for treatment of pain, suffer primarily from constipation but have few other difficulties, as long as they continue to take the drug. Although there are some opioids, such as meperidine, that are metabolized to a stimulant with convulsant effects, most depress the central nervous system. Death from opioid overdose is through depression of respiratory centers in the brainstem. Since tolerance to the respiratory depressant and, therefore, to the lethal effects of opioids develops rapidly, opioid overdose deaths in chronic heroin users may result from the combination of opioid use with other depressant drugs or may occur when the user inadvertently self-administers a relatively uncut sample or an extremely potent synthetic opioid. Opioid overdose is treated by administration of an opioid antagonist (see Chapter 11). Given intravenously, naloxone will restore consciousness and normal respiration rates within seconds to an individual rendered comatose by opioids. Opioid antagonists are so direct and specific that they can be given to patients in a coma of unknown origin to diagnose opioid overdose. In surgical procedures in which large doses of opioid agonists such as fentanyl are used as anesthetics and the patient is artificially respirated, antagonists can be administered following surgery. The central nervous system and respiratory depression produced by fentanyl are reversed and the patient's recovery is speeded considerably.

It is important for emergency room physicians to be acutely aware of the duration of action of the opioid antagonist they administer in cases of opioid overdose. Naloxone's duration is only about one to four hours. If the opioid action outlasts that of the antagonist, the patient could again become comatose and die several hours after administration of the antidote. Naltrexone is an opioid antagonist with a duration of action of as long as 24 hours. It would be more appropriate for treatment of overdose with long-acting opioids.

Although opioids themselves are relatively nontoxic, there is a great deal of public health danger resulting from the abuse of these drugs. The most important reason for this is that many confirmed opioid addicts use the intravenous route of drug injection and share their equipment. Thus, they are at great risk for developing AIDS. The intravenous drug abuser presents a considerable risk to the rest of society as far as AIDS transmission is concerned. Women drug abusers frequently help support their habits by prostitution, increasing the possibility of transmitting the AIDS virus to heterosexual men and their partners. These facts have greatly increased the pressure to find better and more accessible treatment for intravenous drug abusers.

In addition to the risks of contracting AIDS, intravenous injections with unsterile drug and equipment present many other dangers. Hepatitis, serious skin abscesses, deep infections, and endocarditis are among the health problems that result from injecting drugs intravenously without appropriate precautions. The "fad" popularity of Ts and blues, pentazocine and tripelennamine, was accompanied by increased cases of death due to lung emboli caused by intravenous administration of talc, a constituent in the formulation of the tripelennamine tablet.

Drug abusers often buy and use homemade designer drugs of unknown potency and content, synthesized by chemists of varying skill. These drugs may be much more potent than the heroin they are accustomed to using, resulting in overdose deaths such as those seen with China White in the 1980s and with fentanyl in 1991. Or these designer drugs may contain toxic contaminants; the cases of Parkinson's disease caused by administration of MPTP, a contaminant of the opioid MPPP, constitute a particularly sad example. Fortunately, the cause of Parkinson-like symptoms with abrupt onset in young drug-abusing individuals was quickly determined. In other circumstances the problems could become more widespread before they were detected.

REFERENCES

Adams, J. U., and S. R. Holtzman. Tolerance and dependence after continuous morphine infusion from osmotic pumps measured by operant responding in rats. *Psychopharmacology* 100:451, 1990

Arner, S., and B. A. Meyerson. Lack of analgesic effect of opioids on neuropathic and idiopathic forms of pain. *Pain* 33:11, 1988

Crider, R. Heroin incidence: a trend comparison between national household survey data and indicator data. In: Rouse, B. A., N. J. Kozel, and L. G. Richards, eds., *Self-Report Methods of Estimating Drug Use: Meeting Current Challenges to Validity*, NIDA Research Monograph 57, DHHS. Washington, D.C.: U.S. Government Printing Office, 1985, p. 125

Gardiner, K. L., and R. C. Shreckengost. Estimating heroin imports into the United States. In: Rouse, B. A., N. J. Kozel, and L. G. Richards, eds., *Self-Report Methods of Estimating Drug Use: Meeting Current Challenges to Validity*, NIDA Research Monograph 57, DHHS. Washington, D.C.: U.S. Government Printing Office, 1985, p. 141

Henderson, G. L. Designer drugs: past history and future prospects. *J Foren Sci* 33:569, 1988

Hill, H. F., C. R. Chapman, J. A. Kornell, K. M. Sullivan, L. C. Saeger, and C. Benedetti. Self-administration of morphine in bone marrow transplant patients reduces drug requirement. *Pain* 40:121, 1990

Jaffe, J. H. Drug addiction and drug abuse. In: Gilman, A. G., T. W. Rall, A. S. Nies, and P. Taylor, eds., *Goodman and Gilman's The Pharmacological Basis of Therapeutics*, 8th ed. Elmsford, N.Y.: Pergamon, 1990, p. 522

Jaffe, J. H., and W. R. Martin. Opioid analgesics and antagonists. In: Gilman, A. G.,

L. S. Goodman, and A. Gilman, eds., *Goodman and Gilman's The Pharmacological Basis of Therapeutics,* 6th ed. New York: Macmillan, 1980, p. 494

Jaffe, J. H., and W. R. Martin. Opioid analgesics and antagonists. In: Gilman, A. G., T. W. Rall, A. S. Nies, and P. Taylor, eds., *Goodman and Gilman's The Pharmacological Basis of Therapeutics,* 8th ed. Elmsford, N.Y.: Pergamon, 1990, p. 485

Jasinski, D., J. J. Boren, J. E. Henningfield, R. E. Johnson, W. R. Lange, and S. E. Lukas. Progress Report from the NIDA addiction research center, Baltimore, Maryland. In: Harris, L. S., ed., *Problems of Drug Dependence, 1983: Proceedings of the 45th Annual Scientific Meeting, The Committee on Problems of Drug Dependence, Inc.* NIDA Research Monograph 49, DHHS. Washington, D.C.: U.S. Government Printing Office, 1984, p. 69

Rosenbaum, B. J. Heroin—influence of method of use (letter). *N Engl J Med* 285:299, 1971

Watson, S. J., K. A. Trujillo, J. P. Herman, and H. Akil. Neuroanatomical and neurochemical substrates of drug-seeking behavior: overview and future directions. In: Goldstein, A., ed., *Molecular and Cellular Aspects of the Drug Addictions.* New York: Springer-Verlag, 1989, p. 29

Weingarten, H. L. 1-methyl-4-phenyl-1,2,3,6-tetrahydropyridine (MPTP): One designer drug and serendipity. *J Foren Sci* 33:588, 1988

Wikler, A. *Opioid Dependence: Mechanisms and Treatment.* New York: Plenum, 1980

CHAPTER 4

Depressants of the Central Nervous System: Alcohol, Barbiturates, and Benzodiazepines

Alcohol, barbiturate, and nonbarbiturate sedative-hypnotic drugs, and the benzodiazepine minor tranquilizers are a chemically heterogeneous collection of compounds that have a great deal of pharmacology in common. Their profiles of action include disinhibition of behavior and reduction of anxiety following ingestion of small doses, sedation and ataxia following administration of intermediate doses, and anesthesia and coma after taking larger doses. Alcohol, primarily because it lacks potency (large doses of alcohol are required to produce effects), has no clinical application as a sedative; the clinical usefulness of barbiturates as anxiolytic and hypnotic agents has been largely supplanted by the benzodiazepines; the benzodiazepines, in turn, have gained considerable popularity in the treatment of the pervasive problems of anxiety and insomnia. Their popularity is due largely to their effectiveness and demonstrated safety; in contrast to the barbiturates, overdose with benzodiazepines rarely has a fatal consequence.

There are similarities and differences in the characteristics of the abuse patterns among these three classes of drugs. Alcohol, as one of few legally available "recreational" drugs, presents one of the most serious drug abuse problem in the United States. Between 11 and 16 percent of people in this country have a problem with alcohol abuse at some time in their lives. Although use of cocaine and most other "hard" drugs is decreasing among high school seniors, use of alcohol continues to be extremely high. More than 80 percent of this group indicated that they had an alcoholic drink in the last year and one third reported that they had consumed five or more drinks in the past two weeks (Johnston et al., 1989).

Barbiturate abuse occurs in a much smaller number of people, and these drugs are usually abused in conjunction with abuse of other drugs. Benzodiazepines are also usually abused in combination with other psychoactive drugs, but, except in certain specific instances, drug abusers prefer barbiturates to benzodiazepines.

Although the epidemiology of use and abuse of these drugs is different, there are similar pharmacologic sequelae of their abuse:

1. Chronic administration of alcohol, barbiturates, or benzodiazepines can result in physiologic dependence, and the withdrawal syndromes of each of these drugs have many characteristics in common.
2. There is cross-dependence among the three types of drugs, in that the withdrawal signs resulting from discontinuation of one of these drug classes can be specifically attenuated by administration of either of the other two drug classes.
3. The withdrawal signs following discontinuation of alcohol and many of the barbiturates can be fatal, progressing from tremors to convulsions to delirium to cardiovascular collapse.
4. Only moderate degrees of tolerance appear to develop to the effects of these drugs, and there does not appear to be tolerance to the lethal effects of CNS depressants.

ALCOHOL

Alcohol (ethanol, ethyl alcohol, grain alcohol) probably was among the first psychoactive substances to be used by man. It has been postulated that alcoholic beverages were first made in prehistoric times as a result of the (probably) accidental fermentation of honey, grain, or fruit juices, which would yield, respectively, mead, beer, or wine. Stronger alcoholic beverages became possible when the process of distillation was devised, a feat generally said to have been accomplished around A.D. 800 by Jabir iban Hayyan (known as Gerber in the Western world). Like the distillation process, the word *alcohol* is of Arabian origin, the antecedent word usually being transliterated as *alkuhl* (Roueche, 1966).

In addition to ethanol, several alcohols are readily available in the environment. Among these are methanol (wood alcohol) and ethylene glycol, a constituent of antifreeze. These other alcohols can produce intoxication but are metabolized to toxic substances. The breakdown products of methanol are formaldehyde and formate, which can result in metabolic acidosis, blindness, and death. Ethylene glycol is metabolized to glycoaldehyde and then to glycolate, which also produce metabolic acidosis, resulting in renal and cardiopulmonary failure. The same enzyme, alcohol dehydrogenase, that causes ethanol to be metabolized to acetaldehyde is responsible for the initial breakdown of methanol and ethylene glycol. Alcohol dehydrogenase has higher affinity for ethanol than for the other two alcohols, however, so that administration of ethanol, to compete with and retard breakdown of methanol or ethylene glycol to their toxic metabolites, is a common method of treating ingestion of these poisons.

Social attitudes toward alcohol in Western countries differ markedly from those manifested toward other drugs of abuse. Alcohol is a familiar substance for many people, having been present at home from the time of their earliest memories. It is evident that fewer Americans react to alcohol with the same mixture of emotions—revulsion, scorn, and fear—that is commonly elicited by such illicit drugs as heroin and cocaine. Although satisfactory evidence has existed for over 30 years that alcohol can produce physiologic and psychologic dependence (Isbell et al., 1955) and although alcohol-related accidents are the leading cause of death among young adults, today easy access to alcoholic beverages is generally denied by law only to the young and the grossly intoxicated.

Diagnosis and Epidemiology of Use

The many and varied patterns of alcohol consumption comprise a spectrum of such breadth and diversity that the determination of where essentially benign use ends and abuse begins is most difficult. Although abuse of alcohol and dependence on it have been studied more extensively than any other form of drug abuse, no generally accepted definition of alcoholism has been formulated. Disputes regarding definitions center principally on the degree of psychologic dependence an individual must develop to be classified as an alcoholic, but psychologic dependence itself has not yet been defined sufficiently clearly to permit precise measurement. As discussed in Chapter 1, the American Psychiatric Association's definition of substance abuse disorders (DSM III-R), which includes alcohol abuse, consists of a list of potential characteristics that include manifestations of tolerance and physiologic dependence; inappropriate use of the substance (i.e., when it interferes with social, occupational, psychomotor, physical, or mental functioning); frequent preoccupation with seeking or taking the substance; and repeated attempts to reduce use of the substance (Rounsaville and Kranzler, 1989).

Even with the criteria for alcohol abuse neatly laid out, the physician's problem of how to apply them to individuals and the epidemiologist's problem of how to apply them to populations remain. Various test instruments (Meyer, 1988) have been developed in attempts to help health care professionals detect alcohol abuse problems. These need not be complicated, as indicated by the apparent success of three questions in identifying alcoholics in a research clinic. The questions are, "Has your family ever objected to your drinking?" "Did you ever think you drank too much in general?" "Have others (such as friends, physicians, clergy) ever said you drink too much for your own good?" (Woodruff et al., 1976).

For large populations involved in studies of the epidemiology of alcohol use and abuse, the questionnaires are necessarily larger and more involved. The Diagnostic Interview Schedule, which attempts to uncover not only substance abuse, but other psychiatric disorders as well, has been used in some of the more informative epidemiologic studies of alcoholism. This highly structured interview can be administered by trained, nonprofessional individuals, yielding comparable data from different parts of the country, or even from different countries.

Interviews with approximately 3000 individuals in each of six Epidemiological Catchment Areas representing both urban and rural populations within the United States have revealed some interesting statistics about alcohol use and abuse (Robins et al., 1988). At each site and within each age group, rates of ever having met DSM III-R criteria for alcohol abuse or dependence were higher in males than in females. This was more true for the older respondents than for the younger, suggesting that this sex ratio may be decreasing as the younger generation of women learns to drink more like their male counterparts. Interestingly and puzzlingly, it was found that fewer elderly people had ever had an alcohol abuse problem, even though they had had more time to develop one. The reason for this was not clear. Alcohol disorders also appeared to be more common in those with less education.

Helzer et al. (1988), using a similar test instrument, evaluated the prevalence of alcohol-related disorders among people in different cultures. They found the lowest rate in Taipei, Taiwan, the highest rate in Edmonton, Alberta, and intermediate rates in St. Louis, Missouri and Puerto Rico. There was much agreement between this study and that of Robins et al. (1988): Prevalence of alcohol-related disorders was considerably higher in men than in women, particularly in the area of heaviest use, Edmonton; women were slightly older than men at the mean time of onset of alcohol problems; and the lifetime prevalence of alcohol-related problems decreased after age 45.

These studies and others (Fillmore, 1988) make an additional point that is not widely recognized and should be emphasized here: Alcohol disorders have a high rate of spontaneous remission, although this remission is often not stable, indicating the sometimes episodic pattern of alcohol abuse. In men, undesirable drinking behavior appears to start when they are in their 20s. As men age beyond their 30s, if they have not developed undesirable drinking behavior, they are unlikely to do so. Young men are quite likely to show remission from heavy alcohol drinking, however. Furthermore, unwanted alcohol drinking behavior is uncommon among those over 60. This leaves middle-aged (40 to 50 years) men with the greatest likelihood of having a chronic drinking problem. Thus, as reported by Fillmore, "although unwanted drinking behaviors are rare in general population samples among the middle-aged, these are the years in which they are most likely to be chronic" (Fillmore, 1988, p. 64).

Genetics and Alcoholism

It is extremely popular these days to point out that alcoholism is a heritable trait. One of the most common statements is that the offspring of an alcoholic parent is four times more likely to develop alcoholism than is the offspring of nonalcoholic parents. The idea that alcoholism is inherited is one that was popular early in Western history but that lost favor in the 1930s, when the mood of the scientific and medical communities shifted toward the contributions of personality and environmental factors to mental disorders in general. With the return of emphasis on biological contributors to psychiatric disorders came a resurgence of interest in the possibility of genetic contributions to alcohol-related problems. Whereas it is certainly true that alcoholism tends to occur in families, it is not yet certain how much of a contribution to familial alcoholism is made by genetics and how much is made by environment. Studies of adopted-out offspring of alcoholic and nonalcoholic parents have suggested a genetic role in alcoholism (e.g., Cadoret et al., 1980; Goodwin et al., 1973). There are tremendous problems to overcome in studies of this kind, however, not the least of which is the fact that there is no consistent, easily applied definition of alcoholism. Even to attempt to study the genetic contribution to a condition such as alcoholism—which can change through time, can differ tremendously in degree, and is judged differently by different cultures, institutions, and individuals—is to risk drawing inappropriate and perhaps dangerous conclusions. It will be quite a long time before this extremely complex issue has been studied to the satisfaction of all concerned scientists and clinicians and the inherited nature of alcoholism is thoroughly understood.

Pattern of Use

Although epidemiologic studies have given us a fairly clear picture of how problem drinking develops and changes in populations, there is no similar picture of how problem drinking develops or what pattern it takes in individuals. Most likely, this differs enormously among different people, reflecting the differential contributions of, among others, parents, peers, institutions such as church and fraternity, and heredity. One of the early and most thorough descriptions of patterns of alcohol use was made by Jellinek in his book *The Disease Concept of Alcoholism* (Jellinek, 1960). He suggested four types of alcohol intake patterns: alpha, beta, gamma, and delta. The difference among these types of drinkers depends on the amounts consumed and the patterns of consumption. The alpha type drinks in an undisciplined fashion, but not to extreme; the beta type shows weekend binging. These may progress to the delta and gamma types, who drink to the point of physiologic dependence. The gamma alcoholics show "loss of control" of their alcohol consumption after the first drink, but can abstain between bouts of drinking. The delta alcoholics can limit the amount they consume, but cannot abstain from alcohol consumption even for short times. Jellinek was a superb scholar of alcoholism, but he was not an experimental scientist, and he did not actually observe or measure alcohol drinking patterns under controlled conditions. Unfortunately, his postulations have not led to appropriate research on patterns of alcohol drinking and our knowledge on this matter remains limited.

Studies of drinking by alcoholics in laboratory settings indicate that the drinking pattern is frequently episodic, perhaps like that of Jellinek's gamma alcoholic. Episodic patterns of alcohol intake, in which periods of high alcohol intake alternate with periods of reduced drinking, may be quite common in alcoholics; this is the pattern of alcohol consumption that develops in alcoholics under experimental conditions of free alcohol availability (Mello and Mendelson, 1972; Nathan and O'Brien, 1971) and in experimental animals given free access to alcohol (Winger and Woods, 1973). With both types of experimental subjects, signs of alcohol withdrawal may develop when alcohol consumption is voluntarily reduced. Interestingly, craving for alcohol does not seem to develop during alcohol withdrawal, since the subjects do not resume drinking until the withdrawal signs have cleared. The cyclic pattern of alcohol consumption and the apparent lack of desire for alcohol during alcohol withdrawal contrast with the situation of opioid abusers, who take opioids on a regular basis as long as they can obtain the drugs and whose craving for drug increases during periods of deprivation and withdrawal.

Central Nervous System Effects of Alcohol

Nineteenth-century pharmacologists regarded the effects of alcohol on the central nervous system (CNS) as stimulatory in small doses and depressant in larger doses. In this century, alcohol has been regarded as a uniformly depressant drug, with its apparently stimulatory early effects on speech and behavior being attributed to an alcohol-induced depression or disruption of the mechanisms that normally regulate these activities. The disinhibitory effects of low doses of alcohol may lead to stimulation of behavior that is suppressed by punishment or anxiety, for example. Interestingly, recent data suggest that the stimulatory (or disinhibitory) aspects of alcohol contribute significantly to the maintenance of alcohol ingestion by normal (nonalcoholic) subjects. Those who were only depressed by alcohol chose not to drink (De Wit et al., 1989).

One procedure that has proven very sensitive to the effects of small doses of alcohol is the divided-attention task. In this task subjects are asked to look at and respond to an object in front of them and at the same time report the occurrence of events in their peripheral vision. Following ingestion of small amounts of alcohol, subjects continue to respond normally to the central object but are markedly impaired in their responses to the objects in the periphery (Moskowitz and Burns, 1977). Since such responses are essential to accident-free driving, the effects of just one or two drinks on driving may be due to impairment of divided-attention behavior.

The effects of moderate quantities of alcohol may include a weakening of ordinary restraints on speech and behavior, development of euphoria, and increases in self-confidence, as well as reductions in neuromuscular coordination (manifested in speech, gait, and manual dexterity), visual acuity, and perception of pain and fatigue. In addition, reaction time is prolonged; memory, insight, and the ability to concentrate are impaired; and sexual behavior, as manifested in speech and purposive behavior, may become overt. It is difficult, however, to predict the degree of intoxication that any individual will exhibit at intermediate blood concentrations of alcohol. Individual susceptibility to intoxication, or at least to manifesting signs of it, varies considerably. At low blood alcohol concentrations (50 mg/100 ml or less), 10 percent of a population of drinkers appear intoxicated (as determined by trained observers utilizing such criteria as slurred speech, obvious loss of inhibitions, and locomotor difficulties). At levels regarded as significant both medically and legally (e.g., 101 to 150 mg/100 ml), just 64 percent appear intoxicated. Only at levels exceeding 200 mg/100 ml do virtually all drinkers appear intoxicated (Harney and Harger, 1965).

If alcoholics are similarly evaluated, additional variables must be considered. Some degree of tolerance to the effects of alcohol develops in alcoholics, as do patterns of behavior designed to minimize the outward manifestations of intoxication; as a result, alcoholics with blood concentrations as high as 300 mg/100 ml may appear only mildly intoxicated (Mendelson and Mello, 1966).

When blood levels of alcohol exceed 300 mg/100 ml, most drinkers are markedly intoxicated and some are stuporous. As blood concentrations rise to 400 mg/100 ml and above, a state resembling surgical anesthesia develops, that can be succeeded by coma and death from respiratory paralysis. It is commonly said that death occurs at blood levels in excess of 550 to 600 mg/100 ml, but 350 mg/100 ml has been lethal on occasion, and conversely, a few individuals have been reported to be still ambulatory with blood alcohol concentrations of 700 mg/100 ml (Isbell et al., 1955).

An unusual effect of alcohol that is almost certainly related to its central nervous system actions is the occurrence of alcohol-related blackouts, or periods of amnesia for portions of the drinking episode. During the blackout, the individual may appear normal (although drunk) to his colleagues; he is not comatose, but may be ambulatory and coherent. However, he may remember nothing about certain periods of time and may "wake up" in a strange place with no recollection of how he arrived there. Alcohol-induced blackouts are difficult to study and hence are very poorly understood. Whether they are associated with chronic alcohol ingestion or can occur during a single intoxicating bout is not clear. Similar periods of memory impairment have been occasionally reported with short-acting benzodiazepines (Morris and Estes, 1987), typically following the period when their sedative effects have passed. Whether these two phenomena are related mechanistically is not currently known.

MECHANISM OF ACTION

The mechanism of the depressant action of alcohol has still not been definitively determined. Since the pharmacologic effects of alcohol are similar in many respects to those of barbiturates and benzodiazepines, whose actions are relatively well understood, scientists are looking carefully at CNS functions where the actions of these drugs and alcohol may overlap. In particular, attention has focused on a receptor complex associated with the inhibitory neurotransmitter gamma amino butyric acid (GABA). When GABA binds to its receptor, the associated Cl^- ion channels are opened, resulting in a decrease in the activity of a large group of CNS neurons. Benzodiazepine minor tranquilizers have receptors located on this GABA–Cl^- complex. When they bind here, the affinity of GABA for its receptor—and thus its action of damping neuronal activity—is enhanced (Haefely et al., 1985). Barbiturates appear to have their own receptor site on the same GABA–benzodiazepine complex and have a similar mechanism of action. It is generally acknowledged that alcohol, in contrast with the benzodiazepines, does not act at a specific receptor site. Alcohol produces a general increase in the fluidity of membranes (Goldstein, 1983); this results in an altered flow of ions through neuronal membranes and an altered sensitivity of those neurons to electrical activity. One theory, with some substantiating evidence, is that an area of the GABA–benzodiazepine receptor complex is particularly sensitive to the increases in membrane fluidity produced by alcohol. The change in fluidity somehow results in the opening of the Cl^- ion channels associated with the GABA–benzodiazepine receptor, so that the net effect—a decrease in neuronal activity—is generally the same for the three drug types. Since greater understanding of alcohol's mechanism of action may aid in development of potential treatment agents or antagonists, further research in this matter is critical.

TOLERANCE

Though it is commonly said that tolerance to the effects of depressant drugs develops with prolonged use of high doses, this phenomenon has not been investigated extensively. Anecdotal evidence abounds, but only a relatively small number of well-designed experiments have been conducted. No more than a very rough estimate of the magnitude of the tolerance developed is possible at this time. It appears to be a complex situation in which a number of causative factors must be considered in arriving at any tentative conclusion. There is some evidence for a small, short-lived increased rate of metabolism of alcohol as a con-

sequence of chronic administration. There may also be a limited amount of phar-
macodynamic or tissue tolerance, and behavioral or conditioned tolerance
appears able to produce fairly substantial changes in the effects of alcohol following chronic administration. There also appears to be some cross-tolerance
between alcohol and other sedative-hypnotics. Tolerance to the lethal effects of
alcohol does not appear to develop to a significant extent, however.

PHYSIOLOGIC DEPENDENCE AND THE WITHDRAWAL SYNDROME

Physiologic dependence to alcohol develops as a function of the amount of alcohol consumed and the duration of drinking. The relative contributions of degree and duration of alcohol intoxication have been well described in rodents
(Goldstein, 1983). As with the opioids, the degree of withdrawal is a function
of the dose of alcohol given, the duration of alcohol administration, and the
continuity of alcohol administration—if alcohol is given on an intermittent basis
and the animals are sober for relatively long periods of time, the amount of
subsequent withdrawal is less. Although these factors are likely to be just as
relevant in man as they are in mice, the pattern of alcohol use necessary for the
development of physiologic dependence in humans has not been clearly established and remains in dispute. One of the questions is what actually constitutes
alcohol withdrawal. If the headache and dysphoria of a hangover are the initial
phase of alcohol withdrawal, then physiologic dependence on alcohol appears to
develop after only a few hours of moderate intoxication. If, however, tremulousness is the mildest symptom of withdrawal, alcohol dependence is not manifested until several consecutive days of marked intoxication. More traumatic
manifestations of abstinence, such as a psychotic delirium, occurred in the study
of Isbell et al. (1955) after 400 to 500 ml of alcohol/day had been consumed for
48 or more days. It is not known what the minimum amounts and times are for
the development of severe dependence.

It is possible to divide the withdrawal syndrome into three chronological
stages as shown in Figure 4–1. Manifestations of the first stage usually appear
within a few hours after drinking has been sharply reduced or stopped. Blood
alcohol levels at this time may be 100 mg/100 ml or higher (Isbell et al., 1955).
Tremulousness (the "shakes"), weakness, and profuse perspiration are among
the first signs to develop and complaints from the patient of anxiety (the "jit-
ters"), headache, anorexia, nausea, and abdominal cramps may accompany
them. Retching and vomiting may follow. The patient has a flushed face and
injected conjunctiva. He is restless, agitated, hyperreflexive, and easily startled,
but he generally remains alert. In time the tremors become generalized and more
marked. The EEG pattern at this time may be mildly dysrhythmic, with random
spikes and brief episodes of high-voltage slow waves appearing; the degree of
abnormality of the EEG pattern, however, does not appear to be a reliable prog-
nostic sign of whether convulsions will subsequently occur (Victor and Adams,

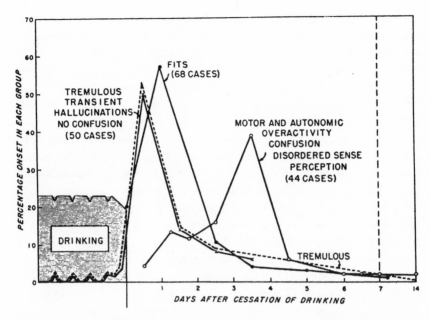

FIGURE 4–1. Pattern of alcohol withdrawal. Following several days of heavy drinking the initial signs of alcohol withdrawal are tremors that can develop even before alcohol has been completely removed from the body. These may be accompanied by mild hallucinations, the "pink elephant" stage of alcohol withdrawal. Tremors and hallucinations always precede the development of convulsions or "rum fits," which, if they occur, will do so within a day or two of cessation of drinking. The most severe aspect of alcohol withdrawal is delirium tremens, which has a peak onset between three and four days after drinking has stopped. (From Victor and Adams, 1953.)

1953). The patient may also begin to "see" or "hear" things (acute alcoholic hallucinosis), often at first only when his eyes are shut but later also when they are open. Insight is commonly retained. For the alcoholic who has developed only a mild degree of physiologic dependence, the withdrawal syndrome may consist merely of the signs and symptoms described earlier, which gradually disappear within a few days.

The second stage, alcoholic convulsive seizures ("rum fits"), appears to develop only in some alcoholics, although the true incidence of seizures during withdrawal has not been determined satisfactorily. In two studies in which a total of 272 alcoholics undergoing withdrawal were observed, the incidence of patients exhibiting one or more seizures was 13 percent (Isbell et al., 1955; Victor and Adams, 1953). The seizures are typically of the grand mal type and may begin as early as 12 hours after abstinence (Isbell et al., 1955; Victor and Adams, 1953) but appear perhaps more often during the second or third day.

The third stage is one of an agitated delirium (delirium tremens), in which auditory, visual, and tactile hallucinations occur, commonly with loss of insight. During this period (often three to four days in length), the patient sleeps little, if at all; he is severely agitated, often completely disoriented, restless, and almost continuously active. Fever, profuse perspiration (to the extent that marked dehydration is possible), and tachycardia can be observed at this time. The patient may describe bizarre delusions. It is typical of withdrawal from central nervous system depressant drugs that the delusions and hallucinations, though individual in nature, are virtually always terrifying to the patient. This is why the patient is continuously agitated and why his behavior may become aggressive toward others or harmful to himself. Though earlier manifestations of alcohol withdrawal can generally be reversed by an appropriate dose of alcohol, barbiturate, or benzodiazepine, once delirium tremens develops, it is extremely difficult to calm the patient by what would be regarded as a safe dose of any CNS depressant drug. Delirium tremens is a potentially fatal disturbance, with death usually being attributed to hyperthermia, or peripheral vascular collapse. Estimates of death rate range from 1 to 37 percent (Harney and Harger, 1965), but a mortality of approximately 10 percent is commonly encountered.

The alcohol withdrawal syndrome usually lasts from five to seven days (Jaffe, 1985). As severe as this syndrome can be and regardless of whether convulsions develop, recovery is usually complete and no persisting medical or psychological sequelae can be detected (Isbell et al., 1955).

Alcohol and the Digestive System

Although it is the interaction between alcohol and the central nervous system that is largely responsible for use and abuse of alcohol, the digestive system is perhaps the organ system next most prominently affected by alcohol. It is this system that alcohol contacts first when it is consumed, that releases alcohol to the rest of the body, and that is largely responsible for removing alcohol from the body through metabolic processes. When alcohol consumption is extreme, the digestive system suffers extremely, and the consequence to the alcohol abuser, as discussed later in the chapter, can be severe.

ABSORPTION, DISTRIBUTION, AND METABOLISM

Though alcohol can be absorbed slowly into the body while in the stomach, the upper portion of the small intestine represents the principal site of its absorption. Here absorption is rapid and virtually complete, so that the rest of the intestinal tract is ordinarily exposed to very little alcohol.

The critical determinant of the rate of absorption appears to be the emptying time of the stomach, which is subject to various influences. The presence of food slows gastric emptying, as do high concentrations of alcohol, which can produce gastric irritation and pylorospasm. The crucial role of the stomach as a temporary impediment to absorption is graphically illustrated by findings made in patients who have undergone massive gastrectomies. These patients usually become intoxicated rapidly with relatively small quantities of alcohol because when they drink, alcohol is delivered almost immediately to the site of its rapid absorption in the small intestine (Goldstein, 1983).

The partition coefficient for alcohol between water and fat is about 0.10 (Goldstein, 1983); consequently, the distribution of alcohol throughout the body at diffusion equilibrium very closely approximates that of water. The rate of entrance of alcohol into various tissues varies directly with the blood supply to the tissue; the concentration in the highly vascularized central nervous system, therefore, rapidly comes into equilibrium with that in the systemic arterial blood. Concentrations in more poorly perfused tissues, such as depot fat and resting skeletal muscle, increase more slowly. It may take 45 minutes or more before the alcohol concentrations in venous blood coming primarily from skeletal muscle approximates that in systemic arterial blood. This explains why a person may become intoxicated very rapidly after consuming a few drinks on an empty stomach (alcohol goes quickly to the well-perfused brain) and then gradually becomes sober over the course of the next 30 minutes (alcohol is distributed to the less-well-perfused organs). This is the same explanation for the finding that intoxication often is more profound during the rising phase of alcohol blood levels than on the descending phase. Blood samples from the forearm vein do not accurately reflect brain levels until equilibrium, a process requiring 30 to 60 minutes.

More than 90 percent of the alcohol absorbed into the body is metabolized, chiefly in the liver. The first step is alcohol's conversion to acetaldehyde, a process that is rate-limiting because of the limited supply of the required NAD cofactor. Attempts to increase the rate of alcohol metabolism by giving substances that are reduced to NAD have not proven very successful. Fructose increases the rate of alcohol metabolism only slightly and then not in all subjects (Goldstein, 1983). Because the rate of alcohol metabolism is limited by cofactor availability rather than by amount of substrate, alcohol is one of few drugs whose elimination is via zero order kinetics. Rate is constant, regardless of the amount of alcohol in the system, until alcohol blood levels are reduced to small amounts.

The second metabolic step entails the conversion of acetaldehyde to acetyl-coenzyme A or acetate, most of which is then oxidized to carbon dioxide; the complete oxidation of alcohol to carbon dioxide and water yields 7 cal/g.

Alcohol not metabolized by the liver is excreted largely unchanged in urine and in expired air. Small quantities may also be found in saliva, sweat, and tears. For medicolegal purposes, a knowledge of the relationship between blood alcohol concentrations and those in readily obtained biological samples is critical. The concentration of alcohol in urine is about 1.25 times greater than that in blood and the concentration in saliva is 1.12 times greater, whereas the concentration in blood is about 2100 times greater than that in alveolar air. It is commonly said that there is a maximal rate at which alcohol can be metabolized (which is typical of enzymatic reactions). The figure cited most often is 7 g (9 ml) of alcohol per hour for a person weighing 70 kg. This should be regarded only as an average value to which individual variations as large as ±50 percent may be encountered. In an experimental simulation of severe chronic alcoholism, it has been found that rates of metabolism can in time become twice the accepted average (Harney and Harger, 1965). This study also indicated that the largest quantity of alcohol that an individual is capable of metabolizing in a 24-hour period is probably in the vicinity of 500 ml (roughly 1250 ml of 80-proof whiskey).

DIRECT EFFECTS ON THE DIGESTIVE SYSTEM

When alcohol is present at concentrations exceeding 15 to 20 percent (which would be the case if any beverage approximately 40 proof or greater were taken undiluted), GI response to its irritant and dehydrating effects can be observed. Gastric secretions and motility are depressed, pylorospasm may occur, and the mucosa becomes hyperemic. The nausea that can occur after the use of alcohol probably stems from GI inflammation. Vomiting is caused by both local irritant and central actions of alcohol (Harney and Harger, 1965).

Prolonged, excessive use of alcohol leads minimally to gastritis, sometimes accompanied by edema and hyperemia of the tongue and buccal mucous membranes. Both motor and secretory activities of the entire GI tract essentially cease during severe intoxication.

In Utero Effects of Alcohol

If a woman consumes alcohol while she is pregnant, she runs the risk that her child will be born with the *fetal alcohol syndrome* (FAS). FAS is thought to occur in one to three of every 1000 births around the world and to be responsible for approximately 5 percent of all congenital anomalies (Sokol et al., 1986). The syndrome is characterized by (1) retarded growth that begins before and continues after birth; (2) a pattern of facial abnormalities, including short palpebral fissures, epicanthal folds, a short nose, a long and hypoplastic philtrum, a thin upper lip, and a flat face; (3) some type of impairment of the central nervous system, such as microcephaly, mental retardation, motor abnormalities, tremors, or hyperactivity. There may also be heart defects, skeletal anomalies, or malformation of the external genitalia. The degree of FAS in children of women who drink alcohol during pregnancy appears to depend on a number of variables. Studies in animals suggest that the amount of alcohol consumed is important, with more severe defects occurring with greater alcohol consumption. Nevertheless, since no clear threshold of alcohol consumption has been established and since individual mothers and fetuses certainly differ, it is clearly unwise for pregnant women to consume any amount of alcohol. Animal studies indicate that the timing of alcohol consumption is also relevant, with the fetus being more susceptible to the teratogenic effects of alcohol early in gestation. Studies in humans, however, indicate that women who are identified as heavy drinkers when they register for prenatal care and who reduce or eliminate their alcohol intake prior to the third trimester as a result of counseling and intervention are less likely to have infants with small head circumference or low birth weight and length. The apparent susceptibility of infants to maternal alcohol consumption during the third trimester was suggested to be due to the fact that this is the time the brain is undergoing its most rapid growth and organization (Rosett et al., 1980). Susceptibility also appears to vary by individual, since identical twins appear to be equally affected by maternal alcohol consumption, whereas fraternal twins may be affected differently. The effects of FAS continue into preadolescence and undoubtedly beyond. Children with more severe early manifestations are those most severely handicapped on 10-year follow-up (Streissguth et al., 1986).

Beneficial Effects of Alcohol

Not all the effects of alcohol are harmful. The appropriate concern with the consequences of overuse of alcohol has tended to make educators, counselors, and physicians paint the drug with an entirely black brush. Recent evidence suggests that there are some health benefits resulting from moderate alcohol consumption (i.e., no more than two drinks per day). As compared to abstainers, the risk of coronary heart disease appears to be less in those who use alcoholic beverages to a moderate extent on a regular basis. This may be due to alcohol's ability to increase blood levels of high-density lipoprotein, resulting in a lower level of low-density, more dangerous lipoproteins. It is also possible that the beneficial effects result from a decreased platelet aggregation and coagulation or from the anxiolytic effects of alcohol that may serve to buffer the effects of stress. Since alcohol is metabolized without the need for insulin, some forms of alcohol may be useful sources of energy for the diabetic. Again, it is important that the alcohol intake be strictly limited. The potential, small health benefits of alcohol (Baum-Baicker, 1985) do not apply to former alcoholics, those with family histories of alcoholism, or pregnant women.

Morbidity

The medical problems associated with alcoholism are evidenced most frequently and with greatest detriment in the digestive system and in the central and peripheral nervous systems. The effects of alcohol in these two quite distinct systems are far from independent, however. Some of the most serious alcohol-related problems of the central and peripheral nervous systems are secondary to malnutrition, which in turn appears to be related in part to decreased absorption of critical nutrients from the gastrointestinal system as a consequence of chronic alcohol ingestion. Malnutrition in alcoholics is also related to their typically poor eating habits (i.e., the substitution of the calories of alcohol for more nutritious foods). Malnutrition per se can result in liver pathology and at one time was thought to be a major contributing factor to the hepatic problems that develop in alcoholics. However, evidence that adequate nutrition does not prevent the liver damage associated with consumption of large amounts of alcohol suggests that alcohol itself is hepatotoxic (Lieber, 1977). In any case, it seems clear that the combination of alcohol's direct effect on the digestive and nervous systems and its indirect effects on nutrient intake and absorption in the chronic alcohol abuser poses greater medical risks than those associated with malnutrition alone.

THE DIGESTIVE SYSTEM

Disturbances in the digestive system are commonly attributed to the collective impact of the direct toxic effects of alcohol; dietary deficiencies, especially of vitamins; and the biochemical disequilibria occasioned by the continuing necessity for metabolism of large quantities of alcohol.

The Gastrointestinal Tract. Morning nausea and vomiting are common experiences for alcoholics. They may be early signs of abstinence, since they can usually be quelled by several drinks and since, in the early stages of alcoholism, gastroscopic evidence of gastritis is not consonant with the magnitude of these symptoms. Irritation of gastric mucosa caused by alcohol usually subsides quickly after intake ceases, but in severe alcoholism, erosion develops to a more serious degree. Gastric or duodenal ulcers are not uncommon and can be sources of serious hemorrhage.

The Pancreas. Alcohol abuse is the primary cause of chronic pancreatitis, although alcohol is unlikely to be involved in acute pancreatitis. Diet also plays a role, with increased risk associated with alcohol abuse in combination with a high-protein diet. The disease results from protein and calcium plugs that develop in the pancreatic ductules, limiting proper pancreatic secretion. In alcoholics, the pain from pancreatitis may be chronic or acute, often depending on the pattern of alcohol consumption. Since alcohol consumption frequently initiates an attack, the best remedy is to stop drinking alcohol (Dimango, 1989).

The Liver. When alcohol is consumed to excess it acts as a nonspecific stressor, producing a sympathomimetically controlled release of fatty acids from adipose tissue and a resulting increase in plasma free fatty acids and liver triglycerides.

Because the liver is devoting much of its efforts to the metabolism of alcohol and levels of NADH are increased because of this metabolism, fatty acid synthesis is increased. Thus, for several reasons, a weekend binge will lead to a fatty liver (Goldstein, 1983).

The relation between this acute fatty liver and the chronic fatty liver, hepatitis, and cirrhosis that can develop in alcoholics is not known. With chronic alcohol consumption, the fat accumulation in the liver is from dietary sources and endogenous synthesis rather than from adipose tissue, suggesting a different mechanism. Cirrhosis, with all its complications, is encountered in about 10 percent of all alcoholics. Its etiology is unknown. Its occurrence in nonalcoholics mitigates against the view that it reflects only the hepatotoxic effects of alcohol. When cirrhosis occurs in alcoholics, it is typically in individuals who have been heavy drinkers for a number of years.

THE NERVOUS SYSTEM

A primary means by which chronic abuse of alcohol causes disturbances in the central and peripheral nervous systems is through alcohol-related thiamine deficiency. The reason some alcoholics have this specific vitamin deficiency is not entirely clear. Chronic alcohol use may lead to increased utilization of thiamine, so that the amount of thiamine in a previously adequate diet becomes insufficient; chronic alcohol use may result in poor absorption of thiamine; alcoholics may be malnourished because of poor dietary habits, and thiamine deficiency may simply be the most obvious result of this malnourishment; or there may be a genetic predisposition in some alcoholics to develop functional thiamine deficiency. Most likely, a combination of these factors, and perhaps others that have not yet been considered, is responsible for the sequelae of thiamine deficiency often observed in long-term alcoholics. Several nervous system disorders that have been described in alcoholics have been attributed to thiamine deficiency.

Alcoholic Polyneuropathy. First and most severely affected in this disorder are the distal portions of the legs, where numbness and pain may develop. In some instances, however, these symptoms may be absent and the diagnosis can be made on the basis of muscular wasting, calf tenderness, signs of impaired motor and sensory innervation, and reduced knee and ankle jerks. Progression of signs and symptoms to the upper extremities may occur in time, and contractures and paralyses may also develop. Even partial recovery may require years, and permanent changes are frequent. Though this syndrome is most likely the result of a vitamin deficiency (most probably thiamine), its etiology remains uncertain. Alcohol itself may have some neurotoxic properties (Haas and Sumner, 1989).

Alcohol Amblyopia. Amblyopia is a bilateral and symmetrical loss of visual acuity for both near and far objects, characterized by a painless blurring of vision, central scotomata, and papillitis. A relatively infrequent occurrence among alcoholics, it stems from nutritional inadequacies, particularly of vitamins, and has been seen in prisoners of war who suffered from malnutrition. The disease is readily reversible in most cases with adequate nutrition (Dreyfus, 1974).

Wernicke's Encephalopathy and Korsakoff's Psychosis. Both Wernicke's encephalopathy and Korsakoff's psychosis appear to be related to thiamine deficiency. They have been known as Wernicke-Korsakoff's syndrome, although the presenting symptoms for the two diseases are quite different. The diseases can be identified on autopsy by specific brain lesions, particularly in the mammillary bodies and periventricular regions, that appear in 2 to 4 percent of all autopsies and in over 25 percent of autopsies of known alcoholics (Martin and Eckhardt, 1985).

The presenting symptoms of Wernicke's encephalopathy include ataxia of gait, mental confusion and disorientation, and, in severe states, hypothermia and coma. Ocular disturbances were once thought to be extremely frequent in Wernicke's encephalopathy (Victor and Adams, 1953) but are found less frequently in current reports (Martin and Eckhardt, 1985). Because of the possibility of Wernicke's encephalopathy, a known alcoholic who appears in the emergency room with ataxia, or coma and hypothermia, should receive an injection of thiamine, along with supportive therapy. If the patient is suffering from Wernicke's encephalopathy rather than alcohol intoxication, the vitamin should reverse these presenting symptoms.

Unfortunately, the symptoms of Korsakoff's psychosis, although also due to vitamin deficiencies, are not readily reversed. These symptoms are primarily memory disturbances. The patient is unable to remember events that occurred a short time before and may lack recall for distant events. He may confabulate, telling marvelous but disjointed stories that appear to be attempts to hide his inability to remember. There is little clouding of consciousness or impairment of intellectual functioning in Korsakoff's disease, although these signs of dementia can occur independently in alcoholics (see later) and can complicate the picture.

Chronic Organic Brain Syndrome. Chronic organic brain syndrome is a true dementia (i.e., an organically based loss of intellectual abilities such as memory, abstract thinking, judgment, or problem solving, or personality changes) that appears as a direct result of alcohol neurotoxicity or as a secondary effect of alcohol abuse. It may be accompanied by dysphasias or apraxias, EEG abnormalities, and such structural changes in the brain as cerebellar and/or cerebral atrophy and ventricular dilatation. The syndrome is relatively common in alcoholics (approximately 9 percent) and is the second most common cause of adult dementia (10 percent) (after Alzheimer's disease—40 to 60 percent) (Martin and Eckhardt, 1985).

Although Wernicke-Korsakoff's disease and chronic organic brain syndrome are described as separate phenomena with apparently distinct causes, most alcoholics with cognitive impairment suffer from some degree of both types of syndromes. Alcohol detoxification should be accompanied by nutritional supplementation. In most cases, some improvement will result, although it will in all likelihood be incomplete.

Although the severe nervous system effects of chronic alcohol abuse are fairly rare, more subtle forms of behavioral impairment are probably more common than was previously thought. Recent data suggest that almost half of detoxified, chronic alcoholics are impaired in their problem solving, perception, and memory skills (Moore, 1987).

Mortality

Ingestion of large quantities of alcohol can result in death. About one third of the deaths attributed to alcohol result from respiratory paralysis produced by an acute dose of alcohol, usually in individuals who are already quite intoxicated. The typical findings on autopsy are edema at the base of the brain and hyperemia of the gastric mucosa (Harney and Harger, 1965). Alcohol in combination with other drugs, particularly other sedative drugs, can be particularly lethal.

Despite the dangers of alcohol overdose, greater alcohol-related mortality results from automobile accidents, private plane and boat accidents, and drownings. The National Highway Traffic Safety Administration estimated in 1988 that nearly one half of fatal motor vehicle accidents were alcohol-related (Fatal Accident Reporting System, 1988), and accidents related to alcohol consumption are a leading cause of death in young adults.

BARBITURATE AND NONBARBITURATE SEDATIVE-HYPNOTICS

After alcohol, the CNS depressants currently subject to most frequent abuse are the barbiturates. Nonbarbiturate sedative hypnotics such as glutethimide (Doriden), ethinamate (Valmid), ethchlorvynol (Placidyl), and methaqualone (Quaalude, Ludes) are also abused, but to a lesser extent, perhaps because of their limited availability. Abuse of such older nonbarbiturate hypnotics as chloral hydrate and paraldehyde no longer poses a significant problem, in part because they are irritating to the mucosa and stomach and have an unpleasant taste and odor. The issue of abuse of the benzodiazepines, nonbarbiturate drugs used in the treatment of anxiety and insomnia, has received considerable public and scientific attention and is discussed in detail in the last section of this chapter.

Patterns of Use

Sedative-hypnotic drugs seem to be more likely than most drugs of abuse to be taken in combination with other psychoactive drugs. The combination of glutethimide and codeine, taken orally ("Loads"), for example, is currently popular among opioid users who may not have ready access to high-quality heroin. "Loads" have apparently replaced "Ts and Blues" (tripelennamine and pentazocine) as the heroin substitute of choice (see Chapter 3). Methadone-maintenance clients often take very high doses of diazepam along with their methadone, reportedly to "boost the high" they get from the opiate, and the combination of sedatives and stimulants is popular among stimulant abusers. Not surprisingly, the drug that is used most frequently in combination with sedative-hypnotics is alcohol. Thus, although there are drug abusers who prefer sedative-hypnotics to other illicit drugs, abuse of this class of compounds may be more prevalent in users who enjoy the "edge" they put on the subjective effects of other psychoactive drugs.

Barbiturates are widely used as "downers"—drugs that can bring one down from a state of normal consciousness or from a state of abnormal excitation produced by stimulant drugs. Thus, they may be taken when the user wants to sleep after a prolonged and exhausting "high" from amphetamine or cocaine, or when he becomes disturbed by the motor manifestations that develop when repeated doses of stimulants are taken at short intervals.

One of the most recent outbreaks of drug abuse involved the sedative-hypnotic drug methaqualone. The short but dramatic story of methaqualone abuse is unfortunately not unique. Methaqualone synthesis was the serendipitous result of an Indian search for antimalarial drugs. The drug's hypnotic actions were quickly recognized and it was promoted as an effective treatment for insomnia. It was advertised extensively to physicians as having distinct advantages over the more commonly used barbiturate hypnotics: It was reported to have a more rapid onset of action, little or no suppression of REM sleep, greater safety, and less abuse potential. The list is reminiscent of the list of the advantages heroin had been reported to have over morphine nearly a century earlier! Because its safety was widely touted, methaqualone's availability was not carefully controlled (Schedule V—unlimited prescription refills in the United States, over the counter in Japan) and abuse of the drug began almost as soon as it came on the market. Methaqualone's popularity was probably enhanced by its reputed aphrodisiac effects. Although some research indicated that the drug had such effects, they were most likely the result of the decrease in inhibitions that most sedative drug produce. Although the drug was rescheduled in the early 1980s to restrict its availability, its abuse continued unabated until the drug was taken off the market completely (Ionescu-Pioggia et al., 1988).

There is no excuse for this mistake to have happened this late in our experience with drug abuse. Excellent procedures have been developed to determine whether a drug is liable to be abused. In the instance of methaqualone, such studies demonstrated that people with histories of drug abuse preferred this sedative over any other sedative-hypnotic tested (Ionescu-Pioggia et al., 1988). Unfortunately, these tests were conducted only after the drug had been marketed and after problems of abuse had become evident. Evaluation of the reinforcing effects of drugs in both humans and animals is a critical part of premarketing drug development and can be used to protect the public from this type of "industrial accident."

The genesis of sedative-hypnotic abuse is probably similar to the genesis of most other forms of drug abuse: The drug is made available through peers or pushers to young people who find it easy to accept or difficult to decline the drug offer. For some of these people, probably because of both environmental and genetic factors, the drug has reinforcing effects and the youth continue to seek it out and take it. This scenario is more plausible than the one that describes sedative abusers as people who were given prescriptions for a drug and who began taking more than was prescribed, finding other sources for prescriptions, and escalating their intake to high levels. Although some patients undoubtedly misuse prescribed sedative-hypnotics, this is more likely due to drug-induced confusion about the amounts already taken, to drug-induced rebound insomnia that encourages more frequent use of hypnotics, and to suicide attempts by those who would not otherwise be classified as drug abusers. With the advent of benzodiazepine hypnotics, which are effective but much safer that barbiturates when taken in high doses, these latter types of misuse have declined substantially. Yet sedative abuse apparently continues much as before.

Among the sedative hypnotics, in recent history, barbiturates have been subject to abuse most frequently, and considerable information about their abuse is available. The remaining discussion will therefore be concerned primarily with the barbiturates; much of the information is applicable to other abused sedative-hypnotic drugs.

Effects of Sedative-Hypnotics

The intoxication produced by barbiturates and other sedative-hypnotic drugs is difficult to distinguish from that produced by alcohol if one cannot detect the odor of alcohol on the breath of the user. Sedative-hypnotics have a capacity similar to alcohol's to release inhibited behavior, and this may account for the increase in aggressive behavior observed in people intoxicated with sedative-hypnotics.

In contrast to alcoholics, barbiturate abusers show stimulation rather than decreases in appetite and do not appear to suffer from malnutrition and malabsorptive phenomena. Thus, organic brain disease, Wernicke-Korsakoff syndrome, polyneuropathies, and G.I. disorders are not associated with barbiturates abusers who do not abuse alcohol concomitantly.

Although barbiturates, like alcohol, are generally thought to have only depressant effects on the central nervous system, many of them produce stimulation prior to the onset of depressant effects. This is particularly obvious when the drugs are given intravenously in doses necessary to produce anesthesia. A paradoxical period of excitement may occur before the subject relaxes into deeper stages of anesthesia. Some compounds with a typical barbiturate structure actually have no depressant effects at all but are convulsants. In some barbiturates, a levorotatory isomer produces sedation, whereas the dextrorotatory isomer produces excitation.

The lethal effects of the most commonly abused sedative-hypnotics result from suppression of respiration; prior to profound respiratory depression, the user passes through increasing levels of intoxication to unconsciousness. Treatment of overdose with barbiturate and nonbarbiturate sedative-hypnotics is primarily supportive. Once any remaining drug has been removed from the patient's stomach, dialysis can assist in removing the drug more rapidly from the blood, but nothing more than assistance in respiration and thermoregulation has proven to speed recovery.

It is interesting, given what is currently thought to be the mechanism of central action of barbiturates, that there is no good, selective antagonist of barbiturate effects. As described in the section on alcohol, barbiturates are thought to have a receptor site on the GABA–benzodiazepine receptor complex. This site is distinct from that of the benzodiazepines but results in much the same effect, that of enhancing the inhibitory effects of GABA. Picrotoxin, a naturally occurring convulsant drug, also binds to this site and acts as an antagonist to barbiturates in electrophysiologic preparations. It is not an effective barbiturate antagonist in the intact animal, however.

Absorption, Distribution, and Metabolism

When taken with the stomach empty, most sedative and hypnotic drugs are rapidly absorbed into the body in the upper portion of the small intestine. Such longer-acting barbiturates as phenobarbital are absorbed more slowly than the more rapidly acting agents (e.g., secobarbital), which explains, in part, users' typical preference for the latter type of barbiturate. The rate of absorption of glutethimide (Doriden) is often erratic, probably because it is so poorly soluble in aqueous solutions.

In contrast to alcohol, about 30 to 40 percent of the barbiturate in blood is bound to plasma protein; thus, drug concentrations in such protein-poor fluids such as cerebrospinal fluid are always less than those in blood. The extent of intracellular protein binding of these drugs roughly approximates that of plasma binding. The water–lipid coefficients for barbiturates are much lower than those for alcohol and differ among the various barbiturates. Those with lower partition coefficients have a more rapid onset of action and a briefer duration of effect (Harvey, 1985). The reasons for this are the same as described earlier for alcohol. More rapidly acting barbiturates readily enter a variety of tissues, including the brain, and are then quickly redistributed into skeletal muscle, depot fat, and the liver (where they are inactivated). Barbiturates also cross the placenta, and a diffusion equilibrium between maternal and fetal blood is established.

The intoxicating effects of the commonly abused barbiturates ordinarily last from four to five hours. To remain continuously intoxicated, therefore, abusers have to take three to four doses of short-acting barbiturates in the course of each day. Though the sensation of intoxication may be gone within hours, it has been observed experimentally that cumulative effects develop upon such a schedule of administration; the severity of neurologic disturbances, it was noted, was minimal in the morning, increased throughout the day, and became maximal in the late evening (Isbell et al., 1950).

The action of the commonly abused barbiturates is terminated principally by means of hepatic metabolism; essentially no unchanged barbiturate appears in the urine. If a hypnotic dose of secobarbital is given to a drug-naive individual, the drug, after reaching equilibrium, disappears from the plasma at a rate equivalent to approximately 2.5 percent of the dose per hour. Inactivation is accomplished principally by mixed-function oxidases located in the endoplasmic reticulum ("microsomes") of hepatic cells. The reaction typically entails oxidation of the larger of the two substituent groups attached to the barbituric acid nucleus at carbon 5; a polar alcohol, ketone, phenol, or carboxylic acid is produced, which appears in urine unchanged or as a glucuronide (Harvey, 1985).

Tolerance

As with alcohol, evidence exists that tissue tolerance can develop to barbiturates, but it has not been well characterized and is not thought to be an effect of large magnitude. There is generally assumed to be little or no tolerance to the lethal effects of barbiturates. There is, however, a substantial metabolic tolerance to the intermediate and short-acting barbiturates. In the process of metabolic degradation, barbiturates enhance the biosynthesis of the hepatic microsomal enzymes responsible for their inactivation. Thus, not only barbiturates, but the many other drugs that are metabolized through this mechanism will be degraded much more rapidly (Harvey, 1985). This type of tolerance will not change the amount of drug necessary to produce a given effect, but it will dramatically shorten the duration of the drug's action. This can be especially dangerous when barbiturates are used chronically for the treatment of insomnia. With the induction of drug-metabolizing enzymes, the hypnotic duration of the drug shortens. Not only does the patient awaken in the middle of the night, unable to return to sleep, but he is likely to experience rebound insomnia. With rebound insomnia, the sleep difficulties are much worse than they were prior to medication; the phenomenon may represent the very early stages of withdrawal. Since the patient expects the hypnotic drug to relieve his insomnia problems, he may take higher doses or take the drug more frequently. This may serve only to worsen the problem of rebound insomnia, and the patient is unwittingly caught in a vicious cycle involving escalating intake of a dangerous drug.

Physiologic Dependence and the Withdrawal Syndrome

The parameters of physiologic dependence to barbiturates have been fairly well elaborated. As with alcohol and opioids, the severity of dependence that develops with chronic administration of barbiturates depends on the dose of the drug and the duration of drug administration. Dependence can be obtained more rapidly with administration of large doses; dependence becomes progressively more severe with increased duration of drug administration, presumably up to some maximum level of severity (Okamoto and Hinman, 1984).

The barbiturate withdrawal syndrome is very much like that of alcohol withdrawal beginning with tremors and diaphoresis and progressing through hallucinosis to convulsions and delirium. It can be fatal. The rate of development of barbiturate withdrawal signs depends on the duration of action of the drug. Termination of chronic administration of a short-acting barbiturate will be followed quickly by the onset of withdrawal signs, whereas longer-acting barbiturates may have a delayed and protracted course of withdrawal.

BENZODIAZEPINES AND OTHER
MINOR TRANQUILIZERS

Minor tranquilizers are prescribed primarily in the treatment of anxiety and, to a lesser extent, of insomnia. The first drug that could properly be called a minor tranquilizer was meprobamate, which came on the market in 1955. It was found to produce problems of abuse that were at least as severe as those produced by barbiturates, and its effectiveness was no better than that of the benzodiazepines, which became available in the early 1960s. Meprobamate is not widely used at the present time, although prescriptions of meprobamate may escalate as tighter controls are placed on benzodiazepines.

Effects of Benzodiazepines

The benzodiazepines, beginning with chlordiazepoxide (Librium) in 1960, followed by diazepam (Valium) in 1963, and subsequently by nine other benzodiazepines marketed in this country for anxiety and insomnia, are among the most widely prescribed drugs in the world. They have several advantages over the barbiturates in treatment of anxiety and insomnia. One is that they can reduce anxiety across a much wider dose range. Thus, it is easier to find a dose of a benzodiazepine that relieves anxiety without producing sleep than it is to find such a dose of a barbiturate. The advantage they have over barbiturates in the treatment of insomnia is that they do not, on chronic administration, produce increased rates of their own metabolism and a shortened duration of action. Although short-acting benzodiazepines (e.g., triazolam) can also produce rebound insomnia, the mechanism is different and the effect is not as severe as it is with barbiturates. Longer-acting benzodiazepines (e.g., flurazepam) do not appear to produce rebound insomnia (Woods et al., 1987).

The greatest benefit the benzodiazepines have over the barbiturates is their margin of safety. Whereas overdoses of barbiturates have been responsible for a large number of accidental deaths, as well as successful suicide attempts, overdoses of benzodiazepines used alone are almost never fatal. On the other hand, benzodiazepines can enhance the sedation produced by other CNS depressants. Such combinations, especially with alcohol, are frequent and are associated with greater risks than the sedation produced by either drug alone.

Patterns of Use

In view of the relative safety of the benzodiazepines and of the assumption, when these drugs were first marketed, that they did not share the dependence potential of the barbiturates, it is not surprising that the benzodiazepines quickly became very popular for treatment of anxiety and related problems. Diazepam was among the 10 most frequently prescribed drugs from the early 1970s to the early 1980s (Baum et al., 1985); during this time, about 9 percent of the adult population of the United States was taking tranquilizers in the course of a year (Mellinger and Balter, 1987). The number of annual prescriptions for benzodiazepine tranquilizers peaked in 1973 (87 million) (Baum et al., 1982), declined until 1981 (55 million) (Baum et al., 1984), and increased slightly after that date (61 million in 1986) (Baum et al., 1987). The widespread use of benzodiazepines raised fears that the country might become "overtranquilized" and that many of those using the drugs might be abusing them. These fears were voiced both in scientific publications and in the public media, particularly around the mid-1970s.

Although it is possible that benzodiazepines have been overprescribed, a recent review of the literature (Woods et al., 1987) indicates that these drugs are not subject to widespread abuse. Numerous studies, both in animals and in normal and anxious humans, have shown that benzodiazepines have little reinforcing effects. Both normal volunteers and anxious patients, given a benzodiazepine for several days and then allowed to take the drug ad libitum, usually choose not to continue to take the drug. Household surveys of drug abuse also find very low rates of abuse of benzodiazepines among the general population (Woods et al., 1987).

People who are more likely to abuse benzodiazepines are people who have abused alcohol or other psychoactive drugs. Experiments in drug preference have found that sedative abusers generally prefer short-acting barbiturates over benzodiazepines but will accept most benzodiazepines in preference to a placebo. Opioid users, particularly those on methadone maintenance, take large doses of diazepam (and perhaps other benzodiazepines) to increase the effect of the opioid. Recent evidence indicates that cocaine users also use diazepam to counter the unwanted aftereffects of the stimulant—which may represent the modern version of the well-known use of barbiturates by amphetamine abusers of a previous generation. Thus, the physician who is considering prescribing a tranquilizer for an anxious patient should be particularly careful to determine whether the patient has a prior or current history of alcohol or drug abuse.

Tolerance and Physiologic Dependence

Since benzodiazepines are sometimes prescribed for chronic administration, there has been an opportunity to gain clinical impressions of the development of tolerance to the effects of these drugs. It is generally acknowledged that tolerance to the sedative effects develops rapidly with these drugs. It is commonly assumed that less tolerance develops to the capacity of these drugs to reduce anxiety; unfortunately, this assumption has not been subjected to rigorous evaluation, and it is therefore unclear whether there is any benefit from taking these drugs on a daily basis for long periods of time to reduce problems of anxiety.

The benzodiazepines can produce a fairly profound, apparently dose-related disruption of the process of remembering. These effects on memory are clinically useful when the drugs are given in large doses as preanesthetics; they are more of a liability in patients who take smaller doses of benzodiazepines for treatment of anxiety and insomnia. The literature indicates that some people who take these drugs on a chronic basis still complain of memory disturbances, suggesting that little tolerance develops to these effects (Woods et al., 1987).

Although psychologic dependence to benzodiazepines does not appear to occur in many patients who have no prior or current problem with abuse of other drugs, physiologic dependence on benzodiazepines does develop in patients and is *not* limited to those with a history of drug abuse. Most patients who take benzodiazepines on a daily basis for three months or longer run the risk of developing physiologic dependence on the drugs. On abrupt cessation of drug administration—perhaps three or more days later, depending on the duration of action of the drug—withdrawal signs may begin to develop. The signs are similar to those of alcohol or barbiturate withdrawal (anxiety, tremor, insomnia) but are usually less severe (convulsions and delirium tremens are rare). Many of the signs of benzodiazepine withdrawal are much like the symptoms for which the drug was originally prescribed. There are also signs that seem specific to benzodiazepine withdrawal, including strange tastes and smells and feelings of depersonalization. These signs can be unpleasant and can be relieved by resuming drug administration. For dependent people, then, development of withdrawal signs may make it difficult to stop taking the drug (Woods et al., 1987). Nevertheless, these people cannot be regarded as "addicts" in the traditional sense of the word, since they usually have little or no craving for the psychologic effects of the drug, simply a need to take it to reduce the dysphoria they feel when withdrawal signs develop. If a decision is made to discontinue benzodiazepine treatment after several months of continued administration, the physician should reduce the dose of the drug very gradually over time and provide support and guidance in working through any withdrawal signs that may develop. Once the drug has been discontinued for a period of several months, the patient can be reevaluated for the original symptoms of anxiety or insomnia. The patient and physician in concert can then decide whether to reinstate drug therapy, perhaps with frequent "drug holidays" to reduce the risk that dependence will redevelop; to switch to another drug that may have less potential for dependence; or to try a course of nondrug therapy.

Other Minor Tranquilizers

New nonbenzodiazepine anxiolytic drugs have been on the market in Europe for several years and are now becoming available by prescription in the United States. The first of these, buspirone, is quite different, in both chemistry and pharmacology, from the benzodiazepines or barbiturates. Buspirone does not produce CNS depression, does not synergize with alcohol, and has little, if any, abuse or dependence potential. It is not clear whether it will prove as effective as the earlier drugs in treating anxiety. Even if it is effective only in alleviating minor anxiety in patients with no prior experience with benzodiazepines, however, it could become an important psychotherapeutic drug. Given the huge market for drugs that reduce anxiety and promote sleep, it is nearly certain that drug companies will continue to attempt to develop more drugs for this condition and we can look forward to the opportunity to evaluate drugs from a variety of chemical classes in the future.

REFERENCES

Baum, C., M. B. Forbes, D. L. Kennedy. Psychotherapeutic drug use: 1973–1983. Presented at the American Psychological Convention Annual Convention. Toronto, 24 Aug., 1984

Baum, C., D. L. Kennedy, M. B. Forbes, and J. K. Jones. *Drug Utilization in the U.S.— 1981: Third Annual Review,* Food and Drug Administration, U.S. Dept. of Health and Human Services, Rockville, Md., 1982

Baum, C., D. L. Kennedy, D. E. Knapp, G. A. Faich, and C. Anello. *Drug Utilization in the U.S.—1986: Eighth Annual Review* USPHS Publication No. PB88-146527. National Technical Information Service, Springfield, Va., 1987

Baum, C., D. L. Kennedy, D. Knapp, J. P. Juergens, and G. A. Faich. *Drug Utilization in the U.S.—1981: Sixth Annual Review,* USPHS Publication No. PB86-179181, National Technical Information Service, Springfield, Va., 1985

Baum-Baicker, C. The health benefits of moderate alcohol consumption: A review of the literature. *Drug Alcohol Dep* 15:207, 1985

Cadoret, R. J., C. A. Cain, and W. M. Grove. Development of alcoholism in adoptees raised apart from their alcoholic biologic relatives. *Arch Gen Psychiat* 1980:37, 561

DeWit, H., J. Pierri, and C. E. Johanson. Assessing individual differences in alcohol preference using a cumulative dosing procedure. *Psychopharmacology* 98:113, 1989

Dimango, E. P. Pancreatitis. In: Kelley, W. N., editor-in-chief, *Textbook of Internal Medicine.* Philadelphia: J.B. Lippincott, 1989, p. 579

Dreyfus, P. M. Diseases of the nervous system in chronic alcoholics. In: Kissin, B., and H. Begleiter, eds., *The Biology of Alcoholism, Vol 3: Clinical Pathology.* New York: Plenum, 1974, p. 265

Fatal Accident Reporting System, 1988: A review of information on fatal traffic crashes in the United States in 1988. National Highway Safety Administration. Washington, D.C.: U.S. Government Printing Office, 1989

Fillmore, K. M. *Alcohol Use Across the Life Course: A Critical Review of 70 Years of International Longitudinal Research.* Toronto: Addiction Research Foundation, 1988

Goldstein, D. B. *Pharmacology of Alcohol.* New York: Oxford University Press, 1983

Goodwin, D. W., F. Schulsinger, L. Hermansen, S. B. Guze, and G. Winokur. Alcohol problems in adoptees raised apart from alcoholic biological parents. *Arch Gen Psychiat* 28:238, 1973

Haas, L. F., and A. J. Sumner. Diseases of the peripheral nervous system. In: Kelley, W. N., editor-in-chief, *Textbook of Internal Medicine.* Philadelphia: J.B. Lippincott, 1989, p. 2433

Haefly, W., E. Kyburz, M. Gerecke, and H. Mohler. Recent advances in the molecular pharmacology of the benzodiazepine receptors and in the structure-activity relationships of their agonists and antagonists. *Adv Drug Res* 14:164, 1985

Harney, R. B., and R. N. Harger. The alcohols. In: DiPalma, J. R., ed., *Drill's Pharmacology in Medicine,* 3rd ed. New York: McGraw-Hill, 1965, p. 210

Harvey, S. C. Hypnotics and sedatives. In: Gilman, A. G., L. S. Goodman, T. W. Rall, and F. Murad, eds., *Goodman and Gilman's The Pharmacological Basis of Therapeutics,* 7th ed. New York: Macmillan, 1985, p. 339

Helzer, J. E., G. J. Canino, H-G. Hwu, R. C. Bland, S. Newman, and E-K. Yeh. Alcoholism: A cross-national comparison of population surveys with the Diagnostic Interview Schedule. In: Rose, R. M., and J. E. Barrett, eds., *Alcoholism: Origins and Outcome.* New York: Raven, 1988, p. 31

Ionescu-Pioggia, M., M. Bird, M.H. Orzack, F. Benes, B. Beake, and J. O. Cole. Methaqualone. *Int Clin Psychopharmacol* 3:97, 1988

Isbell, H., S. Altschul, C. H. Kornetsky, A. J. Eisenman, H. G. Flanary, and H. F. Fraser. Chronic barbiturate intoxication. *Arch Neurol Psychiat* 64:1, 1950

Isbell, H., H. F. Fraser, A. Wikler, R. E. Belleville, and A. J. Eisenman. An experimental study of the etiology of "rum fits" and delirium tremens. *Quart J Stud Alcohol* 16:1, 1955

Jaffe, J. H. Drug addiction and drug abuse. In: Gilman, A. G., L. S. Goodman, T. W. Rall, and F. Murad, eds., *Goodman and Gilman's The Pharmacological Basis of Therapeutics,* 7th ed. New York: Macmillan, 1985, p. 532

Jellinek, E. M. *The Disease Concept of Alcoholism.* New Haven: Hillhouse Press, 1960

Johnston, L. D., P. M. O'Malley, and J. G. Bachman. Drug use, drinking, and smoking: National survey results from high school, college, and young adult populations 1975–1988. National Institute on Drug Abuse. Washington, D.C.: U.S. Government Printing Office, 1989

Lieber, C. S. Ethanol: A twenty year evolution from an "empty" calory engendering malnutrition to a toxic drug. *Acta Gastro-enterol Belg* 48:257, 1977

Martin, P. R., and M. J. Eckhardt. Pharmacological interventions in chronic organic brain syndromes associated with alcoholism. In: Naranjo, C. A., and E. M. Sellers, eds., *Research Advances in New Psychopharmacological Treatments for Alcoholism: Proceedings of the Symposium,* Toronto, 4–5 Oct. 1984. New York: Elsevier, 1985, 295

Mello, N. K., and J. H. Mendelson. Drinking patterns during work-contingent and noncontingent alcohol acquisition. *Psychosom Med* 34:139, 1972

Mendelson, J. H., and N. K. Mello. Experimental analysis of drinking behavior of chronic alcoholics. *Ann NY Acad Sci* 133:828, 1966

Meyer, R. E. Overview of the concept of alcoholism. In: Rose, R. M., and J. E. Barrett, eds., *Alcoholism: Origins and Outcome.* New York: Raven, 1988, p. 1

Moore, D. T. Alcoholic brain damage and behavior. *Alcohol, Drug Abuse, and Mental Health (ADAMA) News,* 13:10, 1987

Morris, H. H., III and M. L. Estes. Traveler's amnesia transient global amnesia secondary to triazolam. *J Amer Med Assoc* 258:945, 1987

Moskowitz, H., and Burns, M. The effects of alcohol and Valium, singly and in combination, upon driving related skills performance. In: Huelke, D., ed., *Proceedings of the 21st Conference of the American Association for Automotive Medicine.* Morton Grove, IL: American Association for Automotive Medicine, 1977

Nathan, P. E., and J. J. O'Brien. An experimental analysis of behavior of alcoholics and nonalcoholics during prolonged experimental drinking: A necessary precursor of behavioral therapy? *Behav Therap* 2:455, 1971

Okamoto, M., and J. J. Hinman. Barbiturate tolerance and physical dependence: Contribution of pharmacological factors. *NIDA Research Monograph* 54, DHHS. Washington, D.C.: U.S. Government Printing Office, 1984, p. 333

Robins, L. N., J. E. Helzer, T. R. Przybeck, and D. A. Regier. Alcohol Disorders in the Community: A Report from the Epidemiological Catchment Area. In: Rose, R. M., and J. E. Barrett, *Alcoholism: Origins and Outcome.* New York: Raven, 1988, p. 15

Rosett, H. L., L. Weinger, B. Zuckerman, S. McKinlay, and K. C. Edelin. Reduction of alcohol consumption during pregnancy with benefits to the newborn. *Alcohol Clin Exp Res* 4:178, 1980

Roueche, B. Cultural factors and drinking patterns. *Ann NY Acad Sci* 133:846, 1966

Rounsaville, B. J., and H. R. Kranzler. The DSM III-R Diagnosis of Alcoholism. In: Tasman, A., R. E. Hales, and A. J. Frances, eds., *Review of Psychiatry,* Vol. 8. Washington, D.C.: American Psychiatric Press, 1989, p. 323.

Sokol, R. J., J. Ager, S. Martier, S. Debanne, C. Ernhart, J. Kuzma, and S. Miller. Significant determinants of susceptibility to alcohol teratogenicity. *Ann NY Acad Sci* 477:87, 1986

Streissguth, A. P., P. P. Sampson, H. M. Barr, S. K. Claren, and D. C. Martin. Studying alcohol teratogenesis from the perspective of the fetal alcohol syndrome. *Ann NY Acad Sci* 477:63, 1986

Victor, M., and R. D. Adams. The effect of alcohol on the nervous system. *Res Publ Assoc Nerv Ment Dis* 32:526, 1953

Winger, G. D., and J. H. Woods. The reinforcing property of ethanol in the rhesus monkey. I. Initiation, maintenance, and termination of intravenous ethanol-reinforced responding. *Ann NY Acad Sci* 215:162, 1973

Woodruff, R. A., P. J. Clayton, C. R. Cloninger, and S. B. Guze. A brief method of screening for alcoholism. *Dis Nerv Syst* 37:434, 1976

Woods, J. H., J. L. Katz, and G. Winger. Abuse liability of benzodiazepines. *Pharm Rev* 39:251, 1987

CHAPTER 5

Depressants of the Central Nervous System: Volatile Solvent and Aerosol Inhalation

Abuse of volatile solvents and aerosols has not captured the attention and concern of the media or the general public in quite the way cocaine or heroin abuse has. In some ways, this is understandable. Solvent and aerosol abuse does not affect nearly as many people as does stimulant and opioid abuse, and most solvents and aerosols have not been thought to produce toxic effects of the order produced by stimulants. Furthermore, since most solvents and aerosols can be easily and inexpensively obtained legally, there is not a great deal of criminal behavior associated with the selling and purchasing of volatile substances. But there are aspects of solvent abuse that should be of continuing concern. One is that solvents are most likely to be used by the youngest members of the drug-abusing community. Boys as young as seven to 10 years of age, as well as young teenagers, are those most frequently found to be sniffing glue or gasoline. Although there are no definitive studies indicating that early exposure to the intoxicating effects of glue and other solvents leads to abuse of other drugs, it is naive to assume that experience with drug-induced euphoria at an early age will have no influence on the propensity of a young man to try other drugs at a later age. Additional concern should surround the increasing number of reports indicating that solvents such as toluene, once thought to have little toxic effect, may produce severe and perhaps permanent neurologic damage. Lastly, statistics indicate that abuse of solvents is not declining among high-school students, even though abuse of stimulants and marijuana are on the decline in this population. Of students who use inhalants at least once per year, there was an increase from 6.2 percent in 1983 to 7.1 percent in 1987 (Johnston et al., 1989). It is therefore important that abuse of this type of intoxicating substance be regarded as a serious problem, requiring the same types of educational and prevention programs as do the "harder" drugs of abuse.

Awareness of the consciousness-altering effects of inhaled compounds is not new. They were appreciated by primitive tribes that burned and inhaled incense and spices to produce mild intoxication as part of religious rituals. In modern times, drug abuse via the route of alveolar absorption dates back to the nitrous oxide and ether "jags" commonly indulged in shortly after the discovery of the euphoric and hallucinogenic properties of these anesthetic agents. Contemporary abuse of volatile substances was first recorded in the literature in 1951 with a description of gasoline sniffing in two boys (Clinger and Johnson, 1951). In subsequent years, increasing numbers of reports about many youths and some adults sniffing such fluids as model cements, lighter fluids, lacquer thinners, and cleaning solutions appeared (Press and Done, 1967). When aerosol products containing chlorofluorocarbons as propellant gases became available, these products were also used to produce intoxication, but inert gases have now largely replaced the environmentally damaging gases as propellants.

In the early 1960s glue sniffing became increasingly popular and a number of deaths related to this practice were reported. The Hobby Industry Association of America and concerned industries acted to remove the two most toxic solvents, benzene and carbon tetrachloride, from those commercially available products most apt to be sniffed or inadvertently inhaled in large amounts. Some companies in the United States, Western Europe, and Australia attempted to reduce sniffing of their products by adding noxious, irritating substances such as oil of mustard or by reducing solvent content. These practices tended to make the products less satisfactory for legitimate users and have been largely abandoned (Kerner, 1988).

The full scope of intentional solvent intoxication in the United States remains undetermined; unfortunately, there are few studies of drug abuse among the very young group. Abuse of volatile solvents is a critical problem in some poor communities, however. Isolated areas such as Native American reservations and small Hispanic enclaves seem particularly vulnerable to the practice of gasoline and glue sniffing, for reasons that are not clear. Studies of Native American young people reflect on the severity of the problem. Lifetime prevalence of inhalant abuse increased from 15 to 32 percent between 1975 and 1983 among adolescent Native Americans living on reservations. More recent measures indicate a decline in prevalence of inhalant abuse, as well as decreases in use of other drugs, but it is too soon to tell whether this trend will continue. Native American youth begin inhalant use when they are quite young, usually between ages 11 and 13. The products used are those most readily available: gasoline, used by 28.4 percent and glue, used by 22.6 percent of Native American adolescents (Beauvais and Oetting, 1988b).

Outside the United States the incidence of solvent abuse varies. Obtaining rigorous data on the prevalence of solvent abuse is quite difficult. Inhalant abusers do not frequently seek treatment, they may not be detected in student surveys if they have dropped out of school, and if they do not have a fixed place of residence, they are not included in general household surveys. Under these conditions, information is subject to considerable error.

Abuse of solvents is a fairly new phenomenon in Southeast Asia and the Pacific. Organic solvent abuse is beginning to be seen in Japan and there is a growing problem of inhalant abuse among the native and poor adolescents of Australia. There appears to be sporadic abuse of inhalants in central and southern Europe. Mexico, on the other hand, has reported wide use of inhalants; it is the drug of choice among extremely disadvantaged adolescents who work and often live on the streets of Mexico City. Twenty two percent of this population reported using inhalants on a daily basis (Medina-Mora and Ortiz, 1988). Inhalant abuse also appears to be a significant problem in many of the countries of Latin America (Medina-Mora, 1988).

PREPARATIONS USED

There are four main classes of inhalants subject to abuse:

1. Volatile solvents including gasoline, paint thinners, cleaning solutions, lighter fluid, and glue. The solvents responsible for the central nervous system effects of these substances are the aromatic and aliphatic hydrocarbons such as benzene, toluene, xylene, and naphthalene. Paint thinners may also contain the esters ethyl and propyl acetate or the ketones acetone and methyl butyl ketone.
2. Aerosols such as spray paint, containing the alcohols methanol, ethanol, or isopropanol.
3. Anesthetic agents including ether, chloroform, methylene chloride, trichloroethylene, and nitrous oxide. Some of these products may be abused by medical personnel who have access to them. Others are contained in oil and grease dissolvers where they are available to the general public.
4. Amyl, butyl, and isobutyl nitrite. Amyl nitrite is a very old vasodilator, used since 1867 to relieve the pain of angina pectoris. It was originally available in small, mesh-enclosed glass ampules, called pearls, that were designed to be crushed by the fingers. The popping sound that resulted caused them to be referred to as "poppers." Amyl nitrite was available only by prescription before 1960 and prescriptions for it have been required since 1969 (Newell et al., 1988). It has clinical use in the treatment of cyanide poisoning. Isobutyl nitrite, with similar pharmacologic properties, is used for a very dissimilar purpose, that of room odorizing (Schwartz, 1988).

All the preceding products contain one or more of a wide variety of volatile substances that have a generalized depressant effect upon the central nervous system similar to that of volatile general anesthetic agents. Toluene outdistances all other solvents in popularity because of its minimal irritant effects, not unpleasant odor, rapid vaporization, and supposedly "good high."

PATTERNS OF USE

Most reported volatile solvent sniffers are boys between the ages of 10 and 15 years. Many offenders are as young as seven or eight years old, however, and many girls and increasing numbers of adults are also known to follow this form of drug abuse. Inhalant use among boys tends to outnumber use among girls by a wide margin in most populations, although among Native American eighth graders, girls are slightly more likely than boys to use inhalants (Beauvais and Oetting, 1988b). Use appears to occur in episodes among the young, with use increasing when a new product suddenly becomes popular, and then declining (Beauvais and Oetting, 1988a). Usually, sniffing as a form of intoxication is given up by the mid-teens and is generally perceived by older adolescents as an unacceptably childish way of getting one's "kicks" (Press and Done, 1967).

Huffers (huffing is the term used if the material is inhaled through the mouth; if the material is inhaled through the nose, the procedure is usually called sniffing) of such semiliquid materials as glues and cements generally squeeze anywhere from one-third of a tube to five tubes of the preparation into the bottom of a paper or plastic bag. The opening of the bag is then held tightly over the mouth and sometimes the nose as well and the vapors are inhaled until the desired effect is produced or the solvent evaporates completely. Liquid materials may be inhaled either directly from the container or from saturated cloth, gauze, or cotton. The solvent-impregnated cloth may be held in the hand and placed over the mouth and nose; more often, it is placed in a bag and sniffed. Mexican street boys may place the material directly on their sleeve to inhale if they see police in the area. Sometimes, beer or wine is drunk to potentiate the effect.

Most aerosol breathers separate the propellant gas from the particulate contents. A variety of techniques has been employed to accomplish this; the can may be held in an inverted position, thus evacuating the gas only; the contents may be prefiltered through a washcloth or rag, theoretically allowing passage of the gas only; or, as with glue sniffing, the aerosol may be sprayed directly onto the sides of a plastic or paper bag, with the gaseous contents alone being inhaled. Other huffers resort to spraying the contents of the can directly into the mouth, without prefiltering.

Volatile solvents are often warmed by cupping the bag in the hands or even holding it over a radiator or hot plate to increase the solvent concentration. It has been estimated that this technique can result in vapor concentrations 50 times the maximum allowable industrial concentration (which for toluene is 200 parts per million). Up to 3.6 mg of toluene has been recovered from 100 ml of air in such a glue-containing paper bag (Press and Donne, 1967).

The huffer usually inhales from his own or, less often, a shared bag until the desired effect is produced; this usually occurs within a few minutes. He may continue to huff off and on perpetuating his state as long as the solvent supply lasts. Excessive, prolonged continuous sniffing of high vapor concentrations will ultimately result in unconsciousness. The user will then relax his grip, so the paper bag falls away from his mouth. Thus, unconsciousness can protect the user from deep respiratory depression, hypoxia, and death. This hazard, however, is greatly increased by the use of a plastic bag. Little ambient air enters the respiratory tract, since the plastic is nonporous and the seal between the mouth and bag is tight. A partial vacuum may even result. Hypoxia develops rapidly and if, in his stuporous state, the abuser fails to remove the bag from his face, he may die. Indeed, along with deaths attributable directly to the toxic effects of halogenated hydrocarbons in some aerosol propellants and cleaning solutions that produce cardiac arrest, plastic bag suffocation is a leading cause of death among volatile solvent sniffers.

Some youths gather for sniffing in groups of from three to ten persons of the same sex, whereas others may carry out their habit alone. Because of the pervasive tell-tale odor, group users, in particular, tend to seek out such areas as abandoned buildings and rooftops where they and their vapors will be undetected. Consequently, in northern cities there may be a decline in glue sniffing in winter months when such areas are physically uncomfortable and evaporation of the solvent is slowed because of the cold. Basements, school lavatories, and locker rooms, as well as an individual's bedroom, are also common locations. The discovery of rags, handkerchiefs, balloons, or plastic or paper bags containing dried films of solvent-containing products should alert parents or teachers. Another significant finding is that of a white powdery ring that appears around the mouth of the forgetful novice glue sniffer, where the bag was held and glue contacted the skin. Also, vapors may be readily smelled on the breath from some distance away for an hour or so after a sniffing episode.

There have been studies made of an unusually large number of adult toluene users in an area of Philadelphia (McSherry, 1988). These people, most between the ages of 20 and 28, come together on a daily basis, often for many hours of the day, to use their drugs, but are otherwise socially isolated. They appear to be on the bottom rung of the social ladder and are physically, sexually, and emotionally abused by each other and by other members of the drug-using community. Many of them are illiterate and have difficulty managing life tasks such as purchasing groceries, traveling on public transportation, and keeping appointments. They are often malnourished, have very poor personal hygiene, are often

lice infested, and have badly decayed teeth. It is not clear whether their inca-
pacities preceded or followed their chronic use of toluene, but it is clear that
they are among the most unfortunate victims of the street.

Gasoline sniffing is also done singly or in groups. Users are more likely to
sniff from a large container, such as the gasoline tank of an automobile, or a 5-
gallon container used to fill lawnmowers or other equipment.

The nitrites are typically inhaled directly from the vial. Nitrites are popular
among adolescents; a report on high school seniors in 1986 indicated that 9
percent of this group had used nitrites at least once "to get high" and that 0.5
percent used them daily (Schwartz, 1988). The pattern of nitrite use by young
people is probably not very different from the pattern of use of other volatile
substances by this group, although most users report inhaling nitrites in isolation
on occasion (Schwartz, 1988).

Nitrite use is not as limited to young people as is the use of glue, however.
Substance abusers in general show a prevalence rate of nitrite abuse of 22 percent
(Lange et al., 1988). Male homosexuals are another group among whom nitrite
use is quite popular; use occurs largely during overt sexual activity (Lange et
al., 1988).

EFFECTS OF VOLATILE SOLVENTS

All materials used in sniffing or huffing contain volatile or gaseous substances
that are primarily generalized central nervous system depressants. As with other
central nervous system depressants such as ethanol and barbiturates, volatile
substances such as toluene produce signs of stimulation at low doses and continuing depression to the point of unconsciousness and death as the dose increases.
Toluene is also like barbiturates and benzodiazepines in that, in rodent models,
it blocks the convulsant effects of pentylenetetrazol and increases rates of behavior that has been suppressed because of punishment (response-contingent delivery of an aversive stimulus) (Wood et al., 1984). Animals also indicate that
toluene has subjective effects like those of barbiturates and benzodiazepines
(Knisely et al., 1990). The onset of action of most solvents is rapid and their
duration of action is short. An exception to this generalization is acetone, which
has a slower onset and longer duration than most other abused solvents (Pyror,
1988). Slurred speech, ataxia, impaired judgment, and feelings of giddiness and
drunkenness accompanied by a marked sense of euphoria are experienced by
almost all users even at the time of their first episode of sniffing.

The immediate effects of euphoria, giddiness, ataxia, slurred speech, perceptual distortions, and so on, usually last for the duration of active sniffing and for
15 to 45 minutes thereafter. The user may then experience one or two hours of
drowsiness and stupor, with the depressant effects gradually wearing off; the
subject then returns to his usual state of consciousness. A number of unpleasant

side effects are also experienced both during use and for variable periods thereafter; these include photophobia, irritation of the eyes, diplopia, tinnitus, sneezing, rhinitis, coughing, nausea, vomiting, diarrhea, chest pain, and vague muscle and joint pains.

Nitrites, which cause profound vasodilation, produce a feeling of warmth and lightheadedness immediately upon inhalation. This phenomenon, called a "head rush" by adolescents, is brief but may result in loss of consciousness due to postural hypotension if the user is standing when he inhales the drug (Schwartz, 1988). The vasodilatory effects of the drug result in short-lived headaches and in pulsatile headaches that may last much longer.

HABITUAL USE OF VOLATILE SOLVENTS

Psychologic Dependence

Many users of volatile substances take the drug repeatedly, generally preferring to sniff a particular product (and even brand). Alternative substances are readily substituted, however, when the product of choice is not available. Compulsive, repeated sniffing has been reported in a number of studies. Indeed, one large-scale user is said to have inhaled up to 25 tubes of glue (21 cc each) daily (Press and Done, 1967).

Tolerance

Studies of the development of tolerance to toluene, nitrites, or other solvents and aerosols are infrequent and reports of tolerance are largely anecdotal. Although these reports support the position that tolerance may develop to the behavioral effects of solvents and aerosols, without carefully controlled studies using animal models, it is difficult to ascertain the parameters of tolerance, that is, the dose and frequency variables that might contribute to tolerance development, or the rate of tolerance development and disappearance. Of considerable interest is whether cross-tolerance exists between the various solvents and aerosols, and between these products and the barbiturates and ethanol, which they resemble.

Physiologic Dependence

There is little to suggest that the practice of volatile solvent inhalation results in physiologic dependence in humans. No substantial evidence of such dependence has been presented and the short duration of action of most solvents probably precludes its development. If physiologic dependence exists at all, it is very mild, occurs only rarely, and cannot be considered to be a significant part of the experience of the vast majority of sniffers. Studies in animals, particularly rodents, where the effects of continuous exposure to vapors from these products can be evaluated, will be helpful in establishing whether physiological dependence can be induced. Since many of these drugs have other pharmacologic actions in common with barbiturates and benzodiazepines, it would not be surprising to find that physiologic dependence with barbiturate-like withdrawal signs develops in these animal models.

TOXIC EFFECTS OF VOLATILE SOLVENTS: MORBIDITY AND MORTALITY

Most exposure to volatile solvents, either within an industrial setting or through abuse, is not exposure to a single substance. Solvents typically contain several volatile agents, which, in combination, may produce more or different toxic effects compared to exposure to a single solvent. In addition, heavy metals such as cadmium and lead are contained in spray paints and leaded gasoline and these metals can have nephrotoxic effects. Because of this exposure to a combination of volatile solvents, it is difficult for the investigator to determine the toxic nature of each one individually when examining the clinical literature.

Aliphatic Hydrocarbons

Hexane, petroleum naphtha, and petroleum distillates have been reported to cause peripheral neuropathy both among those who abuse gasoline and paint thinners and among those exposed in industrial environments. Both sensory and motor neuropathy have been observed, and the classic hexane syndrome includes microscopic evidence of axonal swelling, neurofilament accumulation in axons, and skeletal muscle atrophy (Sharp, 1988).

Acute excessive exposure to fumes of leaded gasoline has resulted in petechial and gross pulmonary hemorrhages, pneumonitis, and bronchitis in factory workers. Chronic industrial exposure may result in anemia, parethesias, neuritis, and cranial nerve paralysis. Lead poisoning produces severe neurologic disorders and is perhaps the most serious problem associated with gasoline sniffing. As lead is removed from gasoline to reduce environmental pollution, lead-induced neuropathies should decrease.

Aromatic Hydrocarbons

Benzene is markedly toxic, producing bone marrow aplasia, anemia, and necrosis or fatty degeneration of the heart, liver, and adrenal glands. Methylated benzenes have been shown to cause ototoxicity (Sharp, 1988).

Toluene is considerably less toxic than benzene, although it is not without hazard. Research on the neurologic toxicity of toluene is inadequate (Ron, 1986), but recent studies using magnetic resonance imaging of brain tissue indicate that a substantial proportion of chronic toluene abusers are at risk of developing atrophy of cerebral, cerebellar, and brainstem white matter (Rosenberg et al., 1988). These neuroanatomic changes may be accompanied by neurologic and cognitive changes indicative of dementia (Filley et al., 1990), and young toluene abusers may be at increased risk of developing depressive illness (Zur and Yule, 1990). Chronic exposure to toluene may also lead to permanent damage to kidney, liver, heart, and lung (Marjot and McLeod, 1989).

Studies of the effects of chronic exposure to toluene in rodents have demonstrated ototoxicity as virtually the only change (Pyror, 1988). Some care must, therefore, be taken in attributing all the damage observed in human toluene abusers to the effects of toluene alone, since, as mentioned earlier, there could be other agents that the humans are exposed to that either enhance the toxic effects of toluene or have toxic effects of their own.

Studies of adult toluene abusers in a Philadelphia area, mentioned earlier, indicate that they may be severely incapacitated, perhaps because of their drug use. Those who have used the drug chronically for five to 15 years tend to show the most severe signs of mental and physical deterioration. They have slow and/or slurred speech; tremors of the hands, feet, and eyelids are frequently observed; their attention span is short; and major physical problems involving the liver, kidneys, or brain are found in many of these people (McSherry, 1988).

Halogenated Hydrocarbons

Trichloroethylene can produce cardiac arrhythmias. This is a well-known hazard when it is used as a surgical anesthetic and it has, moreover, been responsible for several industrial deaths. Acute renal failure, myocarditis, and heart failure following inadvertent excessive exposure to trichloroethylene (as a tile cement solvent) have been described rarely. Hepatic cell dysfunction and hepatomegaly have also been found through industrial exposure and, on occasion, among sniffers of cleaning fluids containing trichlorethylene and trichloroethane (Litt and Cohen, 1969).

The consequences of sniffing trichloroethylene and 1,1,1-trichoroethane, the volatile solvents of many cleaning fluids, have been infrequently studied. Presumably, this is because the incidence of their use is very low compared to that of toluene. A study of 10 adolescent cleaning fluid sniffers indicated that, whereas half were completely asymptomatic, abnormal liver function was found in the other half. Two of the five adolescents also showed kidney dysfunction and two had parasthesias, tinnitus, ataxia, and headaches (Litt and Cohen, 1969).

Trichlorofluoromethane, dichlorodifluoromethane, cryofluorane, and other fluorocarbons are substances that have wide application singly or in combination with other hydrocarbons as pressurized refrigerants and, until recently, as propellants for aerosol spray can products. Fluorocarbons have marked cardiotoxicity and have caused a number of deaths in the United States through induction of ventricular fibrillation and cardiac arrhythmias.

Carbon tetrachloride, chloroform, and ethylene dichloride are highly toxic, injuring all body cells; they can produce central nervous system edema with congestion and hemorrhage, edema of the lungs, heart, spleen, and kidneys, and fatty degeneration of the liver, as well as cardiac arrhythmias. As previously noted, these well-recognized hazards have resulted in the almost complete elimination of these solvents from currently available commercial products.

Ketones

Acetone, cyclohexanone, methyl ethyl ketone, and methyl isobutyl ketone are all highly irritating to mucous membranes and rarely produce any systemic effects other than central nervous system depression. Methyl *n*-butyl ketone has been linked to a severe peripheral neuropathy without reflexes, although other solvents, including toluene and hexane may have contributed to this disorder (Sharp, 1988). Methy ethyl ketone is less toxic than the *n*-butyl ketone, but apparently can enhance the neurotoxic effects of hexane and methyl *n*-butyl ketone (Pyror, 1988).

Esters

Ethyl acetate is said to produce liver and kidney damage, but no chronic toxicity has been found following industrial exposure. Amyl acetate and butyl acetate are not known to produce liver, kidney, or hematologic damage.

Alcohols

Butyl, ethyl, methyl, and isopropyl alcohols are not as volatile as most solvents and therefore are not particularly rewarding compounds for sniffing. Oral ingestion is a more effective route of administration. On inhalation, metabolism and toxicology are largely similar to those of ethyl alcohol. Isopropyl alcohol may cause central nervous system excitation as well as depression. Methyl alcohol must be assumed to be as capable of producing blindness by inhalation as by oral ingestion, but blindness has not been reported to occur from vapors. Liver, kidney, and blood abnormalities have not been reported from any form of alcohol inhalation.

Glycols

All the glycol compounds are highly irritating to mucous membranes and are only rarely implicated in sniffing. Ethylene glycol, found in antifreeze solutions, is metabolized to oxalic acid, which may, with prolonged exposure, give symptoms of oxalosis with impairment of liver and renal functions; it may produce permanent brain damage.

Methyl cellosolve acetate, a solvent used in some liquid plastic cements, produces significant liver and kidney damage.

Nitrites

Methemoglobinemia and normocytic normochromic anemia has been reported in people who are exposed to amyl or butyl nitrites in an industrial setting, but has not been reported among abusers. Studies in animals indicate that prolonged administration of these compounds can result in a number of disorders of the blood and blood-forming organs. Vital organs can suffer oxygen deprivation when maintained peripheral vasodilation causes pooling of blood in the legs and feet and impaired vascular return. Organic nitrites are mutagenic in tests in bacteria (the Ames test) and they are metabolized to N-nitroso compounds, which are among the most potent carcinogens known. In addition, isobutyl nitrite has immunosuppressive effects that may increase the risk of infectious disease and cancer among users (Newell et al., 1988).

A growing concern among homosexual nitrite users is that use of these carcinogenic and immunosuppressive drugs might increase the risk of developing AIDS and Kaposi's sarcoma. A considerable amount of research devoted to this question suggests that such a result is possible, but the contribution of the drug to these disease states is difficult to establish with certainty (Haverkos and Dougherty, 1988). Severe methemoglobinemia, which develops with inhalation of nitrites, can be rapid and malignant if these products are ingested. Death can result (Wood, 1988).

REFERENCES

Beauvais, F., and E. R. Oetting. Inhalant abuse by young children. In: Crider, R. A., and B. A. Rouse, eds., *Epidemiology of Inhalant Abuse: An Update.* NIDA Research Monograph 85, DHHS. Washington, D.C.: U.S. Government Printing Office, 1988a, p. 30

Beauvais, F., and E. R. Oetting. Indian youth and inhalants: an update. In: Crider, R. A. and B. A. Rouse, eds., *Epidemiology of Inhalant Abuse: An Update.* NIDA Research Monograph 85, DHHS. Washington, D.C.: U.S. Government Printing Office, 1988b, p. 34

Clinger, O. W., and N. A. Johnson. Purposeful inhalation of gasoline vapors. *Psychiat Quart* 25:557, 1951

Filley, C. M., R. K. Heaton, and N. L. Rosenberg. White matter dementia in chronic toluene abuse. *Neurology* 40:532, 1990

Haverkos, H. W. and J. A. Dougherty, eds., *Health Hazards of Nitrite Inhalants*. NIDA Research Monograph 83, DHHS. Washington, D.C.: U.S. Government Printing Office, 1988

Johnston, L. D., P. M. O'Malley, and J. G. Bachman. Drug use, drinking, and smoking: National survey results from high school, college, and young adult populations 1975–1988. National Institute on Drug Abuse. Washington, D.C.: U.S. Government Printing Office, 1989

Kerner, K. Current topics in inhalant abuse. In: Crider, R. A., and B. A. Rouse, eds., *Epidemiology of Inhalant Abuse: An Update*. NIDA Research Monograph 85, DHHS. Washington, D.C.: U.S. Government Printing Office, 1988, p. 8

Knisely, J. S., D. C. Rees, and R. L. Balster. Discriminative stimulus properties of toluene in the rat. *Neurotoxicol Teratol* 12:129, 1990

Lange, W. R., E. M. Dax, C. A. Haertzen, F. R. Snyder, and J. H. Jaffe. Nitrite inhalants: contemporary patterns of abuse. In: Haverkos, H. W. and J. A. Dougherty, eds., *Health Hazards of Nitrite Inhalants*. NIDA Research Monograph 83, DHHS. Washington, D.C.: U.S. Government Printing Office, 1988, p. 86

Litt, I. F., and M. I. Cohen. "Danger—vapor harmful"; spot remover sniffing. *New Engl J Med* 281:543, 1969

Marjot, R., and A. A. McLeod. Chronic non-neurological toxicity from volatile substance abuse. *Human Toxicol* 8:301, 1989

McSherry, T. M. Program experiences with the solvent abuser in Philadelphia. In: Crider, R. A., and B. A. Rouse, eds., *Epidemiology of Inhalant Abuse: An Update*. NIDA Research Monograph 85, DHHS. Washington, D.C.: U.S. Government Printing Office, 1988, p. 106

Medina-Mora, E. Inhalant use in Latin America: A review of the literature. In: Arif, A. E., M. Grant, and V. Navaratnam, eds., *Abuse of Volatile Solvents and Inhalants: Papers Presented at a WHO Advisory Meeting*. International Monograph Series, Centre for Drug Research, Universiti Sains Malaysia Minden, Pulau Pinang, Malaysia, 1:76, 1988

Medina-Mora, E., and A. Ortiz. Epidemiology of solvent/inhalant abuse in Mexico. In: Crider, R. A., and B. A. Rouse, eds., *Epidemiology of Inhalant Abuse: An Update*. NIDA Research Monograph 85, DHHS. Washington, D.C.: U.S. Government Printing Office, 1988, p. 106

Newell, G. R., M. R. Spitz, and M. B. Wilson. Nitrite inhalants: historical perspectives. In: Haverkos, H. W. and J. A. Dougherty, eds., *Health Hazards of Nitrite Inhalants*. NIDA Research Monograph 83, DHHS. Washington, D.C.: U.S. Government Printing Office, 1988, p. 1

Press, E., and A. K. Done. Solvent sniffing, I and II. *Pediatrics* 39:451, 1967

Pyror, G. T. Pharmacologic and neurobehavioral aspects of solvent toxicity based on animal studies. In: Arif, A. E., M. Grant, and V. Navaratnam, eds., *Abuse of Volatile Solvents and Inhalants: Papers Presented at a WHO Advisory Meeting*. International Monograph Series, Centre for Drug Research Universiti Sains Malaysia Minden, Pulau Pinang Malaysia, 1:162, 1988

Ron, M. A. Volatile substance abuse: a review of possible long-term neurological, intellectual and psychiatric sequelae. *Br J Psychiatry* 148:235, 1986

Rosenberg, N. L., M. C. Spitz, C. M. Filley, K. A. Davis, and H. H. Schaumburg. Central nervous system effects of chronic toluene abuse—clinical, brainstem evoked response and magnetic resonance imaging studies. *Neurotoxicol Teratol* 10:489, 1988

Schwartz, R. H. Deliberate inhalation of isobutyl nitrite during adolescence: a descriptive study. In: Haverkos, H. W. and J. A. Dougherty, eds., *Health Hazards of Nitrite Inhalants*. NIDA Research Monograph 83, DHHS. Washington, D.C.: U.S. Government Printing Office, 1988, p. 81

Sharp, C. W. Clinical and medical manifestations of volatile solvents. In: Arif, A. E., M. Grant, and V. Navaratnam, eds., *Abuse of Volatile Solvents and Inhalants: Papers Presented at a WHO Advisory Meeting*. International Monograph Series, Centre for Drug Research Universiti Sains Malaysia Minden, Pulau Pinang Malaysia, 1:227, 1988

Wood R. W. The acute toxicity of nitrite inhalants. In: Haverkos, H. W. and J. A. Dougherty, eds., Health Hazards of Nitrite Inhalants. NIDA Research Monograph 83, DHHS. Washington, D.C.: U.S. Government Printing Office, 1988, p. 28.

Wood, R. W., J. B. Coleman, R. Schuler, and C. Cox. Anticonvulsant and antipunishment effects of toluene. *J Pharmacol Exp Ther* 230;407, 1984

Zur, J., and W. Yule. Chronic solvent abuse. 2. Relationship with depression. *Child Care Health Dev* 16:21, 1990

CHAPTER 6

Hallucinogens: Phencyclidine, LSD, and Agents Having Similar Effects

Drugs that produce marked alterations in perceptions of the environment are called hallucinogens. Many drugs that produce behavioral or physiologic changes at small doses produce distorted perceptions if they are administered in large doses. Central nervous system stimulants, anticholinergics, and some steroids are among these drugs. Other drugs, however, produce altered states of consciousness at relatively small doses that induce few additional effects. Three such drugs are phencyclidine (PCP), lysergic acid diethylamide (LSD), and marihuana, which is discussed in the next chapter. The mechanisms of action of these three drugs are markedly different from each other as are the subjective effects they produce. Drugs that are similar to PCP in their mechanism and effect are the anesthetic ketamine, and the D- (unnatural) isomers of some opioid drugs (e.g., dextrorphan). Drugs that are similar to LSD include mescaline, psilocybin, 2,5-dimethoxy-4-methylamphetamine (DOM), and dimethyltryptamine (DMT).

One interesting and perhaps relevant difference between PCP and LSD is that the former but not the latter compound serves as a reinforcer in animals when presented contingent on the animals' response. Since both drugs produce effects that are occasionally or frequently regarded as dysphoric in both normal and drug-abusing individuals, it is interesting that only PCP maintains behavior in animals. Drugs resembling PCP, such as ketamine and dextrorphan, also serve as reinforcers in animals, whereas drugs similar to LSD such as mescaline and psilocybin do not.

PHENCYCLIDINE

Phencyclidine was synthesized in the 1950s as part of a search for general anesthetic agents with novel mechanisms of action. Marketed as Sernyl, PCP had only a brief therapeutic life. Although physicians were intrigued by the drug's effects (analgesia, amnesia, lack of suppression of laryngeal reflexes, little cardiovascular effect, and little muscle relaxation), the postoperative effects of PCP were highly unpleasant for some patients. The mildest complaints were of graphic nightmares; some patients became delirious and showed near mania when the anesthetic effects of PCP began to subside. Because of this "emergence delirium," Sernyl was removed from sale in the 1960s. A closely related drug, ketamine, with similar properties but a shorter duration of action, continues to have wide use in veterinary medicine. It is also popular for use with specific patients, particularly children requiring burn dressing changes.

PCP was first offered for illicit sale in California in the mid-1960s, but only as pills designed to be swallowed (Petersen and Stillman, 1978). The numerous reports of psychotic symptoms caused a decline in the popularity of PCP. The drug reappeared in the early 1970s as a powder designed to be snorted or smoked; this time it sold well, especially to young, white, polydrug abusers. Although use in this population has declined, abuse of phencyclidine among African-Americans and other minorities in major metropolitan areas has been increasing since 1983. Increasing incidence of phenyclidine abuse in St. Louis is shown in Figure 6–1; virtually all this increase is due to escalating use by African-Americans. Problems of phencyclidine abuse have surfaced recently in Washington, D.C., Los Angeles, Chicago, and New Orleans (Poklis et al., 1990). It is not used to any great extent outside the United States.

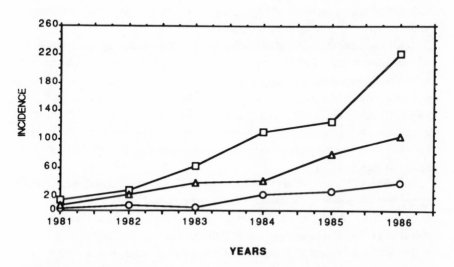

YEARS

FIGURE 6–1. Increased PCP abuse in metropolitan St. Louis, Missouri demonstrated by drug abuse indicators: (□) admission to drug treatment programs, Missouri Department of Mental Health; (△) emergency room episodes, project DAWN; (○) deaths, St. Louis City and County Medical Examiners Offices. (From Poklis et al., 1990.)

Patterns of Use

It is difficult to be certain of the pattern of phencyclidine abuse, since this drug
is often substituted for other drugs, and other drugs are often substituted for it.
Approximately 50 percent of current users indicate that they use the drug about
once per week. In other cases, the pattern of use is more similar to that of the
stimulants: groups of people gather to smoke or snort the drug on a frequent
basis for two to three days. During this time they do little besides take the drug,
and following the "run," they sleep (Jaffe, 1990).

Effects

Ingestion, by smoking or snorting, of approximately 5 mg of PCP produces the
following effects in people: a sense of intoxication, slurred speech, nystagmus,
a rolling gait, and feelings of numbness in the hands and feet. Muscular rigidity,
sweating, apathy, and a blank stare may develop. Users report feelings of depersonalization and disordered thoughts. The image of progressive disintegration
has been offered to capture the psychological effects of the drug (Bakker and
Amini, 1961), indicates a growing inability to process information and a narrow-
ing of awareness. Distortions of body image are particularly common; subjects
report that their arms do not belong to the rest of their body or that parts of their
body are perceived to be floating in space. Even their voices may not seem to
be theirs but to be coming from a distance.

Following intramuscular administration of ketamine, a drug with properties
very similar to those of PCP, subjects have reported sensations of light throughout the body; sensations of floating from room to room, where moving, glowing
geometric figures could be seen; absence of time sense; and dramatic changes in
body perception. Body consistency was described as changed, so that the body
felt as though it was made of dry wood or foam rubber and parts of the body
were felt to be grotesquely distorted or changed in size to very large or very
small (Hansen et al., 1988).

Drowsiness develops with larger doses of PCP, and this may be accompanied
by feelings of isolation, as though other people cannot contact those who have
taken the drug. Amnesia for the period of the drug's action is common. The
period of PCP's effects is usually from four to six hours.

With doses in excess of 5 mg, a more pronounced analgesia is experienced.
Hostile or unusual behavior, which sometimes occurs with smaller doses, is more
apt to be observed with larger ones. Blood pressure is likely to be increased,
along with heart rate. Increased salivation may become evident, as may fever,
repetitive movements, muscular rigidity, and excessive sweating. As might be
expected with a drug whose primary use has been in producing anesthesia, larger

doses result in stupor or coma, although the eyes may remain open and the extremities may continue to move in random or stereotyped patterns.

PCP is easily absorbed via all of its common routes of administration. Hydroxylated metabolites of the drug appear in the urine in the form of glucuronides; some metabolites may have pharmacologic activity, but it is unlikely that they contribute to the effects of phencyclidine itself (Jaffe, 1990). Only a small portion of PCP appears unchanged in the urine. The half-life of the drug in the body is ordinarily around three days (Petersen and Stillman, 1978); this value can be reduced to one day by appropriate treatment in cases of overdose (discussed later).

Tolerance and Physiologic Dependence

Although tolerance has been found to develop to some of the actions of PCP, this does not appear to be a uniform phenomenon. This is not surprising since PCP produces a wide variety of effects. It produces stimulation in some doses in some preparations; in other situations, it has clear depresssant effects. Although the evidence is far from complete, current observations suggest that tolerance develops to the depressant effects of PCP, but little tolerance develops, and perhaps even sensitization occurs, to the stimulatory effects of PCP. Tolerance, even to the depressant effects of PCP, seems to be fairly limited, and can be accounted for in some cases by increased rates of PCP metabolism (Woods and Winger, 1991).

In contrast to the paucity of knowledge about the development of tolerance to PCP, quite a bit has been learned about the development of physiologic dependence on PCP in animals. In rhesus monkeys, removing access to PCP following 20 to 30 days of 4 to 7 mg/kg/day of the drug results in a drug deprivation syndrome that includes piloerection, penile erection, diarrhea, persistent vocalization, abnormal eye movements, ear and facial twitches, hyperresponsiveness, and teeth grinding. These signs can be completely eliminated by administration of 0.25 mg/kg PCP (Balster and Woolverton, 1980). A similar syndrome has been observed in rats given large doses of PCP over the course of several days and then withdrawn from the drug. PCP-withdrawal signs have not been clearly demonstrated in humans, which is not surprising, given the irregular pattern of PCP self-administration in humans. Fairly continuous administration of large doses of PCP has been used to produce dependence in animals, and the minimum rate of drug administration necessary to produce dependence has not been determined.

PCP Toxicity; Overdose

Toxic states are characterized by problems of hostility toward others. Confusional periods, accidents, and death have been attributed to overdoses, but the incidence of such effects is unknown. If coma, convulsions, or psychotic states develop, toxicity is commonly said to be severe. Patients who appear in emergency rooms with PCP overdoses can sometimes present with symptoms nearly identical to acute schizophrenia (Balster, 1987). The similarity between these two states has led some investigators to propose PCP administration as a model of schizophrenia.

Management of patients suffering from overdoses is symptomatic and directed toward hastening urinary excretion of the drug and its metabolites. Continuous gastric suction, maintaining vital functions, and protecting the patient and others from the consequences of faulty judgment and hostile behavior are necessary. Two techniques are used to speed elimination of the drug from the body: acidification of the urine and continuous gastric suction. Administration of ammonium chloride or cranberry juice to get urinary pH below 5.0 is important. The gastric suction is needed because significant quantities of PCP are secreted into the stomach. Suction and urinary acidification typically reduce the half-life of the drug from three days to one day (Jaffe, 1990; Petersen and Stillman, 1978).

PCP toxicity is frequently characterized by difficult behavioral problems for which talking down is rarely a successful remedy. If drug treatment is attempted, haloperidol is preferred by many clinicians. Phenothiazines are believed to augment the atropinelike actions of PCP. Additionally, such patients may require pulmonary ventilatory support of depressed respiration, treatment of fever, and management of excessive salivation by suction. Convulsions may require diazepam, and hypertension may necessitate hydralazine.

The psychotic phase of PCP toxicity may last for several weeks after a single episode of drug use. The psychotic state may follow or be preceded by coma and may be characterized by delirium and paranoid ideation. It has been found helpful to seclude these patients from external stimuli as much as possible. A "flashback" phenomenon, in which a person who has ingested PCP experiences the drug effect several weeks later in the absence of taking any additional drug, has been described with PCP as well as with LSD.

Mechanism of Action

In the past decade, there has been an increased understanding of the neuronal effects of PCP and related drugs. They appear to block specific channels in neuronal membranes through which chloride and sodium ions pass in the process of depolarizing those membranes. The channels that are blocked by PCP are those that are ordinarily activated by the neurotransmitter glutamate. Glutamate is ubiquitous throughout the body and apparently obtains selective activity through the presence of a number of different glutamate receptors. One of these receptor types is referred to as the NMDA receptor (*N*-methyl D-aspartate), since this amino acid was found to activate these receptors selectively. It is the opening of ion channels by activation of the NMDA subset of glutamate receptors that is blocked by the presence of PCP.

One of the most exciting potential clinical uses of NMDA antagonists such as PCP and related drugs is in prevention of much of the neuronal damage that results when the brain is temporarily deprived of oxygen, as in drowning, strangulation, or stroke. In these ischemic conditions, there is a cascading release of glutamate from cells. Glutamate is highly toxic when cell function is compromised and the usually efficient methods of glutamate removal are taxed. NMDA antagonists reduce the ability of glutamate to damage cells, which thereby limits the toxic actions of this neurotransmitter. Unfortunately, the side effects of PCP administration render this drug inappropriate for the treatment of drowning or stroke victims, but the search for drugs with a similar mechanism and fewer side effects may eventually result in a therapeutic agent.

In addition to its ability to block NMDA-specific glutamate effects, PCP appears to interact with the dopamine neurotransmitter system. These effects may be related to the stimulation produced by PCP and may occur by increasing release or decreasing inactivation of dopamine in the central nervous system. This system is less well understood than are the NMDA-related effects of PCP. A connection between these two effects of PCP is possible but has not been confirmed.

LSD

LSD (D-lysergic acid diethylamide, lysergide, LSD-25) (see Fig. 6–2) is a semisynthetic compound that was first prepared by Swiss chemists searching for new drugs derived from naturally occurring constituents of ergot. The hallucinogenic effects of the drug were discovered following an accidental ingestion of minute quantities (Hoffman, 1979). Only the D isomer of LSD possesses hallucinogenic activity; the monoethylaminde-congener produces similar central nervous system effects, although it is considerably less potent. The illicit supply of LSD has easily equaled demand, for amateur chemists have been able to procure readily the starting materials required for the synthesis of LSD and to accomplish the synthesis without great difficulty.

The illicit use of LSD on a broad national scale began in the United States around 1965. A significant impetus for this development was provided by the immense publicity accorded Dr. Timothy Leary and his fulsome (and sometime inaccurate or misunderstood) tributes to the drug's effects. Several large hospitals in Los Angeles have placed the date of the onset of the "LSD-era" as September, 1965. Their psychiatric emergency services, which had previously been seeing patients with adverse reactions to LSD at the rate of about six per year, now began seeing such patients at a rate of 60 to 180 per year and receiving in addition three to five telephone calls of inquiry about LSD for each patient seen (Ungerleider et al., 1966; Ungerleider et al., 1968).

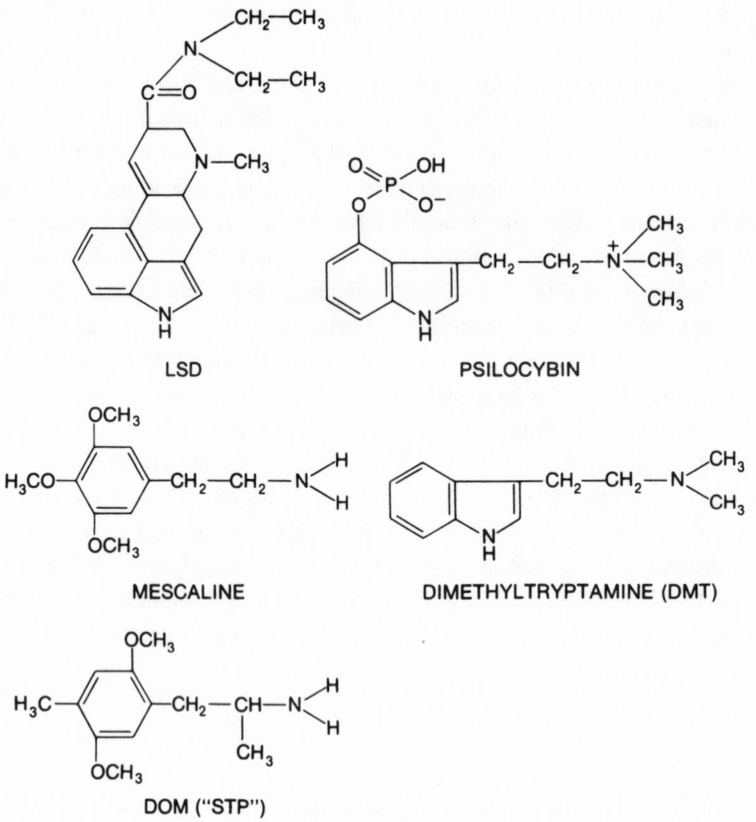

FIGURE 6–2. LSD and similar hallucinogens. The physiologic and hallucinogenic effects of each of these naturally occurring drugs are quite similar, although their chemical structures are remarkably different. LSD is by far the most potent of these drugs, which all appear to produce their effects through agonist actions at one serotonin receptor.

Patterns of Use

LSD is an extremely potent compound. Doses of LSD in excess of 35 μg are effectively hallucinogenic, and "street doses" of the drug range typically from 50 to 300 μg (Cheek et al., 1969). The compound may be provided as a powder, a solution, a capsule, or a pill, the last often having a distinctive shape and color (Smith, 1969). In addition, drops of LSD solution often have been placed on sugar cubes, animal crackers (Ludwig and Levine, 1965), or pieces of blotting paper, which are then offered for sale. LSD is most commonly taken by mouth. Occasionally, tobacco is saturated with an LSD solution and then smoked, but the "high" obtained by this means is generally found to be unsatisfactory. LSD is usually taken infrequently, on a weekly or monthly basis, and usually in the company of friends who are also using the drug. Probably only a minority of drug users take LSD at short and regular intervals for sustained periods of time (i.e., once daily or once every two to three days). Patterns of multiple drug abuse in which LSD played a major or minor role were common when LSD was at its peak of popularity.

Effects of LSD

When taken by mouth, the effects of LSD are perceptible within 30 to 40 minutes. Users state that it may be an hour or so, however, before they are "flying," a term synonymous with maximal psychic effects. The physiologic effects of LSD are most evident one to three hours after administration and are essentially absent after six hours (Forrer and Goldner, 1951; the psychic effects are commonly said to persist for eight to 12 hours (Smith and Rose, 1968).

The physiologic changes produced by hallucinogenic doses of LSD can include slight rises in blood pressure and heart rate (though occasionally bradycardia develops), marked pupillary dilation, cutaneous flushing, increased salivation and lacrimation, conjunctival injection, trembling in the extremities, hyperreflexia, leukocytosis, vomiting, and evidence of a slight ataxia (Ungerleider et al., 1966; Forrer and Goldner, 1951). The intensity of these changes usually appears to be dose related. LSD has not been observed to affect respiratory rate or blood glucose levels (Ungerleider et al., 1966). One possible consequence of the mydriasis produced is varying degrees of photophobia.

The psychic changes produced by LSD apparently vary from one individual to another and from one occasion to another. When the effects are not terribly dysphoric to an individual, they have been described in the following way. Among the earliest psychic effects consistently experienced by users of LSD are feelings of derealization and depersonalization and a loss of body image. These perceptual distortions may produce considerable anxiety in the novice and trigger the onset of a "bad trip." Under the influence of LSD, the individual may feel that he or she is divided into two people: an uninvolved observer and a participating self. Perceptions of color, distance, and shape are altered so that colors appear brighter or more intense; fixed objects, such as chairs or walls, may change in color or shape or appear to move; and bizarre designs may be seen. Experiences associated normally with one sensory modality are translated into another; as a result of this synesthesia, colors may be "smelled," for example, and sounds may be "seen." These perceptual aberrations have been described as pseudohallucinations, illusions, or visions, since the user of LSD typically retains sufficient insight to recognize that these phenomena are drug-induced and often remembers them clearly after the "trip." Under the effects of LSD, the user often loses all sense of time in a jumble of past, present, and future. Concentration sometimes is difficult, and attention can fluctuate rapidly. There is a sense of a profusion of vague ideas pressing for attention, and the user may become engrossed with "philosophical, ethical or highly egocentric issues" (Report of the Special Committee, 1969). This engrossment, coupled with impairment in judgment produced by LSD, may cause the user to believe that he has discovered new truths of fundamental philosophical importance or fresh and significant insights into himself. His descriptions of these "discoveries," however, typically seem unintelligible or nonsensical to those not under the influence of the drug (Report of the Special Committee, 1969; Smith, 1969). Some users become so preoccupied with visions or thoughts that they appear catatonic or stuporous, although their attention can be gained with persistence. Conversely, though less commonly, a user's behavioral pattern may be one of apparently purposeless and disorganized hyperactivity (Report of the Special Committee, 1969).

Less predictable, marked emotional changes may occur "ranging from ecstasy to despair" (Report of the Special Committee, 1969). Emotional lability and suggestibility may be notably enhanced (Smith, 1969). Great euphoria may be experienced without the user being able to explain its origin, and small environmental changes, such as the sun going behind a cloud, may quickly transform the user's mood into one of sadness or despair.

Mechanism

It has been hypothesized for some time that the mechanisms of action of LSD are related in some way to the serotonin (5HT) system in the brain. In the early 1950s, LSD was shown to block some of the effects of serotonin on peripheral tissue. Subsequently, LSD was shown to produce a profound inhibition of serotonin-containing neurons, and it was postulated that LSD's hallucinatory effects were a result of presynaptic suppression of normal (inhibitory) serotonergic activity in the central nervous system. Unfortunately, other drugs, such as DOM and mescaline, which had hallucinatory effects very much like those of LSD, did not have the same ability to suppress serotonin neurons. Furthermore, lisuride, a nonhallucinatory congener of LSD, did produce such suppression. Studies in cats also demonstrated tolerance to the behavioral effects of LSD-like agents but no similar tolerance to this neurophysiologic effect of these drugs (Heym and Jacobs, 1988).

Serotonin has been found to activate a number of receptors; among these are $5HT_2$ and the $5HT_1$ receptors. A better understanding of the possible mechanism by which LSD produced its hallucinatory effects was made when the selective $5HT_2$ antagonists mianserin, ketanserin, and pirenperone were shown to block a wide variety of behavioral effects of LSD. This provided some of the most convincing evidence that LSD acts postsynaptically on specific $5HT_2$ receptors, not presynaptically on serotonin receptors in general, as had been previously thought. Little affinity of LSD has been shown for the $5HT_1$ receptor sites. It thus appears at the present time that the most promising avenue for understanding the neurophysiologic properties of LSD most relevant to its behavioral effects is to consider the drug a 5HT$_2$ agonist. As Heym and Jacobs (1988) point out, however, it is not entirely clear that this receptor is activated by serotonin under normal conditions. Another neurotransmitter in the brain may be more closely related to this system. They also make the point that hallucinogens are complex drugs that have many different effects in the brain. Although one effect has been identified, the others are probably not irrelevant, and we have much to learn about how these various effects interact to give the characteristic changes in sensory perception that are observed following administration of LSD.

Absorption, Fate, and Excretion

LSD is colorless, tasteless, oderless, and soluble in water. Judging from the fact that its effects can be perceived within 30 to 40 minutes after oral administration, we may assume that the drug is absorbed from the gastrointestinal tract fairly rapidly; the extent of absorption is unknown. When the drug is given intravenously, the initially high plasma concentrations in human subjects fall rapidly within the first 30 minutes and decline more slowly thereafter. From these observations, it is possible to calculate that the half-life of LSD in human plasma is approximately 175 minutes (Aghajanian and Bing, 1964). The plasma concentrations of LSD following intravenous injection are higher than those that should obtain if the drug were evenly distributed within the total pool of body water, but little else is known about the distribution of LSD in human tissue.

Likewise, little is known about the metabolism and excretion of LSD in human beings, which is the case, by and large, for all ergot alkaloids and their semisynthetic congeners. The fact that just 50 to 100 µg of LSD can exert effects that may last for 12 hours has led some to speculate that human metabolism and/ or excretion of this compound occurs very slowly; others suggest that LSD may act as a "trigger," setting in motion changes that persist for hours after the drug itself has been inactivated or excreted. The latter speculation stems largely from findings in laboratory animals in which the half-life of LSD in plasma is just 7.5 minutes (Aghajanian and Bing, 1964). Other animal studies have indicated that LSD is inactivated via hepatic oxidation and that little unchanged drug appears in the urine (Pfeiffer and Murphee, 1965).

Tolerance and Physiologic Dependence

Given that the typical pattern of LSD abuse is one of infrequent administration, it is unlikely that either tolerance or dependence would develop in humans. In animal studies, where drug can be given frequently, no evidence has been obtained to suggest the development of physiologic dependence on LSD. Tolerance, on the other hand, has been shown to develop in animal models. It develops quickly and dissipates quickly when frequent drug administration is terminated. Interestingly, cross-tolerance between LSD and mescaline and psilocybin as been demonstrated, but no such cross-tolerance has been described between LSD and amphetamine or scopolamine. Cross-tolerance frequently suggests similar effects, often mediated through the same pharmacologic systems.

Morbidity and Mortality

LSD has a reputation for producing "bad trips" on occasion, even among those who have used the drug previously with no adverse effects. The reason for these reactions is unknown, but they have a multitude of related factors. In clinical situations it has been shown that psychotic episodes lasting for more than 48 hours occur at a rate of from 0.8 to 1.8 per 1000 administrations of LSD (Smart and Bateman, 1967).

ACUTE ADVERSE REACTIONS
Acute adverse reactions refer to untoward responses to LSD that last no more than a few days after the occasion of drug use.

Users of LSD often refer to nonpsychotic adverse reactions as a "bad trip" or a "bummer." In contrast to the enjoyable LSD experience in which the user relishes the perceptual aberrations, knows they are drug induced, and does not feel threatened by them, a bad trip is commonly said to begin in the following fashion: "After taking the drug one can feel it has 'gotten away' from him; that he no longer has control of the psychologic effects he is experiencing. He wants to be taken out of this state immediately" (Smith and Rose, 1968). Such fear may arise from the illusion of spiders crawling over one's body, of being on the verge of falling into a black and bottomless chasm, or of one's hand being purple and believing it will always be so, for example. The most common adverse reaction is a state of acute panic, often accompanied by a fear of imminent insanity. Confusion or psychic depression is also possible. Precipitate flight, such as jumping through a window or the heedless rush across a busy street, represents an attempt to escape the bad trip. Some adverse reactions apparently end as the drug effects subside; others persist as long as a few days (Smart and Bateman, 1967).

The bad trip can also be characterized by a variety of psychotic reactions, some of which disappear as the effects of LSD wear off. A threatening illusion may suddenly seem real (Smith, 1969) and not drug induced; the vision or pseudohallucination of a good trip may dissolve into a true and frightening hallucination.

The development of such delusional states as megalomania and paranoia has led to some of the most bizarre and dramatic episodes associated with the use of LSD. The user may believe himself to be Jesus Christ and designate relatives and friends as various biblical personages. Convinced that he is weightless or that he can fly, the user may jump out of a window. Convinced that he is invincible, he may stab himself (Ludwig and Levine, 1965) or stand in the midst of a busy street attempting to halt traffic (Smart and Bateman, 1967). Though the incidence of attempted and successful suicide among users of LSD is not known, the available evidence suggests that it is "an important complication of LSD administration" (Smart and Bateman, 1967).

Bad trips may be characterized by the development of acute paranoid states that are "transient episodes not extending beyond the period of LSD activity" (Cohen, 1966). Suspicions that others may be plotting against the user are common manifestations of this state. Physical assaults upon others have occurred, including attempted homicide (Cohen, 1966; Smart and Bateman, 1967), but they appear to be relatively rare.

PERSISTENT ADVERSE REACTIONS
Persistent adverse reactions involve untoward responses attributed to LSD that last from weeks to years after a single occasion of use or after repeated use of the drug.

Prolonged Psychotic Reactions. Various persistent psychotic reactions have been attributed to LSD. With or without therapeutic intervention, the duration of these reactions ranges from approximately one week to several years. Obviously, no clear distinction can be made between the psychotic reactions designated as acute and the shortest of the prolonged reactions. In a few instances, the psychic effects produced by a single dose of LSD have persisted long after (three weeks, for example) the probable period of the drug's action. Such reactions have been called persistent hallucinosis (Cohen, 1966).

Schizophrenic reactions seem to be the most commonly encountered persistent psychotic response; a state resembling paranoid schizophrenia has been described most often. Disorders resembling the catatonic and schizoaffective forms of this disease have also been observed. Other psychotic disorders, such as depression, paranoia, "a confused or manic psychosis," and a "motor-excitatory" state, have been reported to be produced by LSD (Cohen, 1966; Smart and Bateman, 1967).

Some of the prolonged psychotic reactions are self-limiting, but the majority require, in addition to hospitalization, the standard modes of treatment for each type of disorder. On occasion, a disorder has appeared to subside only to recur a few weeks later (Smart and Bateman, 1967).

In any consideration of why certain LSD users develop prolonged psychotic reactions, the view is often advanced that they were unusually vulnerable to the drug's effects because of a preexisting psychiatric disturbance. It has become a general, almost reflex explanation for any adverse psychic effect that is apparently drug-induced and that persists long after the drug has ceased to act. It is, in fact, often difficult to distinguish those who develop prolonged psychotic reactions from those who do not on the basis of prior psychiatric history. In their review of untoward reactions to LSD, Smart and Bateman (1967) concluded that "LSD is precipitating prolonged psychoses in many persons who cannot be diagnosed as psychotic, or who have only minor personality disturbances or none at all" (p.1216).

Spontaneous Recurrences of the LSD Experience (Flashbacks, Flashes, Splashers).   Nonpsychotic and, rarely, psychotic components of the LSD experience recur spontaneously in some individuals for as long as a year or more after the last use of LSD. The onset of these incidents may also be triggered by stress, fatigue, or the use of such other drugs as marihuana or a barbiturate (Horowitz, 1969). The duration of the flashbacks is difficult to ascertain, and their frequency is subject to wide individual variation; individuals experiencing as many as five to 10 flashbacks a day have been described. Flashbacks appear to occur most frequently in individuals with a history of repeated use of LSD (Smart and Bateman, 1967).

PEYOTE AND MESCALINE

In the context of drug abuse, peyote is the most common name given to plant preparations obtained from the mescal cactus *(Lophophor williamsii).* The dome-shaped head of this grayish-green, spineless plant is made up of one or more disks (buttons), which have the potential for flowering and contain the principal peyote hallucinogen, mescaline.

Peyote was used by the Aztecs and other Mexican Indian tribes in religious ceremonies for unnumbered centuries before the arrival of the Spaniards. Late-nineteenth-century raids into Mexico by Indian tribes from our Great Plains area, notably the Kiowa and Comanche, resulted in the establishment of "peyote cults" in this country. The use of peyote in Indian religious ceremonies spread rapidly to our Southwest and northward even to tribes across the Canadian border. Adherents to a new faith, whose teachings and ceremonies reflect both pagan and Christian origins, formed the Native American Church in 1918. It now claims several thousand members, each of whom may, according to court rulings, use peyote legally for religious purposes.

Peyote or mescal buttons are brown and hard and are only rarely available in powdered form. They are usually softened by the user's saliva before being swallowed. The buttons contain, in addition to mescaline, 15 beta-phenethylamine and isoquinoline alkaloids. It is thought that all these compounds are pharma-cologically active, which accounts for the common finding that the effects of peyote and mescaline are not identical.

The effects of peyote are slow to develop and, initially, unpleasant. Nausea is common but rarely results in vomiting. Profuse perspiration and static tremors are also among the early effects. The initial phase, lasting one to two hours, is succeeded by the "hallucinogenic" experience, in which visual hallucinations are prominent (brightly colored lights, vivid kaleidoscopic visions of geometrical forms and sometimes of animals and people), color and space perception may be disturbed, synesthesias are experienced, and more rarely, auditory and tactile "hallucinations" occur (Report of the Special Committee, 1969; Schultes, 1969). As with LSD, the user ordinarily retains insight, and the sensorium is otherwise undisturbed. After this phase of the peyote experience, for which mes-caline appears primarily responsible, the user often falls into a deep sleep. The total experience is said to last about 12 hours.

Mescaline was isolated from peyote buttons in 1896, and its structure was determined in 1918. Its chemical resemblance to drugs like amphetamine and DOM (see Figure 6–2) and to the adrenergic transmitter substances epinephrine and norepinephrine has provoked much speculation. Despite its structural simi-larity to amphetamine, mescaline's mechanism of action is likely similar to that of LSD since the two drugs have similar effects, and drugs that reverse the effects of LSD also reverse the effects of mescaline.

Mescaline is usually taken by mouth in a dose of from 300 to 500 mg, indi-cating that it is roughly 1000 times less potent than LSD. The drug offered on the illegal market is obtained either from peyote buttons or, perhaps more fre-quently, from the "basement" chemist. Some of mescaline's initial effects are typical of adrenergic drugs and include perspiration, tremors, a sense of anxiety, and hyperreflexia. The "hallucinatory" effects of peyote and mescaline are re-ported not to differ markedly and, indeed, to resemble greatly the psychic effects of LSD.

There is apparently no physiologic dependence development to mescaline, but tolerance has been reported. The evidence regarding the nature and magnitude of mescaline tolerance is scarce; as with LSD, this drug is rarely taken on so regular a schedule as to afford an optimal opportunity for tolerance to develop. When tolerance to mescaline does develop, cross-tolerance to LSD can be dem-onstrated (Jaffe, 1990).

DOM (STP)

DOM is a synthetic hallucinogen that first came to public attention in 1967, when chemists at the FDA identified it as one of the active constituents of STP (Snyder et al., 1967). The synthesis of DOM was reported in the chemical literature in 1964, and it is likely that this report provided the necessary information for clandestine chemists supplying the illegal drug trade. The original STP was a variety of drug mixtures, and not all of them contained DOM. Nonetheless, STP became a common synonym for DOM.

DOM (2,5-dimethoxy-4-methyl amphetamine) bears a structural resemblance to both amphetamine and mescaline (see Figure 6–2). Pharmacologically, DOM and such related compounds as DOET (2,5-dimethoxy-4-*ethyl* amphetamine) resemble amphetamine only in certain respects; they produce a sense of euphoria, and the user becomes more talkative. Unlike low doses of amphetamine, low doses of these compounds impair rather than improve the ability to concentrate, rarely cause anorexia, and provide a mild "psychedelic experience" (Farnsworth, 1968). Larger doses create effects reminiscent of mescaline and LSD.

The minimal dose of DOM that is unmistakably hallucinogenic is 5 mg for a 70-kg subject (Snyder et al., 1967), which indicates that DOM is roughly 50 to 100 times less potent than LSD. Doses of DOM of approximately 3 mg produce euphoria and "enhanced self-awareness" but only rarely perceptual distortions and "hallucinations" (Snyder et al., 1968). The effects of DOM are perceptible about 1 hour after ingestion (the conventional route of administration), are maximal at three to five hours, and have largely subsided in seven to eight hours (Snyder et al., 1967; Snyder et al., 1968). Only rarely do subjects report residual psychic effects the next day. At least 20 percent of the DOM administered can be found unchanged in the urine; the maximal rate of urinary excretion was found to correspond in time with the peak of the psychic effects (Snyder et al., 1967).

The physiologic changes produced by DOM are largely characteristic of the preceding hallucinogens: Heart rate is increased (15 to 25 beats/minute), systolic blood pressure is elevated (about 15 to 30 mm Hg), diastolic pressure is unchanged, pupillary diameter is increased (about 15 percent), and body temperature rises slightly (about 1°F). Other somatic changes that may occur include paresthesias, nausea, tremors, and perspiration (Snyder et al., 1967).

The initial psychic effects of hallucinogenic doses of DOM resemble those described earlier for low doses of the drug; in addition, some users may experience vivid visual imagery when they close their eyes. As the drug effect intensifies, multiple images may be seen, objects seem to vibrate and to have distorted shapes, visual details stand out more clearly, and contrasts are enhanced. The passage of time seems to slow, the mind can be overrun with a "thousand thoughts" or occasionally be "blank," expression of thoughts can be difficult, and the user is easily distracted. Images are now seen with the eyes open. The predominant emotional tone of the experience is usually a happy one. The user retains insight throughout the experience and is able to recall it clearly later (Snyder et al., 1967).

True hallucinations, paranoid ideation, anxiety, and panic reactions seem rare, even with doses of DOM as high as 14 mg (Snyder et al., 1967). Only limited evidence is available, however, about the effects of pure DOM, and judging from the experiences of users with other hallucinogens, the possibility remains that the use of DOM may result in "bad trips" and psychotic episodes.

PSILOCYBIN

Some Mexican Indians have long regarded certain mushrooms with hallucinogenic properties as sacred; naming them *teonanacatl* (flesh of the gods), the Indians reserved their use primarily for religious ceremonies. The mushrooms used were probably specimens of the genera *Conocybe, Stropharia,* and *Psilcybe* (Farnsworth, 1968).

In 1958, Hofmann, a Swiss chemist, isolated from *Psilocybe mexicana* two compounds: psilocybin (O-phosphoryl-4-hydroxy-N-dimethyltryptamine; see Figure 6–2) and its dephosphorylated congener, psilocin. Psilocybin is the only naturally occurring hallucinogen identified thus far that contains phosphorus. Its structural resemblance to a compound of possible importance in central nervous system function, serotonin has aroused speculation about the role of hydroxylated tryptamines in the etiology of spontaneous mental disease.

Psilocybin is commonly taken by mouth; it is one of the most rapidly acting hallucinogens by this route of administration, with the first perceptible effects appearing 10 to 15 minutes after ingestion of doses of 4 to 8 mg. Reactions often reach maximal intensity at about 90 minutes and do not begin to subside until two to three hours later. The effects of psilocybin usually last five to six hours in all, but doses larger than 8 mg probably have more prolonged duration (Isbell, 1959).

Isbell has provided one of the most complete descriptions of the effects of psilocybin in man (Isbell, 1959). Physiologically, psilocybin causes increases in pulse rate, respiratory rate, and body temperature; dilates the pupils; and increases systolic, though not diastolic, blood pressure. Evidence of central excitation was obtained in Isbell's study by measuring the threshold for elicitation of the patellar reflex, which was found to decrease. As with LSD, mescaline, and DOM, the absolute magnitudes of these changes are not large. When they are expressed as a function of the total amount of change induced by the entire psilocybin experience of some five to six hours, however, the changes are statistically significant (Isbell, 1959).

The psychic (and physiologic) reactions to psilocybin led Isbell to conclude that "LSD-25 and psilocybin are remarkably similar" (Isbell, 1959), though, on a weight basis, LSD is 100 to 150 times more potent. The earliest subjective changes noted by subjects receiving psilocybin were that objects began to look, feel, or seem peculiar and that they experienced mild anxiety. Thirty minutes after the compound had been taken, anxiety was more pronounced, being manifested as dysphoria or specifically formulated fears of impending insanity or death. Changes in mood then occurred (commonly in the direction of elation), and in a seeming paradox, some subjects reported the coexistence of feelings of anxiety and elation. Hearing was said to be keener, but vision was blurred. Perception of sensory stimuli was altered, and as is typical of hallucinogens, visual distortions were most prominent. Feelings of depersonalization were common. The whole body might seem changed in size (being very large or as small as that of a child, for example), or hands and feet might not seem to be part of the body, or they might take on the shape of paws; some subjects could "see" the bones and blood within a body. Remarks about difficulties in thinking and concentrating, and of being troubled by rapid, tumultuous passages of thoughts, were made frequently. Seven of Isbell's nine subjects retained insight throughout the psilocybin experience and remained oriented in regard to time, place, and person. For two of the subjects, however, the visual images gradually became true hallucinations; thereafter, they "felt that their experiences were caused by the experimenters controlling their minds" (Isbell, 1959). Insight returned as the effects of psilocybin waned.

Physical dependence on the effects of psilocybin has not been reported and probably does not occur. Tolerance to psilocybin develops, and when present, cross-tolerance to the effects of LSD and mescaline can be demonstrated (Isbell, 1959).

DMT

DMT (*N,N*-dimethyltryptamine; see Figure 6–2) is representative, in its structure and pharmacologic effects, of the many tryptamine derivatives that have been isolated from the "hallucinogenic snuffs" used by South American Indians (Farnsworth, 1968). These snuffs are prepared from plants of the genera *Mimosa*, *Virola*, and *Piptadenia*. They are not active when taken orally, and one can only speculate about how the Indians discovered an effective route of administration (i.e., the dried plant material is prepared as a snuff to be inhaled or to be blown into the user's nostrils).

Aside from psilocybin, DMT and, rarely, DET (*N,N*-diethyltryptamine) are the only tryptamine derivatives that have been found on the illicit drug market, and then they have been found only sporadically. Compared with LSD, DMT has the principal shortcoming for the user of brevity of action; in the doses commonly available, its effects last for less than an hour and may persist for only 30 minutes. For this reason it has occasionally been referred to as the businessman's hallucinogen.

DMT is either inhaled as a powder or smoked in tobacco, parsley, or marihuana soaked in a solution of DMT. With doses of 35 to 79 mg, the effects of DMT, both psychic and physiologic, closely resemble those of LSD and other hallucinogens (Petersen and Stillman, 1978). These effects develop rapidly and, as noted earlier, are relatively brief in duration. Some investigators feel that DMT more frequently induces a disabling, though nonpsychotic, state of panic than does LSD (Report of the Special Committee, 1969). It may be that the rapid onset of DMT's effects allows the user too little time to adjust to the drug experience, and thereby a feeling of loss of control occurs more readily.

Physiologic dependence on the effects of DMT is not known to develop; it is not known if tolerance develops. Though DMT exhibits the properties described earlier of a typical hallucinogen, individuals tolerant to LSD show little or no evidence of cross-tolerance to DMT (Rosenberg et al., 1964); the apparent absence of cross-tolerance between these two compounds suggests the possibility that LSD and DMT exert their similar effects via different receptor sites.

REFERENCES

Aghajanian, G. K., and O. H. L. Bing. Persistence of lysergic acid diethylamide in the plasma of human subjects. *Clin Pharmacol Ther* 5:611, 1964

Bakker, C. B., and F. Amini. Observations on the psychotomimetic effects of Sernyl. *Compar Psychiat* 2:269, 1961

Balster, R. L. The behavioral pharmacology of phencyclidine. In: Meltzer, H., ed., *Psychopharmacology: The Third Generation of Progress.* New York: Raven, 1987, p. 1573

Balster, R. L., and W. L. Woolverton. Intravenous phencyclidine self-administration by rhesus monkeys leading to physical dependence. *Psychopharmacology* 70:5, 1980

Cheek, F. E., S. Newel, and M. Joffe. Deceptions in the illicit drug market. *Science* 167:1276, 1969

Cohen, S. A classification of LSD complications. *Psychosomatics* 7:182, 1966

Farnsworth, N. R. Hallucinogenic plants. *Science* 162:1086, 1968

Forrer, G. R., and R. D. Goldner. Experimental physiological studies with lysergic acid diethylamide (LSD-25). *Arch Neurol Psychiat* 65:581, 1951

Heym, J., and B. Jacobs. 5HT2 agonist activity as a common action of hallucinogens. In: Rech, R. H., and G. A. Gudelsky, eds., *5-HT Agonists as Psychoactive Drugs.* Ann Arbor: NPP Books, 1988, p. 95

Hansen, G., S. B. Jensen, L. Chandresh, and T. Hilden. The psychotropic effect of ketamine. *J Psychotropic Drugs* 20:419, 1988

Hoffman, A. How LSD originated. *J Psychedelic Drugs* 11:53, 1979

Horowitz, M. J. Flashbacks: Recurrent intrusive images after the use of LSD. *Amer J Psychiat* 126:565, 1969

Isbell, H. Comparison of the reactions induced by psilocybin and LSD-25 in man. *Psychopharmacology* 1:29, 1959

Jaffe, J. H. Drug addition and drug abuse. In: Gilman, A. G., T. W. Rall, A. S. Nies, and P. Taylor, eds., *Goodman and Gilman's The Pharmacological Basis of Therapeutics*, 8th ed. Elmsford, N.Y.: Pergamon, 1990, p. 522

Ludwig, A. M., and J. Levine. Patterns of hallucinogenic drug abuse. *J Amer Med Assoc* 191:92, 1965

Petersen, R. C., and R. C. Stillman, eds., *PCP Phencyclidine Abuse: An Appraisal*. National Institute on Drug Abuse, Department of Health, Education and Welfare Publication No. (ADM) 78-728, Washington, D.C.: U.S. Government Printing Office, 1978

Pfeiffer, C. C., and H. B. Murphree. Introduction to psychotropic drugs and hallucinogenic drugs. In: DiPalma, J. A., ed., *Drill's Pharmacology in Medicine,* 3rd ed. New York: McGraw-Hill, 1965, p. 321

Poklis, A., M. Graham, D. Maginn, C. A. Branch, and G. E. Gantner. Phencyclidine and violent deaths in St. Louis, Missouri: A survey of medical examiners' cases from 1977 through 1986. *Am J Drug Alcohol Abuse,* 16:265, 1990

Report of the Special Committee on Drug Misuse. Non-medical use of drugs, with particular reference to youth, Council on Community Health Care, Canadian Medical Association. *Canad Med Assoc J* 101:804, 1969

Rosenberg, D. E., H. Isbell, E. J. Miner, and C. R. Logan. The effect of *N,N*-dimethyltryptamine in human subjects tolerant to lysergic acid diethylamide. *Psychopharmacology* 5:217, 1964

Schultes, R. E., Hallucinogens of plant origin. *Science* 163:245, 1969

Smart, R. G., and K. Bateman. Unfavourable reactions to LSD: A review and analysis of the available case reports. *Canad Med Assoc J* 97:1214, 1967

Smith, D. E., and A. J. Rose. The use and abuse of LSD in Haight-Ashbury. *Clin Pediat* 7:317, 1968

Smith, D. E. Use of LSD in the Haight-Ashbury. *Calif Med* 110:472, 1969

Snyder, S. H., L. Faillace, and L. Hollister. 2,5-Dimethoxy-4-methylamphetamine (STP): A new hallucinogenic drug. *Science* 158:669, 1967

Snyder, S. H., L. A. Faillace, and H. Weingartner. DOM (STP), a new hallucinogenic drug, and DOET: Effects in normal subjects. *Amer J Psychiat* 125:357, 1968

Ungerleider, J. T., D. D. Fisher, and M. Fuller. The dangers of LSD. *J Amer Med Assoc* 197:389, 1966

Ungerleider, J. T., D. D. Fisher, M. Fuller, and A. Caldwell. The "bad trip"—the etiology of the adverse LSD reaction. *Amer J Psychiat* 124:1483, 1968

Woods, J. H., and G. Winger. Phencylidine and related substances. In: *Drug Abuse and Drug Abuse Research: The Third Triennial Report to Congress from the Secretary, Department of Health and Human Services.* Washington, D.C.: U.S. Government Printing Office, 1991, p. 145

CHAPTER 7

Marihuana and Hashish

The hemp plant *(Cannabis sativa)* grows freely in the temperate and tropical zones of the world. For more than four centuries, man has used this plant for numerous purposes. The most significant commercial use has been the conversion of its stalk fibers into rope, twine, and cord. Hemp was one of the important cash crops in colonial Kentucky, and for more than 100 years thereafter a few counties in this region met the needs of our armed forces for rope fiber. The plant's seeds have been fed to poultry and caged birds. The seeds, when crushed, yield an oil used in the manufacture of paint (to speed its drying) and soap, with the resultant solid residue being fed to cattle or used as fertilizer (Walton, 1938, Chapter 5).

The hemp plant is dioecious (i.e., both male and female forms exist). The male (staminate) plant is typically taller than the female, its flowers are borne in panicles, and it usually dies when its flowering cycle has been completed. The female (pistillate) plant is typically bushier than the male, its flowers are long catkins, and it secretes a clear, sticky resin that covers the flowering tops and adjacent leaves. The function of the resin, it has been postulated, is to retard dehydration of the flowering elements; the hotter the climate in which the plant is grown, the greater the amount of resin usually secreted. Both forms of the plant have large leaves, palmately compound, each with five to seven linear–lanceloate leaflets, which, in turn, have serrated leaf margins. According to chemical analysis, male and female plants have essentially equivalent psychoactive potency. Traditionally, however, the resin-covered flowering tops of the female plant and their adjacent leaves are considered more desirable and in some parts of the world are harvested exclusively (Paris and Nahas, 1984). Chemists and cultivators alike agree that the younger, topmost leaves have the highest drug content and that the stalk, roots, and seeds are virtually drug-free (Paris and Nahas, 1984).

The amount of psychoactive drug content varies tremendously among the nearly infinite varieties of the extremely adaptable marihuana plant; drug content varies as well, depending on the environment in which the plant is raised. Varieties developed for making rope, grown under conditions that favor high fiber content, may contain very little active drug. Varieties developed for drug use but grown under less than ideal environmental conditions, such as domestically grown marihauna, typically have relatively low content of psychoactive compound. Experienced users seek the usually more potent Mexican, Jamaican, and North African varieties.

The two types of *Cannabis* extracts used most frequently in the United States for their psychoactive effects are marihuana and hashish. Of uncertain origin, the word *marihuana* may be simply a variant of the Spanish equivalent of Mary Jane (Marijuana), which was a Mexican slang word for any cheap tobacco but which, by the end of the nineteenth century, referred exclusively to a *Cannabis* extract (Snyder, 1971). The most potent marihuana, containing just the dried flowering tops from a drug-rich variety of hemp plant, is called *ganja* in India and Jamaica (Rubin and Comitas, 1975). Marihuana may also be prepared from hemp plants containing varying amounts of psychoactive drug and may contain widely variable proportions of such other parts of the plant as leaves and stems; such preparations are called *kif* in North Africa, *dagga* in South Africa, *bhang* in India and the Middle East, and *macohna* in parts of South America (Walton, 1938).

Hashish, the Arabic word for "dry grass," usually refers to an extract considerably richer in psychoactive drug than the marihuana preparations described earlier. Hashish often is an extract containing only the drug-rich resin secreted by the hemp plant, which has been obtained by boiling resin-covered parts of the plant in appropriate solvents or by some mechanical means, such as scraping these parts of the plant. In India, this type of extract has been named *charas*. In color, hashish may be brown, gray, or black. It is often sold in America in the form of small cubes. Hashish, like marihuana, is subject to considerable variation in potency from one sample to another. In comparison to the "typical" marijuana sold in America today, it is often said that on the basis of psychoactive drug content per unit weight, hashish is five to 10 times as potent as marihuana (Pillard, 1970).

By weight, hashish may have a tetrahydrocannabinol (THC) content of 5 to 12 percent. The most potent forms of marihuana have a THC content of 4 to 8 percent (exemplified by the *Cannabis* extract from Jamaica called *ganja,* which is more potent than the Indian preparation of the same name). Mexican marihuana typically has a THC content of less than 1 percent, and American hemp usually has less than 0.2 percent. (National Commission on Marihuana and Drug Abuse, 1972; Mechoulam, 1970).

CHEMISTRY

From specimens of *Cannabis sativa,* chemists have been able to isolate and characterize the chemical structure of more than 20 compounds peculiar to this plant; these compounds are referred to collectively as the *cannabinoids* (see Figure 7–1). Two of the cannabinoids exhibit psychoactive activity in animals and people, several exhibit sedative or antimicrobial activity, and the remainder are biologically inert. Dr. Raphael Mechoulam and his colleagues in Israel first isolated and characterized the structure of a psychoactive cannabinoid, 1-Δ-3,4-*trans* tetrahydrocannabinol (THC) in 1964. Using a different labeling system, the compound was later designated Δ-9 tetrahydrocannabinol (see Figure 7–2).

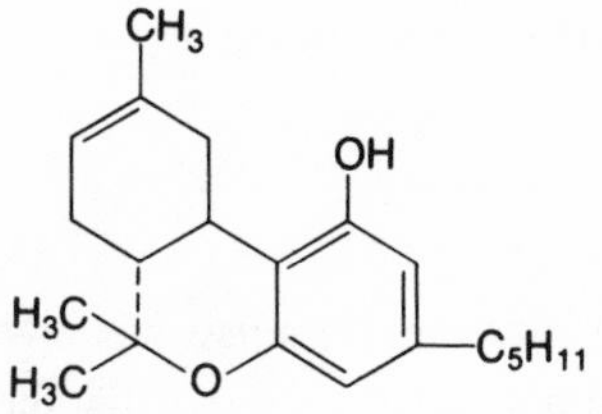

I. Δ$^{1(6)}$-THC

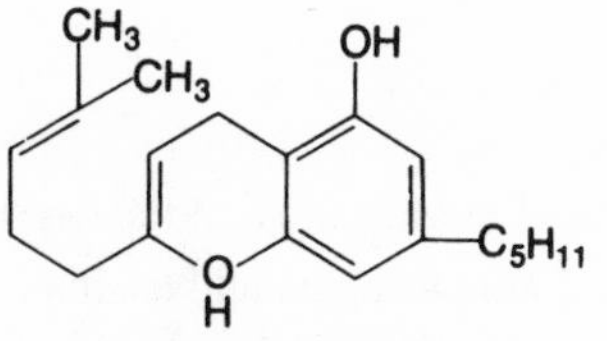

II. CANNABIGEROL

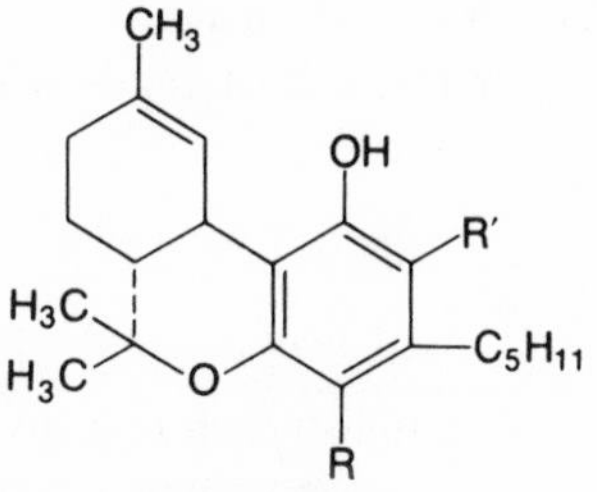

IIIa. Δ^1-THC acid A
        (R=H; R′=COOH)
IIIb. Δ^1-THC acid B
        (R=COOH; R′=H)

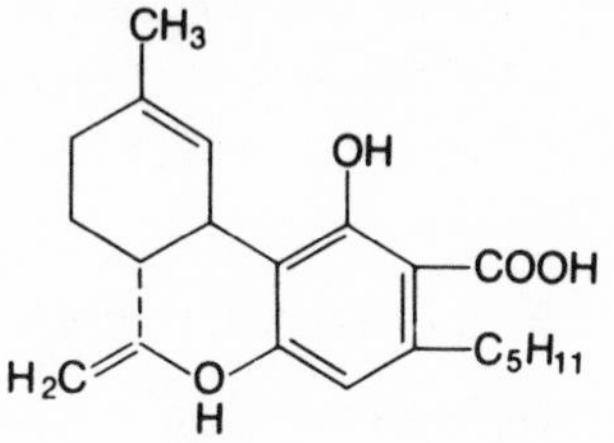

IV. CANNABIDIOLIC ACID

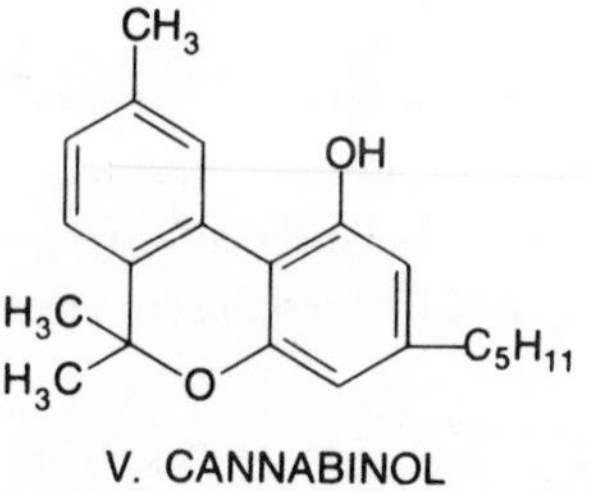

V. CANNABINOL

FIGURE 7–1. Various cannabinoids. Compound I (1-Δ$^{1(6)}$-tetrahydrocannabinol), is a psychoactive substance, exerting effects similar to those of Δ^1-THC. Compounds II, IIIa IIIb, and IV have been postulated to be biosynthetic precursors of Δ^1-THC (Mechoulam, 1970). Compound V is biologically inactive and presumably represents the oxidative degradation of Δ^1-THC.

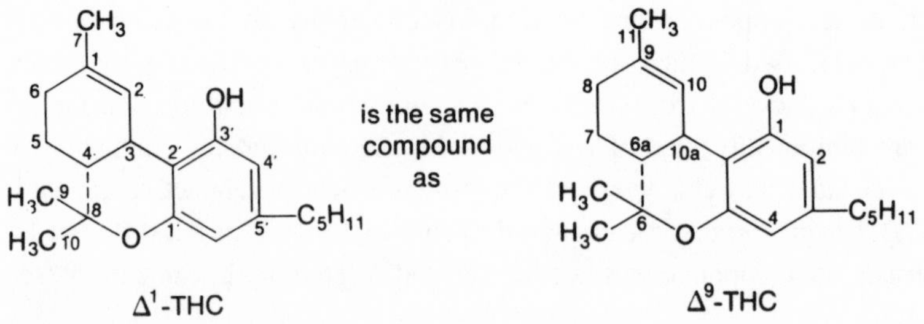

FIGURE 7–2. Structures of the most prevalent psychoactive compound present in cannabis extracts, tetrahydrocannabinol (THC). When the nucleus is numbered as a monoterpenoid would be, the compound is designated Δ^1-THC. When the nucleus is numbered as a pyran-type compound would be, it is designated Δ^9-THC.

Numerous studies have indicated that THC is the most prevalent psychoactive compound in marihuana and hashish, and it is commonly assumed today that the hallucinogenic effects of such extracts are caused largely by the THC they contain. On administration to animals and human subjects, THC faithfully mimics the physiologic and psychologic effects of *Cannabis* extracts (Hollister, 1971). A review of the biosynthesis of the various naturally occurring cannabinoids can be found in Harvey (1984).

ABSORPTION, BIOTRANSFORMATION, AND EXCRETION

Smoking represents the most commonly used route of administration of *Cannabis* extracts in the United States. The cigarettes ordinarily contain 300 to 500 mg of solid material; if the marihuana has a relative THC content of 1 percent, there is obviously 3 to 5 mg of THC in the cigarette. On average, 18 percent of the THC content of a marihuana cigarette are absorbed through the lungs of the smoker; differences in smoking techniques can cause the relative amount absorbed to fluctuate between 10 and 23 percent (Hollister, 1986).

As a route of administration, smoking results in a rapid onset of drug action, with effects becoming perceptible within a matter of seconds, or minutes at most, after inhalation of smoke. The length of interval between inhalation and perception of the effects of THC is probably largely determined by the concentration of drug in the smoke.

The consumption of food or beverages containing THC is a popular practice in some countries, notably India, but an infrequent one in this country. Oral ingestion of THC produces a more variable plasma level of THC than does smoking; the amount of drug absorbed is about one-third of that which would be absorbed by smoking (Harvey, 1984). Onset of drug effect following oral consumption is within 30 to 120 minutes, depending in part on the vehicle in which the THC is contained and in part on the quantity and type of food present in the stomach.

The THC molecule is not ionized and has a high oil–water partition coefficient. Under most conditions these factors ensure that the drug would enter cells very quickly and pass easily through barriers that protect brain and fetal tissue. THC is highly bound to plasma lipoproteins and albumin, however, with only about 3 percent of the total plasma amount being free to pass biological membranes and enter cells. Low concentrations of unbound drug suggest that tissue uptake is limited initially by blood flow. Tissues that are more thoroughly perfused, such as the lung and the kidney, collect the drug initially; it is later distributed to less-well-perfused tissues, such as body fat (Harvey, 1984). The brain does not accumulate as much as other tissues because of the difficulty this highly bound drug has in passing the blood–brain barrier.

Elimination of THC is fairly complicated. Following intravenous administration, concentrations of the drug in plasma decline rapidly over the first hour. This may be a result of a redistribution of the drug to various organs. The elimination half-life has been estimated at 28 hours in experienced users and 56 hours in nonusers. However, THC elimination may have several phases, and studies in animals suggest half-lives of several days in some species (Harvey, 1984).

Regardless of whether THC is administered by the oral route, by the intravenous route, or by inhalation, the greater part of its metabolites is found in the feces (35–65 percent) and the lesser part in the urine (15–30 percent). The percentage unaccounted for after five days of measurement is assumed to be sequestered within the body. The cannabinoids in the feces are thought to enter the intestine as constituents of biliary secretions and subsequently, to varying degrees, to reenter the body via absorption in a lower segment of the intestine (enterohepatic circulation) or to pass on unabsorbed. When THC is given by mouth, some of the fecal cannabinoids may represent unabsorbed drug metabolized by intestinal bacteria.

On administration of radioactively labeled THC to human subjects by inhalation or by intravenous injection, the presence of metabolites of THC (including some that may be equally potent or more potent than THC itself) can be detected within minutes; peak plasma values for the metabolites occur less than 15 minutes after the administration of THC by these two routes.

The variable nature of the level of available psychoactive drug in the brain can be appreciated in this discussion. Metabolism is rapid but may yield active metabolites; enterohepatic circulation may lead to an increase in plasma levels following an initial decrease; plasma binding and many organ depots may serve as reservoirs from which free drug can be slowly released over long periods of time. A more thorough discussion of some of these points can be found in Harvey (1984).

PATTERNS OF USE

A systematic and informative survey of marihuana (and hashish) use in the United States was undertaken by the National Commission on Marihuana and Drug Abuse. Their results, published in 1972, indicated that 14 percent of adolescents between the ages of 12 and 17, and 15 percent of individuals over 18 had used marihuana at least once. This means that, by 1972, an estimated 24 million Americans had been exposed to the effects of *Cannabis* extracts. Although at least half of both age groups used the drug only once or very infrequently, a substantial proportion used the drug often.

More recent reports of drug use among high school seniors indicate that marihuana use in this group peaked in 1978 and 1979. A relatively steady decline has been evidenced since 1980. In 1988, 47 percent of high school seniors reported using marihuana at least once, 33 percent reported use in the last year, and 18 percent reported use in the last month. The 33 percent figure represents a 3.2 percent decrease since 1987. It must be emphasized, however, that vastly more students use marihuana than use any other illicit drug; only use of alcohol and cigarettes exceed use of marihuana in this population.

In parallel with the decrease in use in last year and use in last month is a decline in students reporting daily use. In 1978, daily use peaked at 10.7 percent of seniors sampled. By 1988, this figure had decreased to 2.7 percent. However, 12.8 percent of the seniors reported that they had used marihuana on a daily or near-daily basis for at least a month at some time in the past. Closer analysis of this group of users indicated that it was made up of more males than females and that males used marihuana frequently for longer periods than did females. Those planning on attending college were less apt to use marihuana on a daily basis and engaged in this pattern of use for a shorter period of time (Johnston et al., 1989).

PHYSIOLOGIC EFFECTS

The most consistently observed physiologic changes produced by *Cannabis* extracts or by THC are increases in heart rate and peripheral blood flow, bronchodilation, and injection of the conjunctivae. Changes in blood pressure, respiration, and body temperature are usually minor in magnitude and variable in direction. Pupillary size is unchanged, but intraocular pressure is lowered by THC.

The increase in heart rate seems to correlate fairly well with the dose of THC; this increase may range from changes of questionable significance after small doses to relative increments of nearly 100 percent after large doses (Perez-Reyes et al., 1973; Galanter et al., 1972). The degree of heart rate increase may be related to the psychologic effects of the drug. An intense subjective effect (e.g., euphoria or anxiety) will result in a larger heart rate change than if the effect is somnolence. Heart rate reaches its maximum at 15 to 30 minutes following drug ingestion, remains elevated for 30 to 40 minutes, and declines slowly over the next several hours (Harvey, 1984). The temporal nature of the changes in heart rate is determined by the route of administration and the size of the dose. The temporal characteristics of tachycardia and of the psychologic changes produced by THC show a high correlation when the cannabinoid is given by mouth (Perez-Reyes et al., 1973). When THC is inhaled, however, the peak tachycardia occurs 15 minutes later, and tachycardia has subsided by more than one half at the time (some 45 minutes later) the subjective effects reach maximal intensity (Galanter et al., 1972). Studies suggest that the effect of THC on heart rate is not a direct effect but the result of drug interference with certain reflexes concerned with the maintenance of cardiovascular homeostasis (Beaconsfield et al., 1972).

PSYCHOLOGIC (SUBJECTIVE) EFFECTS

Inhalation of the smoke of a marihuana cigarette is followed within minutes by feelings of well-being, relaxation, and tranquility in most people. The individual who is notably apprehensive, depressed, or angry, however, may become more so under the influence of THC. The user feels intoxicated but typically reports that this feeling can be much more easily suppressed voluntarily than can the equivalent effect produced by alcohol. He may feel fuzzy, dizzy, a bit sleepy, and sometimes "dreamy." He often feels more friendly toward others and finds greater pleasure in their company; a few smokers, however, become quiet and remote. The user typically reports an increased awareness of his environment: vision seems sharper and sounds become more distinct. Many things seem to be humorous, so that laughter comes easily and frequently. By the same token, misfortunes seem more tragic. Human relationships are perceived to have more significance. Not uncommonly, the user feels that he has achieved a novel profundity of thought and an extraordinary acuity of insight; it is rare for objective observers to find much merit in these insights.

Perception of the passage of time is characteristically distorted by THC, so that clock time appears to pass very slowly. Accordingly, after the actual passage of a minute, people under the influence of THC might estimate the length of the elapsed time as only 30 seconds. Feelings of depersonalization, accompanied sometimes by a perception that bodily proportions have changed, also occur, but usually only with larger doses. Colors may shimmer and there may be visual distortions. Visual imagery occurs, though the images may sometimes be seen only when the eyes are closed. As with visions seen under the influence of LSD, the user realizes that the visual phenomena are drug induced.

Reports of feeling "drowsy" or "sleepy" are frequently given by individuals under the influence of THC, and "dreamlike" states may occur. Such a state does not, however, obligate sleep but merely facilitates its onset for the user so inclined. Amounts of THC larger than those in the typical "joints" sold today are more profoundly hypnotic and may irresistibly induce a deep sleep; this is particularly true if the user also is drinking an alcoholic beverage. Studies of the sleep pattern of subjects under the influence of THC have revealed small reductions in the amount of REM sleep in some subjects (Pivik et al., 1972) but do not provide a consistent picture of sleep alteration (Hosko et al., 1973). In regard to sedation and sleep, the effects of THC resemble those of ethanol, the barbiturates, and other generalized central nervous system depressant agents and represent one of the points of sharp contrast between the effects of THC and those of hallucinogens such as LSD.

Although THC is reputed to enhance sexual performance and enjoyment, there is no substantive evidence to support this attribution. Certainly with large doses, behavior of virtually all kinds, including sexual behavior, declines in frequency. At lower doses, sexual fantasies and sexual thoughts may be prominent, and the altered sense of time may contribute to the feeling that orgasm is prolonged. As with many drug effects, the user's expectations and recollections from previous use, as well as the current setting, will play an important role in his behavior following drug ingestion.

As with other types of hallucinogens, paranoid ideation occurs among users of THC. It is rarely reported after or verbalized during the drug experience when relatively small doses are taken, but it can become quite pronounced in some subjects or users who have taken large doses. Panic reactions have been observed as well, particularly in first-time users or in those who take the drug for therapeutic reasons. The changes in perceptions and thinking that are perceived as pleasant by some may be dysphoric in others and can deteriorate into panic or paranoia in still others.

The effects of THC on the intellect (mental processes and responses) and on intellectually directed motor activities (psychomotor performance) have been tested in various ways. As a first approximation, the decrements in cognitive and psychomotor performance appear to be dose related: The larger the dose, the greater the decrement. It has been observed, however, that previous exposure to the effects of THC is also an important factor in this situation. Experienced marihuana users frequently exhibit no decrement in performance even under the influence of fairly large doses of THC, and occasionally their performance improves. The explanation for this phenomenon is yet to be discovered.

It is generally agreed that some loss of what is called short-term, or immediate, memory is a frequent concomitant of intoxication with THC, even for the experienced user. Users report difficulty in completing long sentences; they fear that they will forget what they have started to say so that the ending of the sentence may well be incongruous with its beginning. This specific impairment has also been demonstrated by psychologic tests involving story recall, remembered digits, and the like. Long-term memory is apparently unimpaired. The result may be a "peculiarly disconnected" pattern of speech, characterized by slightly disjointed sentences and abrupt, irrelevant conversational tangents (Pillard, 1970). Performance on tests that require immediate memory and that require the subject to keep a goal in mind while digits are being manipulated mentally is also impaired by THC. Some investigators feel that the impairment in immediate memory plus the altered subjective sense of time affects the user's ability to separate the past, the present, and the future and, thereby, his ability to "locate himself in the continuum of time" (Snyder, 1971, p. 68). This, they suggest, results in the feelings of confusion and depersonalization that sometimes occur in the milder states of THC intoxication and that are more common in more deeply intoxicated subjects.

The impact of THC on an individual's ability to drive a car or fly a plane safely is a matter of widespread medicolegal interest. Unfortunately, it is still not clear how marihuana affects such activities. Certainly, sufficiently large doses will produce marked impairment in an individual's ability to perform psychomotor tasks such as driving a car or flying an airplane. The effects of smaller doses appear to vary, depending on the individual (some were impaired, some showed improvement); establishing a clear relation between blood levels of THC and degree of impairment has also proven difficult (Hollister, 1986). The effects of alcohol on driving ability seem more marked and more deleterious than those of marihuana (Hollister, 1986), although it is difficult to compare the two drugs on the basis of blood levels or subjective effects, so it is difficult to know whether similar doses were administered, or even what would constitute similar doses. Certainly, a combination of marihuana and alcohol would be particularly dangerous in those operating motor vehicles, and such a combination is found fairly frequently among victims of automobile accidents (Hollister, 1988).

Electrical activity of the brain, as recorded by electrodes on the scalp, changes hardly at all during intoxication with THC, though several investigators have noted small decreases in the frequency and voltage of the alpha rhythm on the electroencephalogram. With the aid of subcortically situated electrodes, it was possible to observe changes in the pattern of electrical activity from the septal region during "rushes of euphoria" in a patient intoxicated with marihuana (Hollister, 1971; Low et al., 1973). By and large, however, the use of conventional neurophysiologic techniques has not yet yielded information of value in any sense other than the negative.

MECHANISM OF ACTION

The mechanism of THC's action is not understood. Some theories hold that its effects on the central nervous system are related to its interaction with the lipid component of neuronal membranes, perhaps to increase the fluidity of such membranes, and alter their permeability to critical ions (Hollister, 1988). A similar mechanism has been postulated for ethanol. An important difference between THC and ethanol, however, lies in their ability to produce central effects. THC, despite the fact that it enters the brain very poorly, can produce perceived effects at ingested doses of as low as 0.3 mg. Ethanol, on the other hand, although it enters the brain very rapidly, produces perceived effects only after doses on the order of 7000 mg or more. Drugs with a potency as low as that shown by ethanol are more likely to act in a general way to disrupt membranes. Drugs as potent as marihuana are more likely to act at very selective sites, at drug-specific receptors.

Such receptors have been identified recently in brain tissue by evaluating the ability of series of cannabinoids to displace an extremely potent radiolabeled synthetic cannabinoid from brain homogenates. The potencies with which the drugs in the series displaced the labeled cannabinoid corresponded well with the relative potencies of these drugs in behavioral assays (Herkenham et al., 1990). This, as described in Chapter 3 for opioids, is a critical observation in determining whether a binding site can be considered a functional receptor. This cannabinoid receptor was found to be located in greatest concentration in the nuclei of the basal ganglia and in the hippocampus and cerebellum, a pattern not seen with other drug receptors. Preliminary data suggested that the receptor is coupled to a guanine nucleotide-binding regulatory protein. Thus, more information about potential mechanisms of marihuana's action may be forthcoming in the near future.

PHYSIOLOGIC DEPENDENCE AND TOLERANCE

The issue of whether there are typical physiologic disturbances that follow sudden cessation of THC use has not been clearly resolved despite the long history of chronic use of this drug. This in itself suggests that such withdrawal signs, if they develop, are subtle. Following chronic administration of THC to monkeys, signs indicative of withdrawal included piloerection, photophobia, penile erection, tremor, yawning, increased aggressiveness, and irritability. In man, sleep disturbances, nausea, vomiting, occasional diarrhea, and decreased appetite have been reported (Hollister, 1986). What has not been clearly demonstrated is whether these signs will disappear with the readministration of THC. Without such a demonstration, it is not clear that they are true withdrawal signs (Dewey, 1986).

Tolerance develops to a considerable extent to the effects of THC (Nahas, 1984). This has been most clearly shown in animal studies in which behavior disrupted by comparatively small doses of THC (0.3–1 mg/kg) is not disrupted by much larger doses (180 mg/kg) as a consequence of chronic administration of the drug. Tolerance to Δ9 THC confers cross-tolerance to synthetic cannabinoids as well. Doses well beyond the lethal dose have been given to tolerant pigeons, rats, and dogs without any serious sequelae. There is some evidence that tolerance is not conferred to all actions of THC. Decreases in locomotor activity and in aggressiveness persisted in rodents despite long-term administration of the drug (Nahas, 1984).

In humans, early indications of tolerance were exhibited by increases in the amount of drug used over time. It seems apparent that a naive user could not take as much drug as do some long-term users in Jamaica, North Africa, or Greece, but the nature of the tolerance shown is not understood.

ADVERSE EFFECTS

Acute Adverse Effects

For substances that seem to have been used as extensively and as frequently as the *Cannabis* extracts, remarkably few instances of untoward effects have been reported. The most common adverse reaction to this hallucinogen, as to LSD, is an acute nonpsychotic panic reaction in which the user fears that he is losing his mind. A variant of this panic reaction occurs most often in older, naive users who may interpret the THC-induced tachycardia, in the setting of the other psychic effects, as a sign that they are dying. Another form of nonpsychotic "bad trip" encountered among users of THC (particularly naive users) is an acute depression. Though it is often said that the panicky and the depressed reactions occur most often in the naive user, they have also been encountered in experienced users, particularly if the setting is alien or the dose larger than expected.

The most serious of the acute reactions is a toxic psychosis. Also called an "acute brain syndrome," it has been described as very much like the delirium caused by a high fever (Weil, 1970), in which the patient is disoriented, confused, troubled by true visual and auditory hallucinations, and possibly experiencing feelings of depersonalization and derealization. The patient may be prostrate during this period. By definition, toxic psychoses are self-limiting and end when the THC is metabolized. As a result, sleep ordinarily intervenes after four to six hours and the patient awakes free of psychotic symptomatology.

Although marihuana is generally thought to be free of next-day "hangover" effects, there is frequent reference in the literature on cannabinoids to headaches and hangoverlike feelings. In his review of adverse reactions to marihuana, Weil notes that, "Miscellaneous, mild ill-effects of marihuana (such as nausea, headache and transient paranoia) are familiar to most users" (p. 997). Weil's statement suggests that these mild adverse effects are common concomitants or sequelae to the use of marihuana, but, like most other authors in the field, he has not reported the results of a systematic survey of how people feel "the day after" the use of marihuana or hashish. The transient paranoia and nausea, which might well stem from the feeling of dizziness experienced by many using THC of which Weil speaks, probably occur primarily during the period of intoxication, but it is not clear to what extent headache occurs during intoxication and to what extent it occurs on the morning after. The likelihood of feeling poorly the next day is correlated in individual case reports with the use of large doses and/or the development of acute adverse psychic effects (Weil, 1970).

Persistent Adverse Effects

Few psychotic episodes lasting for more than 48 hours after THC consumption have been reported (National Commission on Marihuana and Drug Abuse, 1972). It is possible that some of the shorter "persistent" psychotic episodes (three to 10 days in duration) may represent iatrogenic prolongations of either toxic psychoses or what were originally nonpsychotic panic reactions (Weil, 1970; Negrette, 1973). This has been accomplished, in view of some psychiatrists, by treating the patients as if they had presented with a full-blown psychiatric emergency, medicating them immediately and admitting them to a psychiatric ward. Repeated medication plus the surrounding presence of truly psychotic patients could serve to convince the patient, as the effects of THC wore off, that he had truly "lost his mind." This could also slow the rate at which he regained his usual degree of contact with reality.

An "amotivational syndrome" has been described by West (1970) in the following way:

> the experienced clinician observes in many of these individuals (i.e., regular users of marijuana for 3 to 4 years) personality changes that seem to grow subtly over long periods of time: diminished drive, lessened ambition, decreased motivation, apathy, shortened attention span, distractability, poor judgment, impaired communication skills, loss of effectiveness, introversion, magical thinking, derealization and depersonalization, diminished capacity to carry out complex plans or prepare realistically for the future, a peculiar fragmentation in the flow of thought, habit deterioration and progressive loss of insight.

Some physicians feel that this syndrome is caused by THC. Investigations of the psychologic and social consequences of patterns of heavy use of THC in various countries have revealed quite different sequelae from one country to another. A heavy user in Jamaica may be a respected minor civil servant, but in Morocco, a man with the same pattern of use may do little more than eat, sleep, and smoke *kif*. Such observations support the view that psychosocial deterioration is not an inevitable consequence of THC use (National Commission on Marihuana and Drug Abuse, 1972). Laboratory studies have not produced any evidence for an amotivational syndrome, and the suggestion has been made that changes in goals and life-styles that frequently accompany a young person's involvement with illicit drugs may account for the behavioral changes observed. Thus, it may be difficult to separate cause and effect in determining the interaction between marihuana use and decreased ambition (Hollister, 1986).

With regard to violent crimes, the stereotyped allegation is that marihuana acts both to release the normal inhibitions against violent crimes and to embolden the individual to commit such acts. It was the finding of the National Commission on Marihuana and Drug Abuse that, "Rather than inducing violent or aggressive behavior through its purported effects of lowering inhibitions, weakening impulse control and heightening aggressive tendencies, marihuana was usually found to inhibit expression of aggressive impulses by pacifying the user, interfering with muscular coordination, reducing psychomotor activities and generally producing states of drowsiness, lethargy, timidity and passivity" (National Commission on Marihuana and Drug Abuse, 1972, p. 72). The commission recognized that it could not assume that the foregoing description of the effects of marihuana applied to all users; it therefore investigated this situation from a diametrically opposite point of view: How many violent crimes have been committed by marihuana users, particularly offenses committed while the user was under the influence of marihuana? The commission found no evidence "to indicate that marihuana was responsible for generating or creating excessive aggressiveness or impulsivity in individuals having no prior history of impulse or personality disorder. The most that can be said is that in these rare instances, marihuana may have aggravated a pre-existing condition" (National Commission on Marihuana and Drug Abuse, p. 73). Within the populations surveyed, the commission could find no significant difference in the incidence of violent criminal behavior when marihuana users were compared with nonusers.

"Flashbacks" have been reported among both users of THC and users of LSD, though the frequency seems very much lower in the former group (Pillard, 1970; Snyder, 1971). Some users find the recurring drug experience to be pleasant, but others regard flashbacks as threatening and disturbing. A few who have used both LSD and THC (on separate occasions) found that smoking marihuana triggers recurrences of the LSD experiences (Weil, 1970).

A variety of somatic disturbances has been observed in long-term users of THC; these include conjunctivitis, chronic bronchitis, hepatic enlargement, arteritis, gastroenteritis, and poor dentition (National Commission on Marihuana and Drug Abuse).

A teratogenic effect of THC has been demonstrated in rats, mice, rabbits, and hamsters; the effects on these animals' litters have ranged from resorption of the litter and stunting of the young to more specific defects, such as phocomelia and encephalocele (Pillard, 1970). Equivalent reports in humans have been confined largely to observations of highly dubious value, such as "increased incidence" of chromosomal "breaks" in leukocytes from peripheral venous blood.

Kolodny and his colleagues (1974) found subnormal plasma testosterone concentrations and oligospermia in young men ranging in age from 18 to 28, during "chronic, intensive" marihuana use (between five and 18 marihuana cigarettes per week). Studies using less-long-term exposure to marihuana have not confirmed these findings (Hollister, 1986). Evidence exists that heavy marihuana use can suppress the development of secondary sexual characteristics in the very young user (Hollister, 1986). The effects of marihuana on the female reproductive system have not been widely studied, but the drug may lead to increases in annovulatory menstrual cycles (Hollister, 1986).

Potential Therapeutic Uses of THC

THC and its synthetic analogs have been evaluated for their ability to suppress severe nausea and vomiting in patients undergoing some types of cancer chemotherapy and for their ability to lower intraocular pressure in patients with glaucoma. Although the drugs are effective in both situations, the side effects, primarily of unwanted perceptual and psychological changes, have limited their clinical usefulness. With further synthetic development, it may be possible to separate some of the potential therapeutic effects from the undesirable central nervous system effects.

REFERENCES

Beaconsfield, P., J. Ginsberg, and R. Rainsbury. Marihuana smoking. Cardiovascular effects in man and possible mechanisms. *New Engl J Med* 287:209, 1972

Dewey, W. L. Cannabinoid pharmacology. *Pharmacol Rev.* 38:151–178, 1986

Galanter, M., R. J. Wyatt, L. Lemberger, H. Weingartner, T. B. Vaughan, and W. T. Roth. Effects on humans of *delta*-9-tetrahydrocanimol administered by smoking. *Science* 176:934, 1972

Harvey, D. J. Chemistry, metabolism, and pharmacokinetics of the cannabinoids. In: Nahas, G. G., ed., *Marihuana in Science and Medicine.* New York: Raven, 1984, p. 37

Herkenham, M., A. B. Lynn, M. D. Little, M. R. Johnson, L. S. Melvin, B. R. de Costa, and K. C. Rice. Cannabinoid receptor localization in brain. *Proc Natl Acad Sci* 87:1932, 1990

Hollister, L. E. Marihuana in man: Three years later. *Science* 172:21, 1971

Hollister, L. E. Health aspects of cannabis. *Pharmacol Rev* 38:1, 1986

Hollister, L. E. Cannabis — 1988. *Acta Psychiatr Scand Suppl* 345:108, 1988

Hosko, M. J., M. S. Kochar, and R. I. H. Wang. Effects of orally administered delta-9-tetrahydrocannabinol in man. *Clin Pharmacol Ther* 14:344, 1973

Johnston, L. D., P. M. O'Malley, and J. G. Bachman. Drug use, drinking, and smoking: National survey results from high school, college, and young adults populations: 1977–1988. National Institute on Drug Abuse. Department of Health and Human Services Publication No. (ADM) 89-1638. Washington, D.C.: U.S. Government Printing Office, 1989

Kolodny, R. C., W. H. Masters, R. M. Kolodner, and G. Toro. Depression of plasma testosterone levels after chronic intensive marijuana use. *N Engl J Med* 290:872, 1974

Low, M. D., H. Klonoff, and A. Marcus. The neurophysiological basis of the marijuana experience. *Canad Med Assoc J* 108:269, 1973

Mechoulam, R. Marihuana chemistry. *Science* 168:1159, 1970

Nahas, G. G. Toxicology and pharmacology. In: Nahas, G. G., ed., *Marihuana in Science and Medicine*. New York: Raven, 1984, p. 109

National Commission on Marihuana and Drug Abuse. *Marihuana: A Signal of Misunderstanding*. First Report of the National Commission. Washington, D.C.: U.S. Government Printing Office, 1972

Negrette, J. C. Psychological adverse effects of cannabis smoking: A tentative classification. *Canad Med Assoc J* 108:195, 1973

Paris, M., and G. G. Nahas. Botany: The unstabilized species. In: Nahas, G. G., ed., *Marihuana in Science and Medicine*. New York: Raven, 1984, p. 3

Perez-Reyes, M., M. A. Lipton, M. C. Timmons, M. E. Wall, D. R. Brine, and K. H. Davis. Pharmacology of orally administered delta-9-tetrahydrocannabinol. *Clin Pharmacol Ther* 14:48, 1973

Pillard, R. C. Marihuana. *New Engl J Med* 283:294, 1970

Pivik, R. T., V. Zarcone, W. C. Dement, and L. E. Hollister. Delta-9-tetrahydrocannabinol and synhexyl: Effects on human sleep patterns. *Clin Pharmacol Ther* 13:426, 1972

Rubin, V., and L. Comitas. *Ganja in Jamaica*. The Hague: Mouton, 1975

Snyder, S. H. *Uses of Marijuana*. New York: Oxford University Press, 1971

Walton, R. P. *Marihuana: America's New Drug Problem*. Philadelphia: J. B. Lippincott, 1938

West, L. J. On the marihuana problem. In: Efron, D., ed., *Psychotomimetic Drugs*. New York: Raven, 1970, p. 45

Weil, A. T. Adverse reactions to marihuana. *New Engl J Med* 282:997, 1970

CHAPTER 8

Central Nervous System Stimulants: Amphetamines, Caffeine, and Related Drugs

Central nervous system stimulants are so called because, in contrast to opioids and central nervous system depressants, stimulants produce heightened awareness, decreased sleep and appetite, and increased locomotor activity. In large doses, they may cause stereotyped activity. When lethal doses are ingested, death is likely to be due to cardiovascular complications or convulsions rather than to depression of respiration.

There are a large number of CNS stimulants from a variety of chemical classes (see Figure 8–1). Cocaine and amphetamine may come to mind first when considering abuse of stimulant drugs, but caffeine is far and away the stimulant most frequently self-administered in Western civilization. The more exotic cathinone is the active ingredient in the leaves of the khat plant, which are chewed for their stimulant effects by large populations in some parts of the world. There is also limited abuse of drugs such as methylphenidate, a stimulant used in treating hyperactive children, and phenmetrazine, a stimulant used in the treatment of obesity. "Designer drugs," such as MDMA (methylenedioxymethamphetamine—ecstasy), of arguable use in psychotherapy, may have some actions in common with stimulants and are subject to limited abuse as well.

This chapter will consider issues related to abuse of amphetamine and caffeine and, to a lesser extent, of methylphenidate, phenmetrazine, MDMA, and khat. Because of the currently more serious nature of cocaine abuse, it will be discussed in the next chapter. It is important to point out that even though cocaine and amphetamine are treated separately here, the two drugs are much more similar than they are different. Their subjective effects, toxicities, and patterns of abuse, as well as the tolerance and dependence they produce, are very much alike. The important difference between these two drugs is their oral availability (amphetamine more so than cocaine), their duration of action (amphetamine is

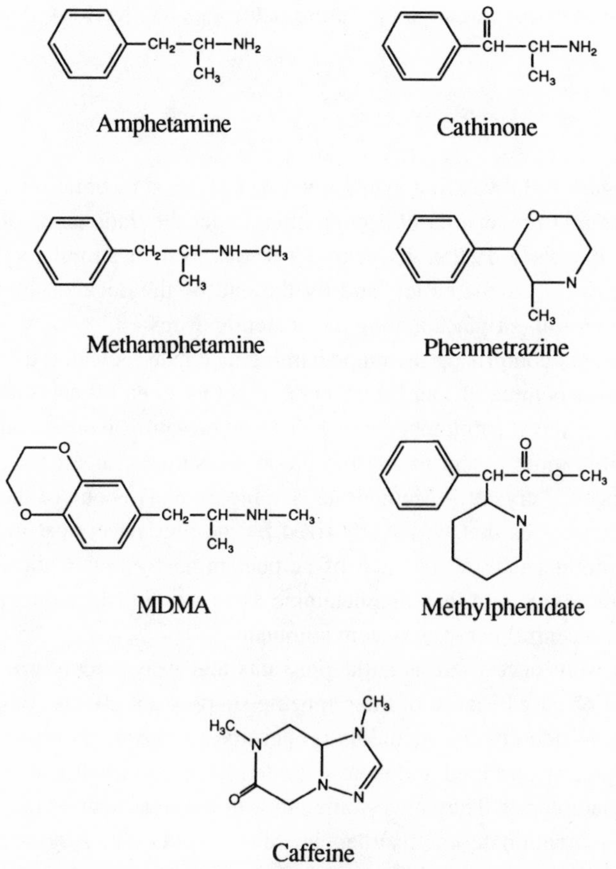

Amphetamine

Cathinone

Methamphetamine

Phenmetrazine

MDMA

Methylphenidate

Caffeine

FIGURE 8–1. Chemical structure of some CNS stimulant drugs. Each of these drugs except MDMA and caffeine has similar psychological effects in humans, and appears to act through catecholaminergic mechanisms. MDMA has some structural similarity to the other drugs, particularly methamphetamine, but its mechanism is apparently through the serotonin system and its effects are different from those of amphetamine. Caffeine has a completely different chemical structure, a different set of effects, and acts as an adenosine antagonist.

longer acting than cocaine), and, at the present time, the sociology of their abuse.

Historically, cocaine and amphetamine have alternated as the stimulant of choice among drug abusers in the United States. The cycle began with cocaine in the 1890s, switched to amphetamine in the late 1930s, and returned to cocaine in the 1980s. Amphetamine, in one form or another, may well present a more serious abuse problem than cocaine at some future date, and we overlook this drug at our peril.

THE AMPHETAMINES

Amphetamine (see Figure 8–1) was first synthesized in 1927 as a racemic mixture; clinical use of the mixture as a nasal decongestant under the trade name of Benzedrine began in the early 1930s. Its central nervous system stimulatory properties became known soon thereafter, and by the end of the decade, amphetamine occupied a prominent place among the analeptic drugs.

Tests of the two isomers comprising the amphetamine racemate indicated that the dextrorotatory isomer is three to four times more potent as a central nervous system stimulant than is the levorotatory isomer. The levorotatory isomer, on the other hand, is a little more potent in altering blood pressure and heart rate. Methamphetamine (speed, "crystal," Methedrine; see Figure 8–1) is one of the many amphetamine derivatives that was synthesized by the pharmaceutical industry following the enthusiastic acceptance of amphetamine by the medical profession. It is slightly less potent than amphetamine as a pressor drug, though clearly more potent as a central nervous system stimulant.

The amphetamines were once used as antidepressants and were widely prescribed in treatment of obesity because of their appetite suppressant effects. Because of their dangerous side effects, including propensity for abuse, their prescribed use has been greatly curtailed and is now limited largely to treatment of the rare condition of narcolepsy. They have some place in the treatment of Parkinson's disease and in attention deficit disorders in children, but other drugs are equally or more efficacious in these disorders, and clinical use of amphetamines is virtually nonexistent.

Patterns of Use

In the late 1930s, soon after it was synthesized and available, scattered evidence was found of amphetamine abuse. The incidence of amphetamine abuse increased after World War II, slowly in some countries like the United States, more rapidly in others like Japan. This increase reflected, in part, the consequences of two war-related events. Millions of doses of amphetamine and methamphetamine in the guise of "awakening drugs" were supplied to service personnel during the war, and after the war, surplus supplies of these drugs were dumped onto civilian markets, most notably in Japan. By 1954, it was estimated that as many as 2 million people (2 percent of the population) were involved in the abuse of amphetamines in Japan (Brill and Hirose, 1969). The drug made available to the Japanese was methamphetamine in injectable form, an extremely dangerous preparation. Not surprisingly, given this formulation, the Japanese pattern of abuse was often one of daily use of stimulants, injected intravenously or sub-cutaneously; the total intake per day in some cases rose to 200 ampules, each containing 3 mg of methamphetamine (Cox and Smart, 1970; Bell, 1967). Governmental programs of strict drug controls and public information about drug abuse have resulted in a notable decrease in the size of this problem.

Relatively mild forms of amphetamine abuse were prevalent in this country to the early 1960s, an increase in methamphetamine use occurred in the late 1960s. Most users fell into one of two categories. In the first category were those who used an amphetamine type of drug only on irregular occasions and usually for a specific purpose of postponing sleep: the student studying for an examination or the truck driver faced with a long trip. Users in the second category typified a more familiar pattern of drug abuse, for their goal was purely hedonistic; they relished the "high" and the enhanced sense of self-confidence that stimulants can produce. In this earlier period Benzedrine inhalers (250 mg of amphetamine per inhaler) were a common source of the drug; once the inhaler was disassembled, the drug-impregnated pledget was removed and ingested, or the drug was eluted into a liquid and drunk. The abuse of Benzedrine inhalers reached such alarming proportions that, in 1949, the amphetamine in these devices was replaced by a drug with weak stimulant properties (propylhexedrine).

Alteration of Benzedrine inhalers meant only greater utilization of the standard medicinal forms of the drug (5- and 10-mg tablets), which were obtained by illegal diversion or, in the case of resourceful users, by deceiving physicians and pharmacists (Bell, 1967). The drugs were almost always taken by mouth, which may account for the fact that drug use often did not escalate. Some users took these stimulants only on weekends in social settings; others felt an almost daily need for them.

Though such mild to moderately severe patterns of oral abuse continue to be exhibited to this day by many users of amphetamine, a new and much more pernicious pattern of abuse gained popularity in America in the 1960s—the "run," in which large doses of amphetamine are injected intravenously or smoked at relatively short intervals for periods as long as six and occasionally 12 days (Kramer et al., 1967). A few years ago, "speed freaks" (those who exhibit this pattern of severe abuse) were thought likely to begin the use of amphetamine during adolescence by taking "bennies" (Benzedrine tablets) or "dexies" (Dexedrine tablets) by mouth (Kramer et al., 1967). The total daily intake escalated and the user was then likely to switch to the intravenous route of administration [high-dose transition (Ellinwood and Lee, 1989)]. It may be more common these days for amphetamine users to switch more quickly to a newly available form of methamphetamine, "ice," which, like crack cocaine, can be smoked for an immediate "high."

With the change from the oral to the intravenous route or to smoking, the pattern of abuse usually becomes most severe. Intravenous use may initially entail doses of 20 to 40 mg taken three to four times a day. In most cases studied, both the dose and frequency of use rapidly increase thereafter. Individual doses taken by "speed freaks" range from 100 to 300 mg and occasionally rise to 3000 mg. For such users the interval between injections or amphetamine smoking often falls to two hours or less (Canadian Medical Association, 1969). An amphetamine user's total daily intake may reach 30 g or more; the equivalent total achieved by the oral route probably rarely exceeds 1 to 2 g (Canadian Medical Association, 1969).

During this compulsive period of drug taking, the individual shows profound stereotyped behavior and eats and sleeps very little (Ellinwood and Lee, 1989). This pattern of amphetamine use eventually leads to physical exhaustion or depletion of the drug supply and the user stops taking drug and "crashes." Users become dysphoric, anxious, and depressed as their blood levels of stimulants decrease. They experience little craving for drug, but may sleep, with or without the help of sedatives, for prolonged periods of time. The withdrawal dysphoria and decreased physical and mental energy may continue for several days or weeks following drug discontinuation. As mood returns to normal, the urge to take the drug returns as well, and if resources permit, users may begin another binge of stimulant use (Ellinwood and Lee, 1989).

Effects of Stimulants

Administration of a single 5- to 15-mg dose of D-amphetamine to a normal individual will result in an increase in blood pressure and heart rate, a decrease in appetite, and a period of increased wakefulness and increased ability to concentrate. Blood glucose increases, as does blood coagulability. Skeletal muscle tension increases, but the musculature of the bronchi and intestines relaxes. Amphetamine produces slight increases in the speed at which trained athletes can run or swim, for example, but it does not increase the speed of untrained individuals, presumably because the drug effect is so small that the amount of variability in performance speed occurring in the untrained subject obfuscates any increases produced by the drug. Much more dramatic enhancement of physical performance by amphetamines is seen when subjects are performing poorly because of fatigue or boredom (Spotts and Spotts, 1980).

These effects of amphetamine also occur in the chronic amphetamine user. Both normal humans and amphetamine abusers report feelings of euphoria, enhanced self-confidence, heightened alertness, greater energy and sexuality, usually occurring within about 30 minutes following oral ingestion of the drug. The user becomes more talkative and often more irritable. He is restless and moves about frequently. An important aspect of the drug's effects is that, during the initial part of a run, reality is not distorted. As the drug's effects wane, feelings of fatigue, letdown, and drowsiness occur; some users may be depressed emotionally, though rarely to any marked extent. Most users commonly fall asleep thereafter and the duration of sleep is not often abnormal.

Except for the speed of onset, the effects of a single dose of intravenous or smoked amphetamine differ only quantitatively from the effects of oral amphetamines. The faster onset and enhanced effects of intravenous or smoked amphetamine or methamphetamine ("ice"), however, increase tremendously the possibility that the user will initiate a run of amphetamine use if sufficient drug is available. A quite different and unpleasant picture of the effects of intravenous or smoked stimulants develops within a run. The early part of a run is usually a period of euphoria, full of rapid and decisive patterns of thought, enhanced self-confidence and self-esteem, and garrulous sociability. Users report being intensely fascinated with their own thoughts and activities, even when they are unpleasant (Kramer et al., 1967). As time passes and use continues, thoughts race through the mind so rapidly that concentration on any one of them is difficult. Abrupt changes in mood replace the unalloyed euphoria of the first day. Frightening visions begin to be seen by many users at this time. Shadows become people, and the user often sees his body as crawling with vermin. Unlike LSD and other drugs classified as hallucinogens, the stimulants produce illusions ordinarily only during the special circumstances of a run, with its prolonged exposure to large quantities of the drug. Recognition that these sensory phenomena are drug-induced is commonly retained, for a time at least (Kramer et al., 1967).

To add to the user's unease and confusion, paranoid symptoms typically develop during a run or binge and gradually intensify with time. These symptoms and the disturbances in sensory perception may be related to the user's awareness of the illegality of drug abuse. Trees, shadows, and parked cars may all be perceived as evidence of police surveillance. Friends may be regarded as informers and rooms may be searched to locate the "bugging" equipment that the user is now sure has been installed. Strangers may be regarded as disguised policemen. Any remark, however casual and even if uttered by a close friend, may be construed as an insult or a threat. The combination of this confused, paranoid state of mind with the feeling of great energy and enhanced physical prowess can lead to explosive outbursts of violent behavior.

The stimulant psychosis is commonly described as closely simulating paranoid schizophrenia. Within a setting of clear consciousness, the individual experiences delusions of persecutions plus visual, tactile, and auditory hallucinations and may exhibit repetitious compulsive behavior (Cox and Smart, 1970; Bell, 1967). The psychosis begins to remit when drug use stops. Its duration is related to the metabolism and excretion of the drug and is therefore shorter for cocaine than for amphetamine. Events that occurred during the psychotic state are usually remembered clearly thereafter (Cox and Smart, 1970).

PHYSIOLOGIC DEPENDENCE ON STIMULANTS

As described in Chapter 1, it is not uncommon to find the term *addiction* used synonomously with physiologic dependence. This has been a most unfortunate confusion in use, particularly in the case of the stimulants. In the past, these drugs have not been thought to produce physiologic dependence and hence have been regarded by some as "nonaddicting." If the term *addicting* is equated with drug-seeking and drug-taking phenomena, however, it is clear that central nervous system stimulants are among the most addicting of drugs.

The question of whether physiologic dependence on stimulants actually develops has not been resolved completely. A few years ago, the deep sleep and the sensations of hunger and fatigue on awakening that followed a run of central stimulant use were regarded as physiologic compensations to be expected after a protracted period of wakefulness, starvation, and continuous activity. Current thinking has changed, however, and the newest version of the psychiatrists' Diagnostic and Statistical Manual (DSM III-R) defines the stimulant "crash" and its aftermath as a true withdrawal syndrome. It is interesting, however, that the withdrawal signs from the slowly metabolized amphetamine are much the same as those from the rapidly metabolized cocaine. With other drugs, such as the opioids and the barbiturates, in which withdrawal signs are more clear-cut, longer-acting drugs typically produce a less severe and more protracted withdrawal. In a true withdrawal syndrome, readministration of the drug in question should rapidly and completely restore the individual to a normal condition. There are few studies of whether cocaine or amphetamine can reverse the withdrawal signs induced by termination of their chronic administration. It would not be surprising to find continued discussion of whether the poststimulant "crash" is in fact a true withdrawal.

TOLERANCE

The nature of tolerance development to stimulant drugs is also unclear. The evidence suggesting tolerance usually takes the form of increases in the amount of drug administered during the course of a run or binge. It is difficult to say, however, whether these observations reflect the development of tolerance, the desire for a more intense stimulant experience, or a combination of the two factors. Tolerance to the cardiovascular effects of the amphetamines and, more specifically, to their vasoconstrictor actions, is strongly suggested by the fact that intravenous users can survive single intravenous doses of 1000 mg or more with only an occasional untoward physiologic effect.

Whether tolerance develops to stimulants may depend on the effect being measured. Studies in animals indicate that the effect of the drug lessens with chronic administration if that effect results in a decrease in the density of reinforcer delivery (Schuster et al., 1966). Thus, the animals appear to learn to overcome the drug effect if doing so causes them to earn more food. No tolerance seems to develop to the stimulant effects of the drug. In other situations, there appears to be an *increased* sensitivity to the effects of stimulant drugs (Robinson and Becker, 1986). There is some evidence that the paranoid psychoses that can accompany high-dose amphetamine use develop with smaller doses in the experienced individual (Ellinwood and Lee, 1989).

Mechanism of Action

Amphetamine has been classified as an indirectly acting sympathomimetic. This means that its actions are related to its ability to release catecholamines from their synaptic terminals, and presumably the behavioral effects of amphetamine are due to central release of catecholamines. Although considerable amounts of research have been devoted to determining how certain aspects of amphetamine's actions are tied to release of specific catecholamines, our understanding of brain function in general is still too poor to permit any conclusive statements to be made. Some current theories have attempted to link the dopamine system to motivational effect of a wide variety of stimuli (Wise and Rompre, 1989). Thus, the ability of amphetamine to release dopamine is thought to be most relevant to the pleasurable effects produced by this drug. Evidence for a dopamine-based effect of amphetamine's addictive actions is, to a considerable extent, based on exclusion of the other catecholamines. Thus, drugs that primarily increase release or block reuptake of serotonin do not have effects or abuse potential like that of amphetamine. Similarly, enhanced release of norepinephrine does not seem to produce the same critical pattern of action as does amphetamine. Enhancement of dopamine levels in synaptic terminals, thought to be the major effect of cocaine, for example, does lead to stimulation, euphoria, and interoceptive effects like those produced by amphetamine.

Absorption and Fate

Amphetamines are absorbed adequately following oral ingestion, upon direct contact with mucosal surfaces and from injection sites. About half of a given dose is inactivated, largely in the liver, by the process of deamination; the remainder is excreted unchanged in the urine. The relative significance of the metabolic and excretory routes as means of disposing of the very large doses common in shooting speed is not known. It is known that excretion is most rapid when the urine is acidic and is relatively slow when the urine is markedly alkaline. The acidotic state resulting from the starvation that prevails during a run can in effect increase the user's drug requirements by promoting amphetamine excretion (Kramer et al., 1967).

Stimulant Toxicity

Certain physical stigmata can mark the chronic amphetamine user. Weight loss (20 to 30 lb or more) is a common finding; this reflects the fact that each run is effectively a period of total starvation. Nonhealing ulcers, abscesses, and brittle fingernails develop, possibly as secondary consequences of malnutrition (Kramer et al., 1967). Bruxism occurs frequently during runs; evidence of this tooth grinding, possibly in conjunction with abraded and ulcerative areas of the oral mucosa, can be detected on appropriate examination.

Amphetamine users who inject their drugs via a parenteral route (most typically the intravenous one) are no more careful of antisepsis than their counterparts in the world of narcotic addiction. As a result, they are subject to the same spectrum of infectious diseases (AIDS, hepatitis, endocarditis, and so on) as the heroin addict; these problems were discussed in more detail in Chapter 1.

The behavioral changes that can develop in chronic amphetamine users are of even greater concern. The drug-induced paranoid reaction and the "hypomanic" absorption in activities can persist in some beyond the period of actual drug use. Perhaps more ominous are the reports of a reduced ability to concentrate and an impairment of memory, particularly for very recent events. These disorders, plus reported difficulties in making mental connections, are manifestations of what has been called the "scrambled brains" syndrome of the amphetamine user or characteristics of the "burned-out" speed freak.

Although it is not known whether these particular disorders represent organic or functional brain damage, it is known that organic brain damage can result from chronic administration of methamphetamine. Following repeated administration of high doses of this amphetamine, experimental animals showed quite selective destruction of the dopamine terminals in the substantia nigra and perhaps a destruction of serotonergic nerve terminals in various brain regions as well (Ricaurte et al., 1984). The mechanism of dopamine terminal destruction seems to be a massive amphetamine-induced release of dopamine accompanied by an inhibition of an enzyme that degrades dopamine. The accumulated dopamine is nonenzymatically converted to a selective neurotoxin that is stored in and destroys dopamine terminals. The effect depends on the dose of drug used and the length of time it is administered.

Although the general behavior of animals that have been given high doses of amphetamine for long periods of time is not abnormal, these animals do appear to have an unusual sensitivity to the effects of drugs such as haloperidol and apomorphine that act through dopamine systems. It is not yet known whether the amount and pattern of amphetamine intake by human users during a run will result in the neurotoxicity that has been shown in animals, but the possibility certainly exists and should be a matter of concern.

KHAT CHEWING AND CATHINONE

Chewing of leaves to extract stimulant alkaloids is not unique to South America and to cocaine. A similar practice has been found in parts of eastern Africa and southern Arabia for hundreds of years. The plant whose leaves are chewed is known as khat *(Catha edulis),* and the material whose effects are apparently maintaining the behavior is (−)-cathinone. The pharmacology and sociology of khat use have been described in detail by Kalix and Braenden (1985). In the traditional pattern of use, young leaves and shoots from the bush are cut early in the day and taken to a nearby market, where they are purchased for use shortly after noon of that day. The potency of the product decreases as the leaf ages, either on the bush or after it is cut, so the most valuable leaves are those that are fresh and young. The users gather in a social group, bringing their khat, and begin to chew the leaves, one by one. The extracted material is swallowed and the chewed leaf is retained in the cheek for further mastication when fresh material is gone. In contrast to cocaine, no lime, ash, or other material is taken with the khat leaves.

The early effects of the drug are to increase socialization and a sense of well-being. Users report a relief from fatigue, increased energy and self-confidence, and feelings of euphoria. After several hours of khat chewing, however, the group of users tends to become more irritable, then more sluggish and depressed. There are some reports of toxic psychoses developing in individuals using particularly potent material.

When khat leaves were originally analyzed to determine the nature of the material that was producing these effects, it was determined that they contained pseudonorepinephrine. This chemical is of quite low potency and did not appear to be able to produce the spectrum of effects observed. It is likely that these early analyses used leaf material that had dried, since it was later found that a new alkaloid, which was named (−)-cathinone, was contained in fresh leaves. Cathinone is chemically similar to methamphetamine (see Figure 8–1) and shares a wide variety of physiologic and behavioral effects with amphetamine and other sympathomimetics. It, like amphetamine, has positive inotropic and chronotropic effects on the heart and produces increases in blood pressure. It also increases metabolic rate and temperature.

In behavioral experiments, cathinone was found to stimulate spontaneous locomotor behavior and to produce stereotyped behavior. Both of these effects are characteristic of amphetamine and cocaine. Cathinone reduces food intake in monkeys and rats, and there is cross-tolerance between cathinone and amphetamine with respect to their anorexigenic properties. Most interesting is the fact that amphetamine and cathinone have similar discriminative stimulus effects in animals; furthermore, cathinone, as amphetamine and cocaine, is self-administered by monkeys.

The evidence therefore indicates that the (−)-cathinone in the leaves of the khat plant is an amphetaminelike material that is appreciated for its euphorigenic properties by those who chew the leaves. It is unlikely that (−)-cathinone will become a serious abuse problem internationally, since the potency of the leaves decreases quickly after harvest and they are therefore difficult to transport great distances. Although cathinone can be synthesized, it is more difficult to make this drug than amphetamine, so it is unlikely, given the very similar effects of the two compounds, that cathinone would replace or compete with amphetamine as a drug of abuse in the United States.

CAFFEINE AND THEOPHYLLINE

Beverages containing methylated xanthines (caffeine, theophylline, and theobromine) have been consumed for over 1000 years by people in China and parts of Africa. In current times it has been estimated that as many as 92 percent of the adults in North America consume caffeine in some form on a regular basis. The longstanding, tremendous popularity of this class of stimulants makes it extremely interesting and important to evaluate these drugs more closely. It must be noted that one reason for the popularity of methylated xanthines over the years must be related to the pervasiveness of these drugs in plants. It is curious that alkaloids of similar structure and function are found in the leaves of *Thea sinensisa,* native to China; in the bark and/or seeds of three varieties of *Paullinia;* in an unrelated holly plant in South America; in *Theobroma cacao* and *Coffea arabica,* also found in South America; and in *Cola acuminata,* located in the Sudan. The function these compounds serve in plants is not known, but it should not be too surprising to find ubiquitous human use of such a ubiquitous alkaloid.

Beverages containing methylated xanthines are used all over the world, with coffee, containing caffeine, being the most popular caffeinated beverage in North America and tea, containing theophylline, being more popular in Europe and Asia. The development of sweetened caffeine-containing cola drinks made caffeine available to children as well as adults; there are few places in the world where these cola beverages are not making money for U.S. manufacturers. And, of course, there is cocoa, containing theobromine, the distinctive and universally appreciated flavor essential to the wide variety of sweetened chocolate temptations. Fortunately, theobromine has very little stimulant property, allowing chocolate to be enjoyed for its flavorful attributes without concern about stimulant side effects.

Patterns of Use

The most frequent pattern of caffeine use by those who drink it on a daily basis is early-morning consumption, followed by a reduced amount of intake during the rest of the day (Griffiths and Woodson, 1988b). In some countries—England and Japan, for example—the drinking of tea can be quite ceremonial and ritualized, occurring at specific times during the day or under specific circumstances.

The amount of caffeine in a cup of coffee or tea varies dramatically, but a typical amount is 85 mg per cup of coffee; 50 mg per cup of tea; 360 ml (12 oz) of a cola soft drink contains approximately 45 mg of caffeine (Rall, 1990). The blood level of caffeine produced by drinking 85 mg of caffeine in a cup of coffee will also vary, depending on whether the coffee is drunk quickly on an empty stomach or more slowly, with or after food consumption (Dews, 1982).

Effects

Caffeine is classified as a central nervous system stimulant. It has been shown to increase rates of behavior in experimental animals (Dews, 1982). Although structurally unlike amphetamine (see Figure 8–1), caffeine can, like amphetamine, reverse some of the behavioral deficits in humans that result from fatigue, boredom, or lack of sleep and can increase feelings of alertness. It can also delay sleep in relatively low doses (approximately 1.5 cups of coffee). In high doses, in nontolerant individuals, it increases blood pressure and heart rate. These effects disappear with chronic administration of caffeine, indicating the development of tolerance (Dews, 1982).

Caffeine has many effects that are quite different from the more typical CNS stimulants, such as amphetamine, cocaine, and methylphenidate, however. Its mechanism of action does not appear to involve changes in dopamine levels, as is true with the classic CNS stimulants. Rather, it acts as an antagonist of the naturally occurring substance adenosine. Adenosine's central actions are not well understood and have been defined, to a large extent, by evaluation of the actions of methylxanthines. Thus, adenosine actions in the central nervous system may include neuromodulation resulting in central nervous system depression.

Although there is some evidence that caffeine has discriminative stimulus properties in common with cocaine and methylphenidate (but less so with amphetamine) in rats (Holtzman, 1986), humans receiving caffeine are more likely to report an increased level of tension, "jitteriness," and anxiety, as opposed to the effects of amphetamine, which include feelings of "well-being" and "euphoria" (Griffiths et al., 1986). Caffeine has considerably less reinforcing effects than amphetamine or cocaine. In animals, caffeine does not maintain the high rates of behavior, as do such drugs as cocaine, amphetamine, and other classic CNS stimulants (Griffiths and Woodson, 1988b). A recent study in normal (non-drug-abusing) humans given a choice between capsules containing caffeine and capsules containing placebo, suggested that caffeine has very little reinforcing effect in this population (Stern et al., 1989). Small doses were chosen no more frequently than placebo, and larger doses were chosen less frequently than pla-

cebo. This stands in contrast to the frequent selection of amphetamine or phenmetrazine capsules in a similar population of normal human subjects. Other studies have emphasized individual differences in liking caffeine-containing
capsules. Some subjects took few of the capsules with caffeine; others always
selected the capsules containing the caffeine (Griffiths and Woodson, 1988b).

PHYSIOLOGIC DEPENDENCE
There is an unusual aspect to the reinforcing effects of caffeine that has only
recently been brought to light. That is the nature of the caffeine withdrawal
syndrome and how it may affect caffeine consumption. It has been known for
some time that, following termination of chronic caffeine consumption, humans
report mild to severe headache and, less frequently, feelings of fatigue and other
signs that may be part of a caffeine withdrawal syndrome. The syndrome typically begins 12 to 24 hours after the last dose of caffeine, peaks at 20 to 48 hours
after the last dose of caffeine, and most frequently lasts about one week (Griffiths
and Woodson, 1988a; Figure 8–2). Few parametric studies have been done, but
the withdrawal signs appear to be dose and duration related, being more likely
to develop in people who have consumed caffeine-containing beverages for long
periods or in large doses.

As has been emphasized throughout this book, there is a poor relationship
between the ability of a drug to produce physiologic dependence and its ability
to function as a reinforcer. It does seem to be the case, however, that self-administration of some dependence-producing drugs can be affected by the presence

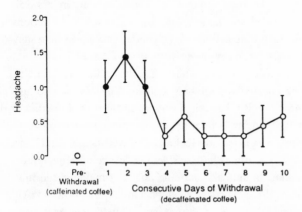

FIGURE 8–2. Caffeine withdrawal. The effect of substituting decaffeinated coffee for
caffeinated coffee on subjects' report of headache. Subjects drank only caffeinated coffee
for an average of 10 days before it was replaced by decaffeinated coffee. Data that are
significantly different from prewithdrawal ratings are shown as filled data points. (From
Griffiths and Woodson, 1988a.)

or impending onset of the withdrawal signs of that drug. One of the best examples of this is the benzodiazepines, which are weak reinforcers in and of themselves but produce physiologic dependence that can make it difficult for some people to stop taking these drugs (see Chapter 4).

A similar situation appears to exist with caffeine. In well-controlled experimental conditions, it has been shown that human subjects who had been drinking caffeinated coffee for one week before being asked to select between caffeinated and decaffeinated coffee selected the caffeinated coffee 92 percent of the time. They reported that the decaffeinated coffee was "weak" and produced fatigue and headache and they did not like it as much as the caffeinated coffee. Those who had been drinking decaffeinated coffee during the prior week selected caffeinated coffee on 50 percent of the choice opportunities and reported no greater liking for one type of coffee over the other. It appeared that the main effect of one week's experience drinking caffeinated coffee was to decrease the liking of decaffeinated coffee, rather than to increase the liking of caffeinated coffee (Griffiths and Woodson, 1988a). Interestingly, and perhaps relevant to understanding the nature of the ability of caffeine to maintain behavior, after several days of drinking decaffeinated coffee, subjects no longer found it weak and unsatisfactory. Furthermore, the number of cups of coffee consumed remained nearly the same, regardless of whether the coffee contained caffeine.

This suggests that humans who are suffering from caffeine withdrawal dislike decaffeinated coffee, presumably because it does not relieve their headache and fatigue. People who are not experiencing caffeine withdrawal apparently have no particular preference, one way or the other, about whether their beverage contains caffeine or not. It thus appears as though caffeine is not a good reinforcer in the nondependent individual, but it can come to serve as a reinforcer if its consumption relieves the distress of caffeine withdrawal. The increasing popularity of decaffeinated coffee, teas, and cola drinks in the United States indicates that caffeine itself may not be necessary to maintain consumption of these types of beverages.

METHYLENEDIOXYMETHAMPHETAMINE (MDMA)

Methylenedioxymethamphetamine is a drug that will probably slip from memory over the next decade, but it is discussed here because it serves as an example of a "designer drug" that received considerable attention in the media in the 1980s. Our legal system of drug control is based on schedules that provide various degrees of restriction of drug availability (see Chapter 12). Each schedule consists of lists of drugs whose availability is limited because of known or suspected abuse potential. Until recently, this system was one of inclusion: a drug that was not listed could have relatively unrestricted availability. Thus, when new drugs are synthesized or old, unscheduled drugs were rediscovered, they might have

been freely available until the legal system found the time and reasons to schedule them. This did not include drugs synthesized by pharmaceutical companies,
since these drugs are tightly restricted until many years of testing demonstrate
their safety and effectiveness. But the clandestine chemist could synthesize a
new compound and make it available to the public; its sale and use were not
necessarily illegal. These drugs are termed *designer drugs,* and although they
have not yet produced much actual damage, they do pose a frightening potential
for harm.

MDMA (ecstasy) is not a typical designer drug, since it was first synthesized
in 1914 by a German drug company, apparently for treatment of obesity.
Through processes that are not clear the drug showed up in California in the late
1960s, in the hands of a few psychotherapists who reported that it was very
useful in helping clients respond to the therapeutic process. People were reported
to have improved psychologic insight, to relate better to others and to themselves, and to show amazing progress in coming to terms with whatever problems brought them to therapy.

California law did not prohibit the use of drugs such as MDMA as long as
there was some assurance that the drugs were made by reputable sources and
their use was physician initiated and supervised. As might be expected, however,
MDMA did not stay within the physician-supervised purview; it soon appeared
on the streets. Clandestine laboratories made and distributed the drug, and demand for it was reported to be widespread in Chicago, Miami, and Boston in
the early to middle 1970s.

A move was made to add this drug to Schedule 1 of the Controlled Substances
Act, the most restrictive schedule, reserved for drugs with no therapeutic potential and high potential for abuse. This would make the drug unavailable for any
but research purposes. Outspoken objections came from psychotherapists, who
felt that an important weapon in treatment of human misery was being taken
from them. The conflict became a media event, with both sides of the argument
being presented by leading spokespersons on talk shows and in the press. The
upshot of this story is that the Drug Enforcement Administration won, the psychotherapists lost, and MDMA is currently a Schedule 1 drug, placed there originally on an emergency basis.

The reaction to MDMA was probably overblown; the drug did not appear to
have great abuse potential. Those who used it to produce changes in mood rather
than to aid in psychotherapy typically took it with low frequency (once per month
was fairly typical). First-time users often were disappointed with the effects of
the drug, and most indicated that they would not bother to take it again. Those
who took the drug frequently reported adverse effects, such as increased muscle
tension and sweating, which served, in effect, to limit drug use (Siegel, 1986).
It appears to have been relatively safe in acute doses, at least on a behavioral
level. Few people have come to emergency rooms because of problems related

to MDMA ingestion. On the other hand, it is doubtful that MDMA would have had any lasting ameliorative effects on the progress of psychotherapy. The goals and processes of this treatment are so poorly defined that it would be most difficult to determine whether *any* intervention was effective.

MDMA is an unusual drug. It is not clearly a stimulant, although it has, in common with amphetaminelike drugs, a capacity to increase blood pressure and heart rate. Moreover, it does not have any potential to produce hallucinations, in contrast to a chemically similar drug, MDA (methylenedioxyamphetamine), although it does produce some perceptual changes in the form of increased sensitivity to light, difficulty in focusing, and blurred vision in some users (Siegel, 1986). Its mechanism of action is thought to be via release of the neurotransmitter serotonin, which, as mentioned earlier, is one, perhaps less important, physiologic effect of amphetamine. MDMA may also release dopamine, although the general opinion is that this is a secondary effect of the drug (Nichols and Oberlender, 1990). The most pervasive effect of MDMA, occurring in virtually all people who took a reasonable dose of the drug, was to produce a clenching of the jaws. Sweating, blurred vision, and ataxia also occurred in most of those who ingested the drug. Some of these negative effects persisted for several days or weeks in some subjects (Siegel, 1986). Thus, it is doubtful that MDMA, even if it were not legally controlled, would develop into a drug with serious abuse problems.

The major interest in the drug currently is related to the neurotoxic effects it produces in animals. A great deal of research on this topic has demonstrated that chronic administration of MDMA results in degeneration of serotonin neurons in the brain. This results in what appears to be a permanent decrease of 40 to 50 percent in brain levels of serotonin (De Souza et al., 1990). The functional results of this decreased serotonin have not been well described, although the serotonin system has been implicated in sleep, sexual behavior, appetite, and mood regulation, and the potential for neurotoxic sequelae to result from frequent use of MDMA is high.

DRUGS USED TO TREAT HYPERACTIVITY AND OBESITY

As indicated earlier, amphetamine has been used in the past to treat attention deficit disorders in children and to produce weight loss in overweight adults. The drug is effective in these disorders but is no longer used because of concerns about toxicity, including abuse. Stimulant drugs such as methylphenidate (Ritalin; see Figure 8–1) are currently used in the treatment of attention deficit disorder, and drugs such as phenmetrazine (Preludin; see Figure 8–1) are infrequently used to treat obesity. These drugs are very similar to the amphetamines in animal studies: They produce increased locomotor activity, have similar discriminative effects, and are reinforcers when delivered via the intravenous route.

Despite their similarity to amphetamine, abuse of these drugs does not appear to be a serious problem at the present time. This is most likely because cocaine and amphetamine are readily available and have developed a reputation on the street for producing the type of "high" that stimulant abusers are seeking. Methylphenidate and phenmetrazine may be less easy to locate and have no particular advantage over the more readily available stimulants.

There are some disadvantages to users of drugs such as methylphenidate related to their formulation. They are available for prescription use in tablet form for oral ingestion. The drug available on the street is usually diverted from the prescription source and is therefore the same tablet, meant to be taken orally. These tablets contain talc as a filler, as is typical for oral medications, but stimulant addicts, seeking a rapid and more powerful effect, prefer to self-administer these drugs intravenously. They often crush the tablet, dissolve it in water, and, after crude filtering procedures, inject it into their veins. Intravenous talc lodges in various organs of the body, primarily the lungs, where it can, over the course of several years, result in pulmonary talc granulomatosis and restrictive and obstructive lung disease. Addicts can be seriously incapacitated by or even, on occasion, die from this disease.

REFERENCES

Bell, D. S. Addiction to stimulants. *Med J Austral* 1:41, 1967

Brill, H., and T. Hirose. The rise and fall of a methamphetamine epidemic: Japan 1945–1955. *Sem Psychiat* 1:179, 1969

Canadian Medical Association. Non-medical use of drugs, with particular reference to youth. Report of the Special Committee on Drug Misuse, Council on Community Health Care, Canadian Medical Association. *Canad Med Assoc J* 101:804, 1969

Cox, C., and R. G. Smart. The nature and extent of speed use in North America. *Canad Med Assoc J* 102:724, 1970

De Souza, E. B., G. Battaglia, and T. R. Insel. Neurotoxic effects of MDMA on brain serotonin neurons: Evidence from neurochemical and radioligand binding studies. *Ann NY Acad Sci* 600:682, 1990

Dews, P. B. Caffeine. *Ann Rev Nutr* 2:323, 1982

Ellinwood, E. H., and T. H. Lee. Dose- and time-dependent effects of stimulants. In: Asghar, K., and E. De Souza, eds. *Pharmacology and Toxicology of Amphetamine and Related Drugs*. National Institute on Drug Abuse Research Monograph 94, Washington D.C.: U.S. Government Printing Office, 1989, p. 323

Griffiths, R. R., G. E. Bigelow, and I. A. Liebsen. Human coffee drinking: Reinforcing and physical dependence producing effects of caffeine. *J Pharmacol Exp Ther* 239:416, 1986

Griffiths, R. R., and P. P. Woodson. Caffeine physical dependence: A review of human and laboratory animal studies. *Psychopharmacology* 94:437–451, 1988a

Griffiths, R. R., and P. P. Woodson. Reinforcing properties of caffeine: Studies in humans and laboratory animals. *Pharmacol Biochem Behav* 29:419, 1988b

Holtzman, S. G. Discrimination stimulus properties of caffeine in the rat: Noradrenergic mediation. *J Pharmacol Exp Ther* 239:706, 1986

Kalix, P., and O. Braenden. Pharmacological aspects of the chewing of khat leaves. *Pharmacol Rev* 37:149, 1985

Kramer, J. C., V. S. Fischman, and D. C. Littlefield. Amphetamine abuse: Pattern and effects of high doses taken intravenously. *J Amer Med Assoc* 201:305, 1967

Nichols, D. E., and R. Oberlender. Structure–activity relationships of MDMA and related compounds: A new class of psychoactive drugs? *Ann NY Acad Sci* 600:613, 1990

Rall, T. W. Drugs used in the treatment of asthma. In: Gillman, A. G., T. W. Rall, A. S. Nies, and P. Taylor, eds., *Goodman and Gillman's The Pharmacological Basis of Therapeutics*, 8th ed. Elmsford, N.Y.: Pergamon, 1990, p. 618

Ricaurte, G. A., L. S. Seiden, and C. R. Schuster. Further evidence that amphetamines produce long-lasting dopamine neurochemical deficits by destroying dopamine nerve fibers. *Brain Res* 303:359, 1984

Robinson, T. E., and J. B. Becker. Enduring changes in brain and behavior produced by chronic amphetamine administration: A review and evaluation of animal models of amphetamine psychosis. *Brain Res* 396:157, 1986

Schuster, C. R., W. S. Dockens, and J. H. Woods. Behavioral variables affecting the development of amphetamine tolerance. *Psychopharmacologia* 9:170, 1966

Siegel, R. K. MDMA: Nonmedical use and intoxication. *J Psychoactive Drugs* 18:349, 1986

Spotts, J. V., and C. A. Spotts. Use and abuse of amphetamine and its substitutes. National Institute on Drug Abuse, Research Monograph 25, Washington D.C.: U.S. Government Printing Office, 1980

Stern, K. N., L. D. Chait, and C. E. Johanson. Reinforcing and subjective effects of caffeine in normal human volunteers. *Psychopharmacology* 98:81, 1989

Wise, R. A., and P. P. Rompre. Brain dopamine and reward. *Ann Rev Psychol* 40:191, 1989

CHAPTER 9

Central Nervous System Stimulants: Cocaine

The first cycle of stimulant abuse in the United States began with cocaine in the 1890s, soon after chemists discovered how to isolate cocaine from the coca plant, making it easy to keep and transport. With no legal restrictions on its use, cocaine appeared in wine, along with caffeine in Coca-Cola, and in many patent medicines. Publicity about the dangerous effects of cocaine, as well as physicians' increasing interest in reducing the number of patent medicines, led to restrictions on the availability of cocaine in the Harrison Narcotic Act of 1914.

Cocaine use continued to a relatively moderate extent among wealthy celebrities and members of the drug cognoscenti, but until the late 1960s, amphetamine and methamphetamine had taken over as the primary stimulants of abuse. At about this time, the dangers of amphetamine abuse ("speed kills") became widely recognized; at the same time the dangers of cocaine abuse had apparently been forgotten. Cocaine was thought to be relatively harmless, in large part because pharmacologists could detect no withdrawal signs when chronic drug administration was terminated in animals. This information was apparently translated to the general populace by the media and government agencies as meaning that the drug did not produce addiction, although those who studied the drug's behavioral effects emphasized the findings that cocaine, like amphetamine, was a very effective reinforcer, which animals would self-administer to the point of marked toxicity.

At this time, cocaine was an expensive commodity, snorted in powder form by those who could afford it; it was a "status" drug, with limited availability, and the number of cocaine abusers was sufficiently small that there was little concern about its potential for danger. In 1983 a most unfortunate event occurred. A glut in the world market for cocaine made the drug more available and cheaper and, more important, a smokable, inexpensive, and very addictive form of cocaine, "crack" cocaine, became available. Abuse of this form of cocaine quickly reached epidemic proportions; in 1985 it was estimated that 22 million Americans had tried crack or other forms of cocaine and that at least 6 million used it on a regular basis (*National Household Survey,* 1987). Although this figure declined to 1.6 million in 1990 (*National Household Survey,* 1991), there was no similar decrease in the number who used cocaine once a week or more—in other words, in those who were chronic crack smokers.

The story of crack abuse in the late 1980s and early 1990s is one of such current interest that it must be researched from the pages of daily newspapers as well as from scientific books and articles. It is a story that has menacing economic, sociologic, and psychologic ramifications, starting on the streets of the poorest neighborhoods in our country and moving to the widest and wealthiest international levels. It is a story about the destabilization of entire governments in Central and South America and about the destruction of many of our inner cities. Cocaine is a drug that locks entire neighborhoods into their homes in fear of the violence of the drug sellers and users, results in the death of scores of young people every night through gang wars and drug overdoses, and causes the premature births of thousands of desperately ill babies, whose futures are often as bleak as those of their drug-addicted mothers.

Yet the ominous story of cocaine abuse is not difficult to comprehend if one understands something of the pharmacology of the drug itself, the legal system that is trying to combat abuse of this drug, and how human behavior can come under the control of a drug such as cocaine. Unfortunately, simply coming to understand some aspects of cocaine abuse and perhaps even being able to predict the future sequelae of abuse of other drugs, will not lead to controlling or eliminating this scourge. The question of how to contain cocaine abuse does not have a simple answer, as should be clear from the inability of current efforts to accomplish this goal. Yet with several influential people now suggesting that cocaine be legalized or at least decriminalized to reduce the violence associated with its international and inner-city trafficking, it may be instructive to look closely at relevant aspects of both the unique properties of this drug and those properties it seems to have in common with other drugs of abuse.

COCAINE PRODUCTION

Cocaine is a product extracted from the leaf of the shrub *Erythroxylon coca,* which is grown primarily in mountainous areas of South America, particularly Peru and Bolivia. Its fascinating, 1000-year-old history of use, from the time of the Incas to some of its more famous nineteenth-century devotees has been well described by Petersen (1977). Typically, cocaine paste is prepared from coca leaves in a forested setting near where the coca is grown and the paste is shipped to Columbia for conversion to cocaine hydrochloride salt. Cocaine is extracted from the coca leaves with an organic solvent, perhaps kerosene in the primitive process, or benzene or petroleum ether in more sophisticated laboratories. Acid solutions are used along with organic solvents to remove alkaloids other than cocaine and nonalkaloid impurities; the acid is finally neutralized with base and the solution dried. The resulting cocaine hydrochloride salt is available as a solid (rock) or in smaller pieces (flake) of relatively pure substance.

Cocaine is shipped through various illicit channels, often in small, private airplanes, or smuggled onto commercial passenger jets or cargo ships, to distribution centers in larger cities in the United States. Although coca is grown in several South American countries, Columbia is the major exporter (approximately 80 percent) of extracted cocaine to the United States and Europe (Brooke, 1989, p. 24) and immigrants from the Dominican Republic appear to be the major initial cocaine distributors, at least in New York City (Williams, 1989).

The local distributor is usually the person who turns the cocaine hydrochloride into "crack" cocaine. This process involves boiling an aqueous solution of cocaine hydrochloride with sodium bicarbonate and then letting the mixture cool into a water-insoluble, base form of cocaine. From this larger mass, smaller pieces can be broken off and packaged for the retail market.

Although it is not known how cocaine dealers developed this simple method for turning the salt form of cocaine into the base form, the reasons for doing so are at least twofold. One was to help cocaine producers in the early 1980s deal with a glut of cocaine. The producers needed to come up with a "new product" that would increase their sales and profit. At the same time, consumers were requesting that a safer form of base cocaine be made available to them. The earlier process of smoking cocaine (free basing) involved combining an aqueous solution of cocaine hydrochloride with a base and then using ether to extract the free base form of cocaine. The ether had to be allowed to evaporate from the mixture before the cocaine could be smoked, and this process was often hastened by applying a flame to the solution. Since ether is extremely volatile, those who were in a hurry to obtain their free base cocaine occasionally suffered severe burns from the exploding ether.

Why was base cocaine in such demand? The answer reflects the increased addictive nature of drug forms that have an extremely rapid onset of action. Cocaine base, in contrast to cocaine salt, releases cocaine vapor when it is burned. The salt form of cocaine, on the other hand, is water-soluble and, as such, is effective following intravenous injections or inhalation through the nose. Although intravenous injection results in a very rapid onset of drug action, the procedure of giving oneself intravenous injections is unacceptable to all but the most hard-core drug users. Snorting cocaine salt produces a satisfying euphoria, but one that has a slower onset. A comparison between blood levels observed over time following administration of either intravenous or inhaled cocaine is shown in Figure 9–1. Smoking cocaine base puts cocaine into rapid contact with the large surface area of the lungs, from where it is carried directly to the brain. Smoking a drug can result in a "high" that is even more rapid than that resulting

SINGLE DOSING, COCAINE

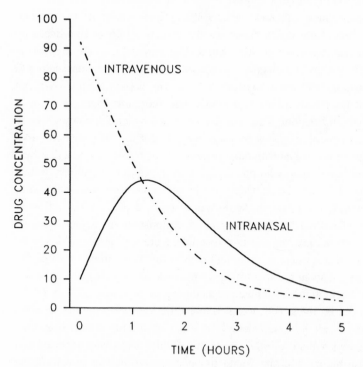

FIGURE 9–1. Comparison of the blood levels of cocaine that develop following either intravenous or intranasal administration of the drug. (From Ellinwood and Lee, 1989.)

from an intravenous injection. Therefore, a drug form that can be smoked has greater reinforcing effects than one that must be snorted or taken by mouth.

The end users of cocaine put pressure on their sellers to come up with a smokable form of cocaine to sell to them directly, so that they would not be subjected to the dangers of preparing free base themselves. The bicarbonate of soda reagent was developed in response. One of the advantages to the buyer, in addition to reducing the dangers of exploding ether, was that free base cocaine was extremely pure. Typically, adulterants of the salt form of cocaine, such as lactose, did not react like cocaine in the process of dissolving and extracting the base form. But the ingenuity of the sellers is not limited to keeping their customers happy; making a healthy profit is of primary importance, and soon an adulterant that could be used during the process of converting cocaine to a base was discovered. This adulterant has the street name of "comeback," since it allows much of the cocaine that is included in the reaction to "come back" when the process is completed (Williams, 1989).

With the development of crack came a nearly ideal situation for stimulant abusers and sellers. Here was a cheap, easily available drug that produced an immediate, intense, but short-lived euphoria. Unfortunately, as the drug scene became perfect for those involved in drug commerce, it became devastating to public health and law enforcement officials. The drug was extremely toxic, not just in terms of the effects it had on the body, but, more important, in terms of the effects it had on behavior. The euphoria produced by smoking crack was so great that the process of searching out, obtaining, and using the drug became of paramount importance to a large number of people. The transmission of diseases, including AIDS, by women who prostituted themselves to make money to buy crack, the babies born to women who were chronic crack users, the gangs fighting for turf on which to establish themselves as crack dealers, the overflow in the courts and jails of crack-related crimes, all demonstrate the addictive nature of crack use. Interestingly, the sellers and suppliers are well aware of this property of base, smokable cocaine. Although distributors often inhale cocaine hydrochloride, they discourage the smoking of crack among themselves, since those who use crack often use so much of their drug supply themselves that there is little left to sell on the streets and therefore little money to pay the supplier. Crack smokers are not dependable employees and are usually cut off from their drug by suppliers (Williams, 1989). At higher levels, it has been reported that Columbian distributors who are found to be using cocaine in any form are summarily shot.

PHARMACOLOGY AND BEHAVIOR

Patterns of Use

Given the serious incapacitation produced by parenteral amphetamine abuse (see previous chapter), it is indeed fortunate that use of this drug declined sharply in the early 1970s. It is equally unfortunate that use of amphetamine was quickly replaced by use of cocaine, in some ways an even more insidious drug than amphetamines. Except for the fact that cocaine is relatively ineffective by the oral route and its duration of action is too short to make it useful to those who simply wish to remain awake for hours at a time, the pattern of cocaine abuse is very much like that of amphetamine abuse. Those who snort the drug typically do so on an intermittent basis, in the company of others who may also be using the drug. Some users, perhaps because of the current ease of drug availability, the low cost, or the switch from snorting to intravenous use or smoking, begin to escalate their dose of cocaine and increase their frequency of use. With the increased euphoria resulting from higher doses or more rapid onset of action comes a greater likelihood of a binge pattern of cocaine use, similar to the amphetamine run. During a cocaine binge, the drug may be injected or smoked as often as every 10 minutes (Gawin and Ellinwood, 1988); food intake and sleep decrease or disappear, social responsibilities are ignored, and all attention is turned to obtaining and using the drug. Animal studies suggest that if there is no limit to the drug supply, self-administration may continue until death occurs. Certainly, there is no shortage of cocaine-related deaths in the human population, but, fortunately, even chronic users usually run out of the drug and resources to obtain the drug before they kill themselves.

When drug use stops, the "crash," an opposite syndrome appears; now the user is exhausted, sleeps a great deal, is more interested in food than cocaine, and is psychologically depressed. He may have little energy and little interest in anything pleasurable, including cocaine. These symptoms may increase in intensity in the week following termination of cocaine use, after which time, the user may feel quite normal, with little interest in resuming drug administration. This phase is unfortunately and inevitably replaced by a recollection of the intense pleasure produced by cocaine and a desire to have that pleasure again (Gawin and Ellinwood, 1988). Thus, as soon as the resources are available, another cocaine binge will begin.

Effects of Cocaine

When cocaine is injected intravenously, when it is smoked, or to a slightly lesser extent, when it is snorted, it produces a sudden rush of intense euphoria. This is accompanied by a sense of well-being—greater self-esteem, alertness, and energy and a general feeling of competence, creativity, and social acceptability. There is unlikely to be any sense of being drugged; rather the experience is that you have become the person you always wanted and knew you could be. As translated from Freud's notes on cocaine, "The psychic effect of cocaine . . . consists of exhilaration and lasting euphoria, which does not differ in any way from the normal euphoria of a healthy person. . . . One is simply normal and soon finds it difficult to believe that one is under the influence of any drug at all" (Byck, 1974).

The most pronounced physiologic effects are an increase in heart rate and blood pressure. Other physiologic changes are similar to those found with amphetamine use, as described in the preceding chapter.

When cocaine is taken chronically, as in a cocaine binge, the effects of the drug intensify as blood levels increase. From increased self-esteem, alertness, and energy, the effects progress to grandiosity, impulsiveness, hypersexuality, compulsively repeated behavior, and increased psychomotor activity (Gawin and Ellinwood, 1988). Anxiety increases to the point of panic and paranoia, with, as in the case of amphetamine, the feeling that people are plotting against you.

These feelings usually disappear quickly when drug use is discontinued, but in some cases they may persist for several weeks (Gawin and Ellinwood, 1988).

PHYSIOLOGIC DEPENDENCE

Until quite recently, it was assumed that no withdrawal signs followed termination of chronic use of cocaine. Although it was clear that experimental animals that had been self-administering cocaine ate a great deal more than usual and slept a great deal more than usual following cessation of cocaine administration, it was thought that this was a normal reaction to having very little food or sleep during the period of cocaine intoxication. The current opinion of many research and clinical scientists is that the hyperphagia, hypersomnia, general malaise, and particularly the anhedonia and depression that were described earlier as following the end of a cocaine binge may in fact be a withdrawal syndrome.

There may be some pressure to describe a withdrawal syndrome for cocaine and other stimulants, since some who are not well versed in the behavioral pharmacology of drugs of abuse seem to think that a drug that does not produce physiologic dependence is not a particularly dangerous drug of abuse. As has been discussed elsewhere in this book, there is little connection between physiologic dependence (and the withdrawal signs that define this dependence) and psychologic dependence or addiction that results in drug seeking and drug taking on the part of those so addicted. Thus, although it appears that, relative to withdrawal from opioid drugs, and even more so from alcohol and barbiturates, the withdrawal from cocaine is quite mild, this should not in any way be construed to mean that the drug has less abuse liability or less risk of addiction than the opioids or sedative drugs.

Research questions on the nature of cocaine withdrawal will certainly focus on the defining conditions of this syndrome. It must be carefully determined, for example, whether further administration of cocaine will relieve the withdrawal signs. The time course of withdrawal from cocaine must also be thoroughly described and compared to the time course of similar withdrawal from amphetamine, for example. With other psychoactive drugs, the longer the duration of action of the drug, the more delayed the withdrawal signs, and the more protracted they are. Withdrawal from cocaine and amphetamine are similar, but whether they differ in latency of onset or duration, as they should if they are "true" withdrawal, has not, to our knowledge, been measured.

It is commonly thought that the presence of drug withdrawal leads to an increase in the reinforcing effects of that drug, since further administration may terminate aversive withdrawal signs as well as producing the usual reinforcing effects. There are few good studies of this phenomenon, but it would appear to be the case with opioid drugs and less true, or even untrue, for ethanol. Since cocaine, several other stimulants, and ethanol are self-administered in a binge pattern, in which users terminate drug administration on their own and may abstain from drug use for some period of time following termination, it is possible that these drugs do not gain in reinforcing strength during withdrawal. An increase in reinforcing strength during withdrawal is *not* a defining characteristic of withdrawal, since withdrawal and reinforcement are independent phenomena, but the question of changes in reinforcing strength of a drug during withdrawal is a very interesting one and must be answered for cocaine as well as for other drugs of abuse.

TOLERANCE

There is considerable confusion about whether the effects of cocaine decrease (tolerance) or increase (sensitization) when the drug is administered chronically (Johanson and Fischman, 1989). Much research in animal subjects has been devoted to asking these questions, and although there are exceptions to most of the following statements, data support the general contention that sensitization develops primarily to unconditioned behaviors such as locomotor activity, stereotyped behavior, and convulsions. When conditioned behavior, such as food-maintained operant behavior, is studied, tolerance to chronically administered cocaine is more likely to develop. Tolerance, but not sensitization, can develop when cocaine is delivered in a constant infusion; sensitization occurs only if there are intervals between drug delivery. There is limited evidence to suggest that larger doses of cocaine are required to produce tolerance than are necessary to produce sensitization (Johanson and Fischman, 1989).

The previous chapter on amphetamine put forward the hypothesis that tolerance to this stimulant was more likely to occur if that tolerance produced an increase in the density of reinforcement. Thus, if the immediate effect of the drug on operant behavior were to suppress responding and therefore decrease the rate of food delivery, then tolerance to this effect would be expected to develop. There have been a few studies in animals that support this hypothesis as far as cocaine is concerned as well (Johanson and Fischman, 1989).

There have been some very interesting studies of the development of tolerance to the subjective effects of cocaine in human subjects. Subjects, who are recruited as being frequent users of cocaine, report positive subjective effects following the initial delivery of intravenous or intranasal cocaine. On subsequent presentations of requested cocaine, there is a reduced subjective effect, even though blood levels of cocaine are at or above the levels that produced positive subjective effects initially. Significantly, tolerance of this sort does not develop to blood pressure increases produced by cocaine; people continue to request additional cocaine, report little subjective change once they have taken it, yet show increases in blood pressure as a consequence of cocaine administration (Johanson and Fischman, 1989).

TOXICITY

In contrast to amphetamine, cocaine apparently does not produce permanent alterations in neuronal tissue; however, it is certainly not without severe toxic effects. The psychotic state that develops during chronic cocaine use and the depression and more subtle psychologic changes that follow a period of chronic use are evidence of toxicity. The lethal effects of cocaine abuse, however, are more frequently due to myocardial infarctions. The mechanism by which cocaine use leads to heart attacks in young, healthy individuals has not been determined, but knowledge of how cocaine acts on the cardiovascular system has provided some general clues. One possibility is that cocaine produces a spasm of coronary vessels, causing a decrease in blood supply to the heart. Cocaine may also increase the heart's use of oxygen at the same time it is reducing the availability of oxygen to the heart. Furthermore, the local anesthetic effects of high-dose cocaine may lead to alterations in the electrical conductivity of the heart and to potentially fatal arrhythmias (Johanson and Fischman, 1989).

Cocaine's ability to produce short-term increases in blood pressure, as well as its vasospastic effects, may also be involved in strokes, both ischemic and hemorrhagic, that have been observed in cocaine users. Convulsions can also occur following administration of large doses of cocaine (Johanson and Fischman, 1989). Recent reports indicate that chronic smoking of crack can result in lung damage, with a condition that looks like pneumonia, but where no infectious organism can be detected. The cause is not yet known, but suggestions include the breakdown of the lung alveoli, because of the direct effects of deeply inhaled cocaine, a restriction of blood flow to the lungs caused by the vasoconstrictive nature of cocaine, by the alkaline substances used in free-base extraction or the adulterants used to cut crack (Patel et al., 1987).

IN UTERO EFFECTS

There is wide publicity and concern about the many "cocaine babies" being born to women who have used large amounts of cocaine during their pregnancies. Cocaine crosses the placenta with ease, so the fetus of a woman smoking crack or snorting cocaine is exposed to the drug and is vulnerable to its toxic effects. Cocaine may increase uterine contractility; cases of onset of labor with abruptio placenta have been reported in women coincidental to an injection of intravenous cocaine (Chasnoff et al., 1985). Cocaine babies tend to weigh less, have decreased head circumference, and suffer from hyperirritability relative to babies born of drug-free mothers. As with other toxic effects of cocaine, the mechanisms by which the drug produces changes in the fetus are not known. A restriction of blood flow to the fetus due to the vasoconstrictive effects of cocaine has been suggested as one possibility (Johanson and Fischman, 1989). Malnutrition in mothers who eat little during cocaine binges could certainly contribute and, since cocaine easily crosses the placental barriers, a direct effect of cocaine, perhaps altering dopamine levels during fetal development, is extremely likely. Furthermore, since many pregnant women who abuse cocaine also take a variety of other drugs, the infant born of these pregnancies may suffer from the effects of exposure to a variety of chemical insults, making it difficult to pinpoint the exact cause of any of the number of problems that these infants must contend with.

Mechanism of Action

Cocaine acts to prevent released dopamine from being taken back up into the neuronal cell; dopamine reuptake is the most important means of terminating the effects of dopamine, and disruption of this mechanism produces marked increases in extracellular dopamine levels. Cocaine appears to accomplish this inhibition of dopamine reuptake by acting on specific receptors (Madras et al., 1989), whose recent discovery may eventually provide greater understanding of cocaine's mechanism of action. The neuroanatomic location of cocaine's effects may be critical; it is currently postulated that certain areas of the limbic system, particularly the nucleus accumbens, may be the site of action of cocaine that is most important for its reinforcing effects (Wise, 1984).

Although the fact that both amphetamine and cocaine lead to increased levels of nervous system dopamine strongly implicates this neurotransmitter in the abuse of these drugs, many aspects of the relation between dopamine and abuse of central stimulants remain unclear. Not all drugs that block dopamine reuptake are subject to abuse in humans (e.g., nomifensine) or in animals (e.g., mazindol). Furthermore, some drugs that act directly on the dopamine receptor thought to be primarily linked to the effects of central stimulants are not subject to abuse (e.g., quinpirole) and drugs that block this site have complicated and difficult-to-interpret interactions with cocaine. Although the dopamine system is one of the most thoroughly researched neurotransmitter systems in the central nervous system, it is much more complicated than the opioid system described in Chapter 3 and remains poorly understood.

It must also be kept in mind that the depth of our understanding of the relatively simple opioid receptor system has done little to reduce abuse of these drugs. Although it is important to continue to investigate the mechanisms of action of cocaine, amphetamine, and dopamine, this work should not necessarily be expected to lead to an understanding of why these drugs are abused or how abuse can be treated. Abuse is a complicated behavioral phenomenon that will yield very slowly to a combination of pharmacologic and psychologic intervention.

Cocaine is also an effective local anesthetic that was once used extensively in eye surgery. It has the advantage of also having vasoconstrictive effects, which tend to keep the drug in the area where its anesthetic effects are needed. Its mechanism as a local anesthetic is by blocking initiation or conduction of nerve impulses in the area where the cocaine is applied. This effect accounts for the numbness that occurs in the nose of people who snort cocaine and the numbness in the mouth of those who chew coca leaves. In attempting to discover whether the local anesthetic effect of cocaine contributes in any way to its likelihood for abuse, researchers have looked at the ability of a number of other local anesthetics to function as reinforcers in research animals. Although most of them were ineffective, one, procaine, maintained even more behavior than did cocaine itself (Woods et al., 1987). Procaine is not thought to share dopamine-releasing functions with cocaine, suggesting that some other mechanism of procaine's action is responsible for its CNS effects. The possibility that cocaine may share some of these effects with procaine, and that a combination of these unknown properties and release of dopamine may be responsible for the unusual degree of psychologic dependence produced by cocaine, should be considered in attempting to understand and treat cocaine abuse.

Absorption and Fate

Cocaine is unusual in that it is metabolized in the blood as well as the liver. Cocaine has a very short plasma half-life (approximately 40–60 minutes) (Johanson and Fischman, 1989). Cocaine is well absorbed following administration by virtually any route. Although not typically taken orally, the drug is effective by this route. An all-too-frequent example of the effect of oral cocaine occurs with "body packers," people who place huge amounts of cocaine into plastic bags or condoms and swallow them as a means of transporting the drug across international borders, with the expectation of retrieving the contents at a convenient time and place. If one or more of the bags break, however, the massive release of cocaine frequently results in death, since even the drugs and equipment available in a well-equipped emergency room are rarely sufficient to counteract the effects of several grams of intragastric cocaine.

Legalization of Cocaine?

There is a movement afoot, proposed, surprisingly, by a few prominent and influential politicians, academicians, and judicial personnel, to legalize cocaine. Its impetus appears to be concern about the violence associated with cocaine trafficking, the economic impact of cocaine import and purchase in this country, and the inability of our criminal justice system to control the cocaine problem. These concerns are similar to those that were raised in opposition to ethanol prohibition. It appeared impossible to prevent illegal manufacture of ethanol then, in much the same way it appears impossible to prevent illegal import of cocaine now. There was considerable violence associated with turf battles between bootleggers for the opportunity to sell illegal ethanol then, as there is considerable violence committed by drug gangs fighting over neighborhoods in which to sell cocaine now. Since these problems were reduced or eliminated by revoking prohibition, it is thought that legalizing cocaine would have similar ameliorative effects. The courts and jails would be unburdened and freer to deal with more "serious" crimes. Taxes on cocaine would bring increased government revenues. The buying and selling of cocaine would produce more jobs, more income, more income tax for the government. The violence associated with illegal cocaine would disappear.

Fortunately, more rational thinking is resisting this approach to "controlling" the cocaine problem. Again using the comparison of ethanol prohibition, it should be pointed out that ethanol use and the medical and social problems associated with abuse of ethanol were much reduced during ethanol prohibition. Despite the easy availability of bootleg ethanol, many fewer people drank ethanol when it was illegal; its illegality was a significant deterrent to its use for a majority of the population. Therefore, it can be expected that if cocaine were legalized, the use of the drug would increase markedly. It might be safe to assume that, as with ethanol, virtually everyone would try cocaine at some time in their lives.

It has been estimated that 20 percent of the people who try cocaine become regular users of the drug and that 5 percent of those who try cocaine become compulsive users of high doses. The progression from controlled use to uncontrolled use appears to depend on increased access to the drug or to a change from snorting to intravenous or smoked routes of administration. If the drug were legalized and easily available, it is reasonable to expect that there would be a greatly increased number of frequent users of cocaine. If only 50 percent of the 200 million inhabitants of the United States tried cocaine, there would be 20 million regular cocaine users in comparison to the 3 million regular users currently thought to exist. Five million people would be compulsive users of cocaine.

It is an error to think, however, that these people would be comfortably supplied with their drug and essentially out of harm's way. Although that may be true to a certain extent with legally supplied opiates such as methadone, it is certainly not true of alcoholic individuals. With ethanol and cocaine, the drug *is* the harm, and the toxic effects of cocaine are much more severe even than those of ethanol. Physiologic effects, as mentioned earlier, can be lethal (e.g., heart attack, stroke, or convulsions). Of greater consequence is the behavioral toxicity of the drug. Cocaine produces a binge pattern of self-administration. During a binge of cocaine use, an individual is absolutely preoccupied with taking the drug; he may harm himself by not eating or sleeping or by picking at "bugs" on his body. He may harm other people if he develops a toxic paranoid psychosis. After a binge, he sleeps and eats and does very little else. This pattern of behavior is not compatible with the type of behavior that society needs and approves of. Cocaine addicts, even those who might have legal access to their drug, are not going to be working, thinking, productive members of society. The cost they would extract from that society would be beyond its ability to pay. The thought of having 5 to 20 million people in this country wasting their lives in states of cocaine intoxication or cocaine withdrawal ought to bring those who favor legalization of cocaine to their senses. If they believe that neither they nor their friends nor the members of their family would ever get involved in cocaine use, even if it were legal, and the rest of the world be damned, then they should look carefully at the drugs they and their friends and family currently use— ethanol, nicotine, caffeine—the legal drugs. Why do they suppose personal immunity from this even more insidiously dangerous drug, were it to become legal as well?

REFERENCES

Brooke, J. *The New York Times,* August 27, 1989

Byck, R. Cocaine Papers: Sigmund Freud. New York: Stonehill, 1974

Chasnoff, I. J., W. J. Burns, S. H. Schnoll, and K. A. Burns. Cocaine use in pregnancy. *N Engl J Med* 313:666, 1985

Ellinwood, E. H., and T. H. Lee. Dose- and time-dependent effects of stimulants. In: Asghar, K., and E. De Souza, eds., *Pharmacology and Toxicology of Amphetamine and Related Drugs.* National Institute on Drug Abuse Research Monograph 94, Washington D.C.: U.S. Government Printing Office, 1989, p. 323

Gawin, F. H., and E. H. Ellinwood. Cocaine and other stimulants: actions, abuse and treatment. *N Engl J Med* 318:1173, 1988

Johanson, C.-E., and M. W. Fischman. The pharmacology of cocaine related to its abuse. *Pharmacol Rev* 41:3, 1989

Madras, B. K., R. D. Spealman, M. A. Fahey, J. L. Neumeyer, J. K. Saha, R. A. Milius. Cocaine receptors labeled by [³H]beta-carbomethoxy-3 beta-(4-fluorophenyl) tropane. *Mol Pharmacol* 36:518, 1989

National Household Survey on Drug Abuse: Population Estimates 1985. DHHS Pub No. (ADM) 87-1539. Rockville, MD: National Institute on Drug Abuse, 1987

National Household Survey on Drug Abuse: Population Estimates 1990. Rockville, MD: National Institute on Drug Abuse, 1991

Patel, R.C., D. Dutta, and S. A. Schoenfeld. Free-base cocaine use associated with bronchiolitis obliterans organizing pneumonia. *Ann Intern Med* 107:186, 1987

Petersen, R. C. A history of cocaine. In: Petersen, R. C., and R. C. Stillman, eds., *Cocaine, 1977,* National Institute on Drug Abuse Research Monograph 13. Washington, D.C.: U.S. Government Printing Office, 1977, p. 17

Williams, T. *Cocaine Kids: The Inside Story of a Teenage Drug Ring.* Reading, MA: Addison-Wesley, 1989

Wise, R. A. Neural mechanisms of the reinforcing action of cocaine. In: Grabowski, J., ed., *Cocaine: Pharmacology, Effects, and Treatment of Abuse*. National Institute on Drug Abuse Research Monograph 50. Washington, D.C.: U.S. Government Printing Office, 1984

Woods, J. H., G. Winger, and C. P. France. Reinforcing and discriminative stimulus effects of cocaine: Analysis of pharmacological mechanism. In: Fisher, S., A. Raskin, and E. H. Uhlenhuth, eds., *Cocaine: Clinical and Biobehavioral Aspects*. New York: Oxford University Press, 1987, p. 21

CHAPTER 10

The Medical Diagnosis
of Drug Abuse

An individual may come under medical scrutiny as a result of drug abuse in a variety of ways: as a comatose or psychotic patient brought into a hospital emergency room; as an individual who is or has been convulsing; as a reckless driver apprehended by the police; as an inattentive, drowsy youngster from a classroom; as a patient with an HIV- or hepatitis-positive blood test; or as an individual who, though in contact with reality, is manifesting changes in his usual pattern of behavior. In all but the infected patient described here, the drug is still present in the individual when the physician sees him and drug use can be detected by measurement of serum or urine levels. These are the easy cases, where the patient himself may be sufficiently frightened by the sequelae of his drug use to ask for help, or where drug use can be established definitively and the patient referred for drug-abuse treatment.

A more difficult situation arises when distraught parents bring their adolescent child to their pediatrician or family practitioner with concerns about the child's possible drug use. In these cases, it is inappropriate for the physician to play the role of detective, using his medical skills to try to determine whether the young person is using drugs and which drugs he may be using. Not only does this put the physician in an antagonistic position with respect to his or her patient and reduces the possibility that he or she can win the patient's confidence and proceed to help him, but it is probably also futile. A person who uses almost any drug on an occasional basis or who uses fairly innocuous drugs such as marihuana on a frequent basis cannot be "found out" through a medical examination if he is not currently under the influence of the drug. Drug abuse is not always diagnosable, particularly in its early stages, when the patient might be most easily helped.

This chapter is intended to inform physicians about changes that they *may* see in their patients, particularly their young, otherwise healthy patients, that might lead them to suspect drug abuse. When such evidence is uncovered in the process of a standard physical examination, the physician should be encouraged to question the patient gently, in as nonjudgmental manner as possible. Even without such evidence, nonjudgmental questions about use of licit drugs (prescribed drugs, tobacco, and ethanol), use of soft drugs (marihuana or hashish), and exposure to more problematic drugs (cocaine or heroin) should be a routine part of any physical examination. Further questions may be necessary to determine whether the use is sufficiently frequent to suggest the need for intervention. Unfortunately, our knowledge is insufficient at the present time to give the physician strong guidelines as to how to determine when the combination of amount of drug use, the type of drug being used, and the age of the patient indicate that intervention is warranted.

Unless they are specifically trained to deal with such matters, physicians should not undertake to treat drug abuse in their patients. Drug treatment programs typically involve counseling, contingency management, drug detection capability, and perhaps individual or group therapy. These matters are best handled by well-trained, experienced drug-treatment professionals. The physician should, on the other hand, investigate available intervention programs to determine their philosophies, procedures, and success rates. He or she may be called on to determine which of several intervention programs are most appropriate for an individual patient and he or she should be able to discuss the various treatment strategies that are available in his or her community. If none is available, or if those available do not seem to fit the needs of the patients, the physician may need to encourage the community to recruit effective drug-abuse treatment specialists.

HISTORY

In taking a history, the physician must be acutely sensitive, not only to the actual content of the patient's answers to questions, but to the manner in which they are answered. Patients with drug-related problems may attempt to conceal them. They may not feel that the reason for seeing the doctor is related to their drug use; they may wish to avoid the potential moral judgment of the physician; or they may be concerned that they will be required to stop their drug-taking behavior, a situation that causes them considerable ambivalence. Alternatively, patients may be seeing the physician specifically because of drug-related problems. They may desire help in reducing or stopping use of drugs, or they may have come to the physician because of pressure brought by family, employer, or the legal system, related to their drug use. In either case, the manner in which the patient answers questions related to drug use (denial, rationalization, or evasion) may be an important aspect of the history taking (Arif and Westermeyer, 1988).

The physician may gain important information by making specific inquiries about past medical problems. Changes in food intake or sleep patterns, or problems of emotional lability should be particularly noted. A family history should include questions about drug intake by family members, as well as questions about any psychological difficulties that may exist in the family. A social history should raise issues about problematic interactions with parents, spouse, or employer, indications of financial or job-related problems, school problems, and any interactions with the law. Reports of arrests because of driving while intoxicated, wife or child abuse, disorderly conduct, or possessing illicit drugs should raise flags to the history taker to probe the possibility of drug abuse more carefully (Arif and Westermeyer, 1988).

The actual drug-use history probes the use of licit drug initially, with questions of whether the individual smokes, and if so, how much, and whether he or she drinks alcohol or takes prescription drugs, and if so how much. Questions about the use of illicit drugs can follow these inquiries. The physician's attitude is important during this interview. If he or she seems hurried or even nervous about such questions, the patient is much less likely to respond truthfully. When positive answers result from these questions, further evaluation of the patient's attitude towards his or her drug use may provide useful information. Is the patient concerned about his or her drug use; do family members express their concern about this use (Arif and Westermeyer, 1988)?

PHYSICAL EXAMINATION

Appearance

In general, there is little by way of appearance that sets the drug user apart from the rest of the population. Nutritional status can indicate a drug problem if the person is a frequent user of cocaine or amphetamine, or a long-term alcoholic. It would be difficult to overlook drug abuse of sufficient magnitude to produce marked weight loss, and the patient would probably not deny such a severe problem. Poor personal hygiene, including dental hygiene, may suggest preoccupation with drug taking.

Pupil size also can indicate possible drug use. Pinpoint pupils suggest recent opioid administration, whereas mydriasis is more indicative of stimulant use. Prescription drugs or pathologic conditions also can alter pupil size, however, and the patient should be questioned carefully about all drug use to avoid inappropriate attributions.

Sensorium

Generally, it can be expected that most drug abusers will arrange their schedule of drug administration so that their anticipated arrival at the doctor's office or clinic will not coincide with evident drug effects. Therefore, dulling of affect, drowsiness, nodding, slurred speech, agitation, uneven gait, and so on will rarely be present. Occasionally, a provocative adolescent may have just smoked marihuana or taken a barbiturate or an amphetamine prior to being seen and will demonstrate the appropriate pharmacologic consequences. Such a youth, however, is likely to boast openly of his use of drugs, so that his altered level of awareness is readily explained.

The frequent opioid user may well be seen under the influence of a drug. He may have the typical nodding, drowsy, withdrawn appearance and entirely detached attitude plus pinpoint pupils, or he may have a milder form of these symptoms, in which he may relate to the situation at hand but demonstrate a diminished attention span and difficulty in verbalizing consecutive coherent thoughts. Nonetheless, it is not unusual to find the opioid user in a state of equilibrium, apparently alert and normal. Alternatively, the dependent user who has been unable to get his usual dose on time may display agitation, irritability, anxiety, sweating, lacrimation, some degree of mydriasis, and a desire to conclude the examination as quickly as possible because he anticipates or is actually experiencing early symptoms of withdrawal.

The alcoholic may also reveal his situation by giving evidence of some degree of intoxication. Symptoms include slurred speech, inappropriate affect, diminished attention span, and similar evidence of central nervous system depression. If such depression exists, the patient's breath probably will have the characteristic odor of alcohol. Indeed, only with alcohol, the rare paraldehyde ingestion, and volatile solvent inhalation will the breath have a significant odor. Should the long-term alcoholic present with the cerebral changes that occur in Wernicke's encephalopathy or Korsakoff's psychosis, his condition will be manifested mentally and neurologically, even in the absence of recent alcohol intake.

In summary, though most casual or intermittent drug users will not demonstrate alterations in their sensorium or level of consciousness when examined, a few users of hallucinogens and a few chronic alcoholics may give evidence of psychotic changes in the absence of recent drug ingestion. One should keep in mind that these changes can easily be confused with those seen in the many individuals who develop psychoses unrelated to drug abuse. On any occasion, the particular drug effects observed are, of course, direct manifestations of the particular drug, the dose, the route of administration, the amount of time that has elapsed since administration, and the individual's own level of tolerance.

VITAL AND OTHER SIGNS

The circumstances attending a visit to a doctor's office and a physical examination are in themselves anxiety producing for some patients. This anxiety alone can easily produce mild to moderate tachycardia, tachypnea, and/or hypertension in susceptible individuals. Therefore, possible physiologic responses to psychic stress should be taken into consideration when evaluating abnormalities in vital signs as possible indications of drug abuse. Nevertheless, rapid heart rate and increased blood pressure that is maintained throughout the examination period in an otherwise healthy adolescent should raise the possibility of recent stimulant use.

Blood Pressure

It has been reported that experimental chronic opioid administration results in slightly elevated systolic and diastolic blood pressures, but the levels are not above acceptable normal limits. Greater but transient elevations of 15 to 30 mm Hg are seen during acute heroin withdrawal. Amphetamine ingestion may also result in mild to moderate hypertension at the time of intoxication and for variable periods thereafter. With barbiturates, tranquilizers, and volatile solvents, blood pressure changes roughly parallel the degree of central nervous system depression that exists but to a lesser and more variable degree than respiratory changes. Hallucinogens, particularly those that have strong adrenergic effects, such as LSD, will produce increases in blood pressure and heart rate. It is unlikely that LSD would produce such increases without, at the same time, producing obvious changes in the patient's behavior.

Pulmonary Ventilation

For opioids, sedatives, hypnotics, and volatile solvents, as with all central nervous system depressants, depression of pulmonary ventilation is a prime pharmacologic manifestation and is directly related to the degree of drug intoxication present at any moment. Amphetamine ingestion readily produces tachypnea. No characteristic alterations of respiration occur with hallucinogen use.

There is no evidence to suggest that ventilatory changes continue after a drug has been detoxified either completely or to a blood level compatible with an individual's level of tolerance.

Pulse Rate

Alterations in pulse rate most readily identify amphetamine abuse, which results in a tachycardia directly proportional to the degree of overall toxicity experienced. Some narcotic addicts also demonstrate slight increases in pulse rate, which are often further increased during acute withdrawal. Users of hallucinogens and marihuana, in particular, may also show pulse rates up to 150. Since pulse rate is highly variable, except under basal conditions, and can be most sensitive to emotional factors that produce psychogenic tachycardia, the finding of an elevated pulse rate is essentially meaningless in the diagnosis of drug abuse.

Though bradycardia may well be a manifestation of an overdose of depressant drugs, it is doubtful that blood levels of opioids, barbiturates, or tranquilizers in a given patient compatible with his being able to accomplish an ambulatory visit to a doctor's office would result in any significant slowing of the pulse rate.

Temperature

Temperature elevations do not occur in uncomplicated drug abuse, with the sole exception of toxic doses of atropinic drugs. When a known or suspected drug user is febrile, he must be evaluated for possible related infections or such foreign-body reactions as hepatitis, tetanus, septicemia, endocarditis, sterile or infected abscesses, and thrombophlebitis. It is also possible that some of the adulterants used to "cut" drugs are pyrogenic.

Integument

Of all the signs of drug abuse, the ones most often considered pathognomonic are the various manifestations and complications of skin puncture. Formerly held to be characteristic of opioid addiction and still largely manifest by this group, they may also result from the injection of any drug administered by the parenteral route.

Heroin purchased on the street, as noted in Chapter 3, is generally "cut" with such adulterants as talc, quinine, and lactose. Capsules or tablets of commercially prepared drugs intended for oral use, including amphetamines and barbiturates, as well as drugs of "underground" manufacture, also contain inert and often irritant binders. Aseptic techniques are rarely observed in the preparation of underground drugs. Only minimal attention, if any, is paid to antiseptic conditions by the injector. Filtration of insoluble material is incompletely accomplished, if at all, by passing the dissolved material through a wad of cotton or gauze. When the drug is injected, therefore, both chemically irritant materials and infecting agents may enter the body, causing local abscesses, thromboses, and scarring. Most pure drugs, when properly prepared for injection, appropriately diluted, and administered under sterile conditions do not usually produce skin lesions. Thus, evidence of multiple intravenous injections would not be demonstrated by an opioid-abusing health care professional.

The lesions caused by "skin popping," or subcutaneous injection of opioids, are often located in such readily accessible areas as the arm and thigh. They may occur anywhere on the body, however, even in sites out of the patient's reach. (The drug would have been injected by a companion in such instances.) To avoid detection, some "skin poppers" have resorted to less frequently revealed areas, such as the lower abdomen.

In examining a person who regularly uses the subcutaneous route for drug administration, one may find a great variety of lesions. There will be the puncture mark itself, either fresh or healing, with or without underlying tissue involvement. In the early stages of an untoward local reaction, there can be heat, swelling, and erythema of varying degrees, progressing in some instances to outright abscess formation, rupture, and drainage. When the reaction progresses beyond a mild local inflammatory stage and, possibly even when sepsis does not occur, the local tissues may be sufficiently injured to result in permanent scarring manifested by two types of lesions: first, a hyperpigmented, flat, round, ovoid macular area with indiscrete margins ranging in size from 1 to 3 cm or more and, second, a round or ovoid "punched-out" depression with well-defined borders 1 to 5 cm in diameter. In the latter lesion, the skin often appears atrophic and shiny and may be depigmented as well (Sapira, 1968).

The "mainliner," or intravenous user of drugs, also develops progressive signs at the site of the veins used, with the added complication of venous thromboses. The sites selected are generally those of the antecubital fossa and forearm. Additionally, a desperate addict in search of a patent vein or trying to hide his habit may resort to other areas of the body he can reach, including abdomen, legs, and feet. Even the external jugular vein, the sublingual veins, and the dorsal vein of the penis have been utilized.

The mildest cutaneous signs of intravenous injection are fresh, healing, or healed puncture marks frequently with minimal but distinct hyperpigmentation over the vein after multiple venipunctures throughout an extended period of time. It is unlikely that a casual, intermittent "mainliner" would demonstrate these permanent changes in pigmentation, though recent injection sites may well be evident.

The most prominent signs of chronic intravenous drug abuse are frequently referred to as "railroad tracks." Resulting from repeated puncture of the skin overlying a vein, this lesion may extend over the course of the vein from 2 to 20 cm in length appearing as an atrophic, flat, sometimes pigmented scar transversed by multiple fine cross marks. In the long-term user, such lesions often provide a detailed anatomical survey of the accessible superficial venous system (Sapira, 1968; Shuster and Lewin, 1968).

Acute lesions, such as local abscesses and acute thrombophlebitis, also occur and may prompt the user to seek medical help. It is safe to say that if an adolescent or young adult presents with an acute subcutaneous infection, abscess, or thrombophlebitis in regions accessible to self-injection and if recent systemic medical treatment can be ruled out, drug abuse must be suspected as a prime cause (Louria et al., 1967).

There is a type of skin lesion that is sometimes considered pathognomonic of chronic heroin use: the "rosette" of cigarette burns consisting of some 10 to 20 circular or linear scars on the anterior chest wall. Such burns occur when the user "goes on the nod" with a cigarette dangling from his mouth, which, as the head droops down, makes contact with the skin. The analgesia induced by the drug blunts pain reception and reflex withdrawal (Sapira, 1968). Cigarette burns between the fingers may be seen in alcoholics and opioid and barbiturate users as well as users of other generalized depressant drugs.

Lymph Nodes

Regional adenopathy related to the site of injection is commonly encountered. Many chronic drug users employing systemic routes of administration demonstrate small, firm, discrete, nontender, palpable axillary and/or epitrochlear nodes or even inguinal nodes if the lower extremities are a frequent site of injection. The most likely cause of the adenopathy is a regional reaction to the contaminants commonly present in illicit substances. Autopsies performed on addicts have revealed a 75 percent incidence of generalized glandular enlargement, particularly in the area of the pancreas, liver, and duodenum (Sapira, 1968). The meaning of this finding is not clear.

Eyes

Miosis is generally one of the physical signs characteristic of heroin intoxication. The failure of a contracted pupil to dilate in a darkened room when vision is fixed on a far object is highly suggestive of recent opiate intake. Pinpoint pupils will be seen in the individual only during the time of intoxication; normal pupillary size and responsiveness gradually return as the drug becomes detoxified and excreted. In the chronic heroin user, some tolerance may develop to the pupillary effects of heroin, and lesser degrees of miosis will be seen. Therefore, eye signs can be a less sensitive indicator than is generally believed. Dilation of the pupil is an early sign of withdrawal in the opioid-dependent user.

Mydriasis occurs with hallucinogen intoxication (excepting marihuana) and is a predictable pharmacologic action of such sympathomimetic drugs as amphetamines and cocaine. It is a common finding in the individual acutely intoxicated with these drugs, but it is uncommon in the ambulatory patient who does not demonstrate other features characteristic of these drugs. Individuals experiencing mydriasis and a resultant intense photophobia may wear dark glasses indoors. One should, however, make sure that such a patient has not received medically induced mydriasis, as in the treatment of glaucoma or iritis, and is not either wearing prescription lenses or following a costume fad in wearing tinted glasses.

Pupillary changes do not occur with the use of barbiturates, marihuana, alcohol, and most solvents.

Sustained nystagmus on lateral gaze will occur during intoxication by such generalized central nervous system depressants as barbiturates and after PCP administration. This phenomenon has not been reported with drugs in other categories commonly implicated in abuse.

Scleral injection occurs during marihuana smoking and has been reported to persist for up to two years thereafter without further drug use. Since scleral injection is a common finding during physical examination of many patients for a variety of reasons (from vernal conjunctivitis to exposure to smog), it cannot be considered an informative abnormality per se in the diagnosis of drug abuse.

Scleral icterus in the previously healthy adolescent and young adult can be considered as highly indicative of hepatitis. Since hepatitis is a frequent, and at times nearly epidemic, complication of the use of contaminated needles, drug abuse must be considered a leading cause in such individuals. In addition, scleral icterus may be a sign of toxic hepatitis because of inhalation of volatile solvents containing chlorinated hydrocarbons.

Nose

The finding of a perforated or severely ulcerated nasal septum can be considered almost pathognomonic of persistent cocaine sniffing. The vasoconstricting effect of this drug on the mucous membranes, with chronic application, can result in tissue ischemia, necrosis, and ultimately, septal perforation. This lesion also has been reported among some heroin sniffers but not among users who inhale volatile solvents.

Glue, heroin, or Methedrine sniffing may produce a reactive rhinitis manifested by a nasal discharge and reddened mucosae. Increased nasal secretions also occur on opioid withdrawal. The physical signs, however, would not differ from those caused by an upper respiratory tract infection or allergic rhinitis.

Mouth and Throat

Many chronic users of drugs pay little attention to oral hygiene and have rampant dental decay. But since a far larger segment of economically deprived individuals than just the addict population receive unsatisfactory dental care, the finding of major neglect is probably more suggestive of poverty than of drug abuse.

Some amphetamine users have been reported to experience uncontrolled bruxism. If clinically noted or historically reported by others to occur during waking hours, such an observation should lead to the consideration of abuse of this type of drug. Grinding of the teeth during sleep, however, is common for many individuals, users or nonusers, and cannot be considered significant in the diagnosis of drug abuse (Cox and Smart, 1970).

Chest

Though percussion, auscultation, and x-ray of the chest in both the casual and chronic drug user generally are unremarkable, pulmonary function studies in chronic heroin users may demonstrate decreased lung volume and decreased diffusing capacity (Sapira, 1968). Such insoluble binders of tablets and adulterants of heroin as talc and starch can, when injected intravenously, travel to the lungs to produce multiple pulmonary thromboses and/or granulomas. With repeated body insults of this nature, diminished pulmonary function and, ultimately, pulmonary hypertension may result. Such findings are unlikely in the intermittent and casual drug user (Louria et al., 1967).

Pulmonary infection may also be an indicator of drug abuse. Injection of microorganisms present in contaminated and unsterile material can produce either localized pulmonary abscesses or more diffuse pneumonic processes. Such an infection is particularly apt to be staphylococcal, although a variety of other organisms, including fungi, may be implicated. In the heroin "mainliner" who becomes acutely ill with pulmonary disease, the edema of overdosage must be differentiated from pneumonitis of bacterial origin (Sapira, 1968; Cherubin et al., 1968).

Pneumocystis carinii was a very rare form of pneumonia prior to the outbreak of the AIDS epidemic. This opportunistic infection is the primary early affliction of the immunocompromised AIDS patient, and the AIDS patient is likely to be an intravenous drug user. Thus, a diagnosis of *pneumocystis carinii* should raise the possibility of drug abuse. However, the problems associated with the patient's drug abuse are dwarfed by the problems associated with his or her HIV-positive status. The most urgent situation here is that he or she receive available therapy for the various infections that can be expected and that appropriate counseling and drug-abuse treatment regimens are undertaken to reduce the risk that this individual will pass the AIDS virus to companions through the group use of contaminated needles and syringes.

Heart

Alterations in cardiac rate were discussed earlier under vital signs. Bacterial endocarditis, either right- or left-sided, is a common finding in the drug user and should be considered in any individual suspected of even casual parenteral drug abuse who presents with a fever of unknown etiology. Conversely, the diagnosis of bacterial endocarditis in an individual with no prior evidence of heart disease, valvular lesions, or congenital anomaly should at least raise the suspicion of illicit drug injection. Of course, bacteremias and even septicemias occur frequently with injection of contaminated material without the development of endocarditis.

Right-sided endocarditis has been found to involve the tricuspid valve only. Often silent, without clinically detectable abnormalities, this condition may not make itself known until embolization produces septic pulmonary infarcts. Left-sided disease may involve both the mitral and aortic valves and generally produces classical symptoms of valvular disease and systemic emboli (Sapira, 1968; Cherubin et al., 1968).

Though elevated S-T segments have been noted in the electrocardiogram of a significant number of chronic opioid users and multiple premature atrial–ventricular beats have been noted in some amphetamine users, these findings are not sufficiently specific to warrant their addition to the diagnostic armamentarium of drug abuse. Periarteritis has been detected in a few heavy amphetamine users; whether a causal relationship exists is unclear (Citron et al., 1970).

Abdomen

An enlarged liver and/or abnormal liver function tests (with or without clinical jaundice) should raise the suspicion of viral hepatitis. As previously noted, the occurrence of this disease in the adolescent or young adult should make one suspect "mainlining" or "skin popping" in the absence of known contact, ingestion of contaminated foods, or a possible iatrogenic source. For the most part, hepatitis transmitted via contaminated needles and blood products is hepatitis B. One may be able to detect the presence of the Australia antigen if the test is performed early in the course of the disease or if the patient is a carrier. Hepatitis A, however, may also be transmitted by needles, as well as by the fecal–oral route. Thus, though the incubation period and laboratory data may point to one viral agent or the other, both must be considered as possibly secondary to contaminated needle use.

In urban areas frequented by drug-abusing youths and young adults, hepatitis incurred through the use of contaminated needles is endemic, if not epidemic, and is seen far more frequently than that contracted by the fecal–oral route. Such considerations must be applied to urban and suburban middle-class populations as well. Some cases of hepatitis may be due to unrecognized drug abuse but are erroneously attributed to other causes. Many individuals develop hepatitis, of course, without an evident source and without being a drug user.

In addition to the overt forms of liver disease, it has been reported that approximately one-third of opioid users present with an enlarged liver, elevated transaminase levels, and/or abnormal flocculation tests even in the absence of a clinical history of hepatitis or jaundice. These findings have been variably interpreted as indicative of a chronic or intermittent anicteric hepatitis or of the chronic hepatotoxic effects of one of the adulterants used in diluting heroin. Experiments with pure morphine have not reproduced these chronic liver findings, and opioids are not believed to exert a specific toxic effect on the liver (Sapira, 1968).

Alcoholic liver disease, arguably progressing from fatty liver and hepatitis to cirrhosis, is one of the most serious complications of chronic alcohol consumption, and chronic alcohol consumption is the most important cause of liver disease in the United States. Although each of the components of alcoholic liver disease is diagnosed from microscopic examination of liver biopsy material, indication of potential alcoholic liver disease on a general physical examination comes from findings of an enlarged liver. In more advanced cases, the patient may have fever, anorexia, jaundice, hepatic tenderness, an enlarged spleen, and ascites. Occasionally, alcoholic liver disease has no symptoms (Crabb and Lumeng, 1989).

Kidney

Though uncommon, a number of instances of focal or generalized glomerular sclerosis have been reported in association with chronic heroin use (Rao et al., 1974). The precise genesis of these lesions, however, is unclear. In the vast majority of chronic drug users, there are no specific renal findings. But the incidence of proteinuria and a nephrotic syndrome is sufficiently higher in heroin users than in the general population to suggest a significant relation.

Various clinical pictures have been observed, ranging from a relatively stable mild proteinuria to relatively rapid and progressive disease. Most characteristic is a nephrotic syndrome with proteinuria, edema, hypoalbuminemia, and hypercholesterolemia. A high percentage of these individuals develop renal failure and die. Biopsy findings tend to relate membranoproliferative glomerulonephritis with the milder forms of disease and focal and segmental sclerosis with the nephrotic picture.

Endocrine System

Virtually all drugs of abuse have been found to produce endocrine changes. Cocaine, for example, alters plasma prolactin and growth hormone levels and the response of thyroid-stimulating hormone to thyroid-releasing hormone (Di Paolo et al., 1989). Marihuana reduces gonadotropin-releasing hormone, which results in decreased levels of LH and FSH and a decrease in testicle and seminal vesicle weight in the male (Harclerode, 1984) and changes in ovulation in the female (Smith and Asch, 1984). Long-term male alcohol abusers may suffer from feminization, with testicular atrophy, loss of male-pattern body hair, and gynecomastia. Women with chronic alcoholism may have irregular menses (Crabb and Lumeng, 1989) and may be sterile. Although these endocrinological changes were once thought to be secondary to alcohol-induced impaired liver function and a consequent decreased ability of the liver to metabolize sex steroids, more recent evidence suggests a direct, albeit complex, role of alcohol on the hypothalamic–pituitary–gonadal axis (Van Thiel, 1981).

Women who chronically take drugs, particularly heroin, often experience menstrual irregularities, sometimes to the point of secondary amenorrhea. Fertility is also reduced, along with viability of the conceptus; these disturbances are manifested in subnormal rates of conception and elevated rates of spontaneous abortion, stillbirth, premature birth, and "small-for-date" babies. The role of poor nutrition and casual, if not frankly neglectful, life-style of the typical chronic drug user as well as the effects of the drugs themselves are undoubtedly both contributory (Gaulden et al., 1964).

Despite the possibilities of morphologic, biochemical, or functional changes in endocrine function produced by drugs of abuse, it is unlikely that a physician will diagnose drug abuse based on endocrinologic findings. For some drugs, the changes are minor; for other drugs they follow long-term drug use that would most likely be detected by another observation at an earlier date. Since menstrual irregularity is common among adolescent girls and not uncommon among young women in general, it cannot be taken as a specific indication of drug abuse.

Nervous System

Neurologic findings that would contribute to the diagnosis of drug abuse are, with several exceptions, those referable to the specific central nervous system effects of the drug involved and the degree of intoxication or withdrawal that may exist at the time examined. In the alert, oriented, nonintoxicated individual, there are usually no suggestive neurologic abnormalities. Exceptions are the persistent neuropathy that has been reported following glutethimide administration, the neuropathy associated with alcoholism, and the tremors that may continue for variable periods following amphetamine intoxication.

Summary

The critical factors that point toward or confirm the diagnosis of drug abuse are the following: a positive or highly suspicious history by the patient or concerned observers, the finding of drugs or apparatus for administering drugs on the patient or among his belongings, the presence of intoxication at the time of examination with concomitant disturbances in thought processes characteristic of the drug or drugs involved, the discovery of typical skin lesions, and the detection of drugs or metabolites of drugs in blood or urine. Other physical findings, as described, may collectively lead clearly to a diagnosis of drug abuse. Taken singly, however, this will be of little assistance.

Though one or more of the preceding findings is generally present in the examination of a chronic drug user, the casual drug user more often than not will not present with historical or physical findings that will establish a firm diagnosis. Thus, we again emphasize that establishing a relationship of mutual trust and confidence between physician and patient can be most constructive in creating an atmosphere in which the actual facts of an individual's drug use may come freely into the open.

LABORATORY DETECTION

Procedures for detecting specific drugs in serum or urine are in demand with the increase in employee drug-screening programs and the necessity of monitoring drug use in patients in drug treatment programs. The most popular procedure currently is enzyme-multiplied immunoassay technique (EMIT). This procedure is sensitive to a wide range of abused substances, including cannabinoids (marihuana), cocaine and its metabolites, barbiturates, methaqualone, phencyclidine, amphetamines, and opioids. Enzyme immunoassay techniques for specific drugs are available in kit form, for rapid evaluation of urine samples. Because false-positive results with any evaluation procedure can have severe consequences to an individual, all drug-positive specimens should be further evaluated with more specific analytical measurement devices, such as gas chromatography and mass spectrophotometry.

REFERENCES

Arif, A. and Westermeyer, J. *Manual of Drug and Alcohol Abuse: Guidelines for Teaching in Medical and Health Institutions*. New York: Plenum, 1988

Cherubin, C. E., B. Baden, F. Kavaler, S. Lerner, and W. Cline. Infectious endocarditis in narcotic addicts. *Ann Intern Med* 69:1092, 1968

Citron, B. P., M. Halpern, M. McCarron, G. D. Lundberg, R. McCormick, I. J. Pincus, D. Tatter, and B. J. Haverback. Necrotizing angiitis associated with drug abuse. *New Engl J Med* 283:19, 1970

Cox, C., and R. G. Smart. The nature and extent of speed use in North America. *Canad Med Assoc J* 102:724, 1970

Crabb, D. W., and L. Lumeng. Alcoholic liver disease, In: Kelley, W. N., editor-in-chief, *Textbook of Internal Medicine*. Philadelphia: J.B. Lippincott, 1989, p. 592

Di Paolo, T., C. Rouillard, M. Morissette, D. Levesque, and P. J. Bedard, Endocrine and neurochemical actions of cocaine. *Canad J Physiol Pharmacol* 67:1177, 1989

Gaulden, E. C., D. C. Littlefield, O. E. Putoff, and A. L. Seivert. Menstrual abnormalities associated with heroin addiction. *Amer J Obstet Gynecol* 90:155, 1964

Harclerode, J. Endocrine effects of marijuana in the male: Preclinical studies. In: Braude,

M. C., and J. P. Ludford, eds., *Marijuana Effects on the Endocrine and Reproductive Systems*. NIDA Research Monograph 44. Washington, D.C.: U.S. Government Printing Office, 46, 1984

Louria, D. B., T. Hensle, and J. Rose, The major medical complications of heroin addiction. *Ann Intern Med* 67:1, 1967

Rao, T. K. S., A. D. Nicastri, and E. A. Friedman. Natural history of heroin-associated nephropathy, *New Engl J Med* 290:19, 1974

Sapira, J. D. The narcotic addict as a medical patient. *Amer J Med* 45:555, 1968

Shuster, M. M., and M. L. Lewin, New York: Needle tracks in narcotics addicts. *NY J Med* 68:3129, 1968

Smith, C. G., and R. H. Asch. Acute, short-term and chronic effects of marijuana on the female primate reproductive function. In: Braude, M. C., and J. P. Ludford, eds., *Marijuana Effects on the Endocrine and Reproductive Systems*. NIDA Research Monograph 44. Washington, D.C.: U.S. Government Printing Office, 82, 1984

Van Thiel, D. H. Hypothalamic-pituitary-gonadal function in liver disease. In: Messiha, F. S., and G. S. Tyner, eds., *Endocrinological Aspects of Alcoholism*, Basel: S. Karger, 1981, p. 24

CHAPTER 11

Management of Selected Clinical Problems: Pharmacologic Aspects

Some of the clinical problems encountered in drug users, including acute drug intoxication or withdrawal symptoms, are direct consequences of drug use. Others are not uniquely related to the drug but result from the life-styles and drug-taking habits of those who use the drugs. Infectious diseases that result from sharing unsterile needles provide an example of the latter problem. This chapter is concerned with detection and management of some of the problems in the first category—problems that are directly attributed to the drug being used and that therefore differ, depending on the nature of that drug. These problems include acute drug intoxication and overdose, withdrawal signs in drug-deprived dependent patients, and the unfortunate situation of babies born to drug-abusing mothers. Also discussed in this chapter is the issue of the use of drugs as adjuncts in rehabilitative programs for drug users.

OVERDOSE

Opioids

The possibility of a drug overdose must be considered when a patient presents in an emergency room in a severely depressed state for which no other explanation is obvious. Information from associates may help in determining whether drugs are involved and, if so, what type of drug, but often this information is only marginally helpful. Fresh needle marks are suggestive of recent drug use, but the drug in question may not necessarily be an opioid. Various patterns of pulmonary ventilation may be present when the patient with an opioid overdose is first seen: tachypnea or dyspnea may be observed as well as varying degrees of ventilatory depression, including apnea. If the patient is seen in the early stages, respiration may still be essentially normal. The pulmonary pathology typical of opioid overdose, pulmonary edema and congestion, can be manifested by rales, frothy sputum, and, radiologically, as a diffuse bilateral infiltrate. It may be detectable when the patient is first seen, or its onset can be delayed for as long as 24 hours after that time, and in some patients it may never develop to an observable degree (Steinberg and Karliner, 1968; Louria et al., 1967). Pulmonary function may also be compromised by the aspiration of secretions or gastric contents (Steinberg and Karliner, 1968). Pupillary miosis, when present in conjunction with other significant findings, is perhaps the most reliable sign of opioid overdose; in severely hypoxic individuals, however, the pupils will probably be dilated.

Treatment often must be initiated, because of the gravity of the situation, before there can be significant resolution of questions pertaining to differential diagnosis. It is important, therefore, to be aware of the various possible sequelae to the use of opioid antagonists and to make provisions for them. The initial dose of naloxone is customarily 0.4 to 0.8 mg by vein. If a response is to be obtained from this first dose, it will be evident within several minutes thereafter at most. The goal of naloxone therapy is to restore pulmonary ventilation to a safe level; it should not be given until full consciousness is recovered, for reasons to be discussed shortly. Wholly satisfactory responses to the *initial* dose of naloxone occur only infrequently, and after a period of 20 to 25 minutes, the initial dose may be repeated, if necessary, until the patient has received a total of 5 to 10 mg of the drug. If no favorable effect has been produced by this cumulative dose, the possibility of opioid overdose can be regarded as highly doubtful.

If pulmonary ventilation is improved by naloxone, a tentative diagnosis of opioid overdose can be made. In such instances, however, three untoward developments may occur. The duration of action of the antagonist may be shorter than that of the opioid. Thus, unless the patient is carefully watched and the antagonist given again when necessary, the patient's status can, within several hours, revert to that present initially. The etiology of pulmonary edema and congestion of opioid overdose remain unknown; they impede oxygenation of the blood and are not reversed by opioid antagonists. Moreover, pneumonia from aspiration or other causes may develop shortly after admission or within the next several days. The action of opioid antagonists in regard to respiration is probably largely, if not wholly, a central one, restoring the sensitivity of the medullary respiratory center to carbon dioxide. Airway problems and those pertaining to the diffusion of gases across pulmonary capillaries remain and require appropriate attention. Finally, many victims of heroin or methadone overdose are opioid dependent. Once evoked by an opioid antagonist, the withdrawal syndrome cannot be easily alleviated; probably because its onset is so abrupt, it is commonly severe and may include convulsions. The indiscriminate use of opioid antagonists in an opioid-dependent individual can produce a severe withdrawal syndrome. Though it is true that the dose of antagonist required to improve pulmonary ventilation may also elicit some withdrawal signs, they will, in most cases, be relatively mild and preliminary manifestations of withdrawal. If withdrawal symptoms appear, it would be prudent to attempt to achieve satisfactory pulmonary ventilation by mechanical means rather than by further doses of the antagonist. The finding that many heroin users today have a limited degree of dependence owing to the grossly diluted drug they receive probably accounts for the fact that relatively few reports in the literature about heroin overdose describe the development of severe, antagonist-induced withdrawal syndromes during treatment. If the patient is a participant in a methadone maintenance program, he may have a high degree of physiologic dependence on opioids, since he has been receiving 30 to 120 mg of methadone daily. Injudiciously large doses of opioid antagonists will provoke intense manifestations of withdrawal in the high-dose methadone.

Barbiturates and Other Central Nervous System Depressants

Overdose with barbiturates is more likely in individuals attempting suicide than in people who abuse these drugs. In either case, however, the patient may have ingested a number of drugs, and they may be interacting to the detriment of the patient's health and the physician's ability to treat. A person deeply comatose with severely depressed respiration should be given an opioid antagonist, as mentioned earlier. If the response is unsatisfactory, the possibility of barbiturate overdose must be considered. Unfortunately, there is no specific antagonist for this drug class, and although there are stimulants that counteract some of the depressant effects of these drugs, they do more to confuse the picture than to aid the patient; their use is not recommended. If there is any likelihood that benzodiazepines have been ingested, the specific antagonist flumazenil can be given. Although benzodiazepines themselves rarely produce coma or life-threatening depression, when they are taken in combination with ethanol or barbiturates, they can have additive or synergistic effects that can be usefully attenuated. As with opioid antagonists, if flumazenil does improve the patient's consciousness, it should be given at one- to two-hour intervals, since it is considerably shorter acting than long-acting benzodiazepines such as diazepam. Flumazenil also has in common with opioid antagonists the ability to produce withdrawal signs in dependent individuals. It should therefore be used judiciously until the patient's status can be determined. Flumazenil has no effect on barbiturate- or alcohol-induced depression.

Treatment of barbiturate or alcohol overdose is symptomatic. The symptoms consist primarily of CNS depression, respiratory depression, and resulting cardiovascular and renal complications. Blood gases should be measured, since respiration may be either slow or rapid and shallow, but blood oxygenation may be inadequate in either case. A patent airway should be established and oxygen administered. These patients are at risk for developing pneumonia and should be evaluated daily for such an occurrence. If cardiovascular collapse is likely, intravenous fluids and blood pressure stimulators can be of great help. If renal failure occurs, hemodialysis should be initiated. Through heroic, supportive measures and good nursing care, 98 percent of patients that present with barbiturate overdose will survive (Rall, 1990).

Stimulants

Overdose with stimulants such as cocaine or amphetamine produces a particularly frightening situation. The list of possible toxic sequelae to ingestion of large doses of cocaine is long.

> In addition to psychiatric disorders, the more common serious toxic effects induced by cocaine include cardiac arrhythmias, myocardial ischemia or infarction, myocarditis, high-output congestive heart failure, dilated cardiomyopathy, cerebrovascular spasm with transient neural ischemia or infarct of brain or spinal cord, intracerebral hemorrhage, aortic dissection, rhabdomyolysis with acute renal and hepatic failure, disseminated intravascular coagulation, convulsions, hyperpyrexia, and respiratory depression [Jaffe, 1990, p. 542].

Unfortunately, there is no specific treatment for cocaine overdose, and symptomatic management of symptoms is the most appropriate way to proceed. Studies in animals suggest that calcium channel blockers and dopamine-D1 antagonists may help prevent cocaine deaths (Jaffe, 1990). Further evaluation of these and other agents may result in better treatment of this condition.

The patient with amphetamine overdose may present with a different set of symptoms if he or she has been taking large doses over a period of several days. Paranoid ideation in these individuals may be marked and difficult to distinguish from paranoid schizophrenia. Blood or urine tests should be requested to determine whether drugs are involved in cases of paranoid psychosis, and acquaintances should be questioned closely if they can give a picture of the patient's activities over the previous days and weeks. In any case, the behavioral manifestations can be suppressed fairly effectively with antipsychotic drugs such as chlorpromazine or haloperidol.

DRUG WITHDRAWAL

Opioids

Heroin withdrawal is not ordinarily a life-threatening situation, usually consisting of flulike symptoms, as described in Chapter 3. Nevertheless, it can be extremely uncomfortable to an opioid abuser, who may show markedly increased craving for his drug during the period of withdrawal. Frequently, opioid-dependent persons are treated with an opioid agonist either in anticipation of gradual withdrawal of all opioids or in anticipation of continued administration of the opioid as an important part of treatment of the addictive behavior.

Methadone is currently the most popular opioid, both for opioid "detoxification" and for treatment of heroin abuse. Methadone was first synthesized in Germany and introduced into general medical use as an opioid analgesic in the late 1940s. Though the chemical structure of this drug differs substantially from that of morphine, the actions of these two drugs are qualitatively identical, and cross-tolerance and cross-dependence between these two drugs and other opioid analgesics exist. Behavior and subjective sensations are reported to be very similar to those produced by morphine. From the pharmacologic point of view, methadone must be considered as virtually identical with most other chemical classes of opioid analgesics, including heroin, with two significant exceptions: It is effective orally, and it acts for longer periods of time than heroin or morphine.

METHADONE WITHDRAWAL

Withdrawal from opioids in the dependent individual is generally best managed with the patient in the hospital, although, increasingly, ambulatory programs are being established for this purpose. Persons with a small "habit" of two to three bags of heroin a day can often be withdrawn easily without recourse to opioid substitution. Substantial degrees of dependence, however, warrant alleviation of the withdrawal syndrome with methadone substitution, whereby detoxification is virtually symptomless.

The patient is observed after the intake of opioid stops, and if significant symptoms appear, an initial dose of 15 to 20 mg methadone is given orally. Additional doses of 10 to 15 mg every four to six hours can be given if symptoms are not suppressed or if they recur. After 24 to 36 hours, the daily methadone requirements can be calculated easily by adding up the total number of milligrams given. Immediately thereafter, this dose (given in two divided doses) is reduced by 20 percent each day; this schedule is usually well tolerated. Most patients can be detoxified in less than 10 days and generally feel well thereafter or experience only very mild withdrawal symptoms for a few additional days (Jaffe, 1980).

SHORT-TERM METHADONE STABILIZATION

Short-term maintenance is usually employed as an ambulatory procedure in carefully selected cases where multidisciplinary services providing evaluation and motivation are available or where a well-motivated patient is awaiting entry into a rehabilitation project. A stabilizing, single daily dose is determined on the basis of the patient's symptoms, starting with 20 mg of methadone per day. The patient must come to the doctor or clinic daily, should receive his drug in liquid form, and should be observed drinking it to avoid diversion of the drug to others.

Central Nervous System Depressants

In contrast to opioid withdrawal, withdrawal from barbiturates or ethanol can be fatal. Fortunately, treatment of barbiturate or ethanol withdrawal is straightforward, involving the prompt administration of benzodiazepines if signs progress beyond the initial phase of tremors, nausea, anxiety, and sweating to preconvulsive or actual convulsive episodes. The benzodiazepines of choice are usually those, such as diazepam, with relatively long durations of action and good anticonvulsive properties. Since most long-acting benzodiazepines are metabolized to active drug in the liver and since the liver of an alcohol-dependent person may be impaired, there is a possibility of drug accumulation in these patients. Oxazepam, lorazepam, or triazolam, which do not have active metabolites, may be more appropriate if accumulation is to be avoided (Kranzler and Orrok, 1989). The long duration of action not only means less frequent dosing, but also indicates a gradual metabolism and a "self-tapering" quality that can be quite useful in the treatment of withdrawal signs. Diazepam is among the most popular and effective benzodiazepine for this condition. An initial dose of 10 mg is recommended, given either intravenously or intramuscularly. The patient should be watched carefully and additional diazepam should be administered in three to four hours if it seems necessary. Therapy may continue for several days, followed by a gradual tapering of diazepam; frequently, drug administration beyond the first day is not necessary (Kranzler and Orrok, 1989).

In addition to benzodiazepines to prevent or lessen the anxiety, tremors, and hallucinations of alcohol withdrawal, vitamins, especially thiamine, should be given parenterally, along with intravenous glucose solutions. Because alcoholics frequently are malnourished and may have compromised liver function, they can suffer from hypoglycemia and vitamin deficiencies. They should be encouraged to eat well-balanced diets, but this may be difficult during the period of ethanol withdrawal. Fortunately, benzodiazepines have an effect of increasing food intake in experimental animals. If this occurs in humans, it may help the recovering alcoholic regain appropriate nutritional status.

Stimulants

Cessation of chronic administration (a "run") of cocaine or amphetamine results primarily in depression, increased appetite, and long periods of sleep. There is rarely any need for any drug treatment for these signs, which arguably constitute a stimulant-withdrawal syndrome. Stimulant withdrawal is followed by a return of desire to self-administer the drug; this craving has been considered as part of the withdrawal sign by some. Treatment of this aspect of cocaine withdrawal has been attempted with antidepressant medication (Jaffe, 1990). The success of this treatment in the general population of cocaine abusers remains untested.

TREATING INFANTS BORN OF DRUG-ABUSING MOTHERS

There is strikingly little information and apparently almost no research on how best to treat infants born of mothers who have abused drugs during their pregnancy. The apparent lack of anything more than modest attention to the problem of developing useful treatment interventions for perinatal drug exposure may be related to the fact that most of these infants and their mothers are of lower socioeconomic status, that the conditions themselves seem extremely difficult to treat, or that the environment where these infants grow up often appears even more devastating than the early drug exposure, making the situation seem hopeless.

Opioids

The problem of dealing with infants born to mothers who have used opioids, including mothers on methadone maintenance therapy, has been with us for a relatively long time. These babies, in addition to being of low birth weight, are often hyperactive, possibly because of the discomfort of undergoing opioid withdrawal. Neonatal opioid withdrawal signs include "irritability and excessive and high-pitched crying, tremors, frantic sucking of fists, hyperactive reflexes, increased respiratory rate, increased stools, sneezing, yawning, vomiting, and fever" (Jaffe, 1990, p. 535). Despite the increased sucking response, these infants often have difficulty feeding, because of uncoordinated sucking and swallowing reflexes. Opioid withdrawal is more life-threatening in infants than it is in adults, since babies who are eating poorly, are vomiting, and have diarrhea can become dehydrated and show disrupted electrolyte balance much more easily than adults. If left untreated, the majority of these infants will die (Finnegan, 1988).

Withdrawal signs will develop within 24 hours in babies whose mothers were using short-acting opioids such as heroin; onset may be delayed for several days in babies of methadone-maintained mothers. The time of the last administration of opioid by the mother also determines the time of onset of withdrawal in the infant. Recent administration of heroin may delay neonate withdrawal and increase its severity (Finnegan, 1988).

Many neonatology textbooks recommend no treatment unless the infant's symptoms seem severe. If they are severe, they suggest phenobarbital and/or chlorpromazine to reduce the hyperactivity and to keep the infant as comfortable as possible. It is not clear what purpose these medications serve except to produce nonspecific sedation. Tincture of opium or paregoric is also suggested, and these drugs, because of their opioid content, should produce a more specific control of withdrawal signs, if, indeed, these are what the infant is suffering. Both tincture of opium and paregoric contain alcohol, which will have its own sedating action but is probably not in the best interest of the child. Common sense suggests that small, tapering doses of morphine or methadone would be useful in treating opioid withdrawal in neonates. It is rare to find such a recommendation in clinical texts, but it is unclear whether this is because these "obvious" drugs have not been found to be satisfactory or whether they have not been tried.

Alcohol

The fetal alcohol syndrome, as described in Chapter 4, is defined primarily in terms of morphologic abnormalities and by the mental retardation that becomes evident as the infant develops. There are few descriptions of overt ethanol withdrawal signs in infants born of ethanol-dependent mothers, although they may appear more "jittery" than normal infants (Streissguth et al., 1980). It seems unlikely that the fetus could avoid such dependence, given that ethanol's access to the fetus is unobstructed. Infants born of ethanol-abusing mothers should be evaluated for signs of fetal alcohol syndrome and observed as well for signs of ethanol withdrawal. Tremors and diaphoresis are among the most obvious early signs in adults and may occur in infants as well. Electrolyte balance should be checked if vomiting and/or diarrhea develop or if sweating seems profuse. It is likely that the mother was poorly nourished, particularly if she received little prenatal care, and vitamin replacement therapy could be beneficial in both mother and child.

Should preconvulsive signs develop, phenobarbital may be the most appropriate treatment drug, one with which neonatologists are familiar and that they have been advised to use with other drug-withdrawal signs. It is probably not necessary to readminister phenobarbital if no further signs develop and if the convulsions do not reappear. This drug is long acting and self-tapering and should outlast the most severe of the ethanol withdrawal signs that develop in infants.

Stimulants

As with treatment of neonates exposed to other centrally acting drugs, there is no universally accepted treatment and, in fact, little suggested specific treatment for infants born of mothers who have abused cocaine or amphetamines. Infants of cocaine-abusing mothers are more likely to be born prematurely than infants of opioid-abusing mothers (Finnegan, 1988), and this adds additional complications to a situation that is already severely compromised. The urgent problem in this case is treatment of signs of drug toxicity rather than dealing with drug-withdrawal signs. Long-term effects of maternal drug abuse in these children remain a question and a concern. Careful monitoring and symptomatic intervention in cases of cardiac arrhythmia, renal failure, changes in body temperature, and changes in blood pressure are currently the only available advice. As in the cases of maternal opioid or alcohol abuse, it may be desirable to give these infants gentle attention and careful monitoring but to keep extraneous stimulation to a minimum. Quiet, dark nurseries may reduce the hyperirritability that is common among these children.

PHARMACOLOGIC MANAGEMENT OF DRUG ABUSE

Opioids

METHADONE MAINTENANCE

In 1965 Dole and Nyswander first reported their success in treating heroin abuse with the use of methadone "blockade" (Dole and Nyswander, 1965). In subsequent years "methadone maintenance" programs based on their experience and protocol have become widespread. Currently, this approach appears to be gaining acceptance progressively (though not without criticism) as the method with the highest potential of all known therapeutic modalities for alleviation of opiate-related crime and for restoration of the confirmed opioid user to a productive life.

The fundamental principles of methadone maintenance depend on the drug's oral efficacy, its long duration of action, and its pharmacologic kinship with heroin that results in the production of "sufficient tolerance to methadone to block the euphoric effect of an average illegal dose of diacetyl morphine" (Dole et al., 1966). Although "cross-tolerance" between methadone and heroin is usually described as the mechanism by which methadone reduces or prevents the effects of heroin and other opioids, the meaning of such cross-tolerance is rarely stated. One might expect that tolerance to the reinforcing effects of methadone would mean that larger doses of the drug would be required to maintain drug-taking behavior. If cross-tolerance to heroin's reinforcing effects developed as a result of methadone's chronic ingestion, ordinary doses of heroin would not provide the subjective effects that they had before and heroin self-administration might not be maintained. However, there has never been any demonstration that tolerance develops to the reinforcing effects of any opioid, and if such tolerance does develop, it is not clear why methadone would be uniquely effective in producing it. Thus, it is safe to say that the mechanism of methadone's ability to suppress heroin self-administration has yet to be determined.

In the initial phase of establishing methadone maintenance, the drug is given in small, divided doses of approximately 10 mg twice daily, the dose being titrated so as to be large enough to alleviate withdrawal symptoms and small enough to avoid oversedation and excessive urinary retention or constipation. The dose is increased gradually over four to six weeks to a maintenance level of 80 to 120 mg/day in a single dose. Although some methadone-maintenance programs have insisted on using smaller doses of methadone, the success rate, measured as reduction in heroin abuse, of methadone programs appears to vary directly with the dose of methadone used (Gerstein and Harwood, 1990). With doses in this range, patients have been found to function normally, have minimal side effects, generally experience no craving for heroin, and are refractory to the "rush" produced by the usual street dose of heroin.

The second phase is a long-term ambulatory period of approximately one year. Outpatients return to the clinic daily, receive their drug dissolved in fruit juice, and are observed to drink it. Their urine is tested to ascertain whether they have been using any illicit drugs. Those individuals who evidence sufficient responsibility are given several days' supply of methadone dissolved in juice to take home, diminishing the frequency of clinic visits and thus enabling some to take jobs or return to school. Generally, such a step has proven satisfactory, since the drug is in an inappropriate vehicle and is too dilute for intravenous injection. Patients with small children at home must be cautioned about the risk that the child may drink the methadone-laced fruit juice, and special containers or labels may be necessary to reduce this possibility.

The third and last phase currently is an indefinite period of time when the patient has been stabilized as a productive member of society. Medically, treatment resembles that in the second phase; at least one dose of medication must be taken in the clinic per week and one urine specimen must be checked. The regimen appears medically safe with few complications. The most troublesome side effect has been persistent constipation, which is generally managed satisfactorily with hydrophilic colloids or other laxatives and occasional enemas. Reduction of libido also occurs. Amenorrheal women usually have experienced an eventual return of normal menses, and a number have conceived and delivered normal infants while on methadone maintenance.

Ideally, under all phases, supportive services are readily available and are related to the needs of the individual patient. Only a few have been found to need little more than medical supervision. Most need substantial support, guidance, and assistance in developing job skills and in resolving personal problems. The conclusion that there should be a much more structured program of ongoing therapy and a wider range of supportive services (Conner and Kremen, 1971) cannot be disputed. Such individual counseling is expensive, however, and with limited financial support for methadone programs and more need for such programs, the issue of whether to provide a large number of clients with methadone and little counseling or a smaller number of clients with drug and more counseling therapy is particularly worrisome.

The success of methadone maintenance seems clear. In controlled studies measuring illicit heroin in urine, criminal activity, and engagement in socially productive activities, clients in methadone maintenance programs have consistently done better than those not taking methadone (Gerstein and Harwood, 1990). Since methadone's beneficial effects are specific for opioids, however, methadone clients can still get effects from nonopioid drugs. In some parts of the country, benzodiazepines have been particularly popular among methadone clients, and cocaine is abused with some frequency among those in methadone treatment programs (Jaffe, 1990). Of course, the success of methadone can be somewhat limited if serious abuse of drugs such as cocaine becomes predominant.

ANTAGONIST AND PARTIAL AGONIST TREATMENT

Theoretically, long-acting opioid antagonists such as naltrexone should provide better protection against the reinforcing effects of illicit heroin than does methadone. Opioid antagonists, by occupying the same receptors that opioid agonists occupy, reduce the opportunity for the agonist to bind and produce its effect. Antagonists have no effect other than to bind at these receptors; the net effect of antagonist administration is to cause a dose-related reduction in the potency of the agonist to produce an opioid effect. Antagonists have not been successful in treating the vast majority of opioid abusers to which they have been given. Opioid abusers typically stop taking this medication after one or two months and revert back to their previous opioid habit. It is likely that this happens because the antagonist, in contrast to methadone, lacks any opioidlike subjective effects and therefore does not reduce the craving the patient has for opioids. The user, unless he is highly motivated, prefers the effects of heroin, which he can perceive and enjoy within a day or so of stopping antagonist administration.

One drug of potential therapeutic use combines the effects of both agonist and antagonist drugs. This drug, buprenorphine, has limited agonist effects, is reinforcing in animals under some circumstances, but has a long-acting antagonist component that can serve to prevent the effects of illicit opioids. It produces few withdrawal signs on its own and can be used to attenuate withdrawal signs in opioid-dependent individuals who have initiated some withdrawal signs. Buprenorphine can precipitate withdrawal in highly dependent clients. Although it has not been adequately evaluated for its therapeutic effects in large groups of opioid abusers, it is an extremely promising compound that should be of considerable practical and theoretical interest over the next several years.

Alcohol

No drugs are available that antagonize the reinforcing effects of alcohol, and it is unlikely, given the mechanism of alcohol's actions, that one ever will be identified. It is not unreasonable to assume that benzodiazepines could be used in alcoholics as a substitute for alcohol in much the same way that methadone is used as a substitute for heroin. Benzodiazepines would have the advantage of not producing the toxic effects on the gastrointestinal, hepatic, and central nervous systems that alcohol does. Moreover, they would not reduce food consumption and lead to malnutrition in subjects who took them frequently. Interestingly, most reviews of the subject do not recommend benzodiazepines for treatment of alcohol abuse beyond their undeniable advantage during withdrawal (Kranzler and Orrok, 1989). Whether alcoholics would take benzodiazepines to the exclusion of alcohol is unknown, but doubtful. The combination of alcohol and benzodiazepines could produce more severe behavioral deficits than either alone, and this might represent a serious complication of prescribing benzodiazepines as part of the treatment of alcohol abuse.

Disulfiram (Antabuse) is a drug that inactivates aldehyde dehydrogenase and blocks the hepatic oxidation of acetaldehyde. If disulfiram has been taken, alcohol consumption will be followed by increased blood levels of acetaldehyde and the "acetaldehyde syndrome" will develop. This consists of vasodilation, facial flushing, throbbing headache, nausea and vomiting, diaphoresis, increased heart rate, orthostatic hypotension, blurred vision, and dysphoria. If severe enough, this reaction can lead to heart failure, convulsions, and death. Mild reactions, after small amounts of alcohol (a single drink), will last from 30 minutes to several hours.

If people with chronic drinking problems take disulfiram regularly, they drink alcohol less often. This has been demonstrated to be the case in at least one experimental study (Kranzler and Orrok, 1989). The difficulty with disulfiram therapy in alcoholics is similar to the difficulty of antagonist therapy in opioid abusers: getting those who need to take their medicine to continue to take their medicine. Compliance with disulfiram therapy is hard to obtain over long periods of time. Disulfiram is probably most effective when it is used in conjunction with other forms of treatment of alcoholism, such as behavioral therapy (Kranzler and Orrok, 1989; Azrinetal, 1982).

Treating alcohol abuse with psychotherapeutic drugs in an attempt to resolve underlying psychologic problems, such as depression or anxiety, has been suggested (Kranzler and Orrok, 1989). Although some data suggest that antidepressant, antianxiety, or antipsychotic drugs may reduce alcohol consumption in alcoholic patients (Kranzler and Orrok, 1989), these data are insufficient to point to clear therapeutic approaches even in selected patients.

Stimulants

There is probably no greater need in the area of drug abuse at the present time than that for a drug that reduces self-administration of cocaine and other stimulants. A great deal of federal money has been devoted to developing and testing potential therapeutic interventions in cocaine abuse. To date, none appears particularly promising. A couple of avenues have been taken to approach this problem. One is to evaluate potential antagonists of cocaine's effects. Since cocaine's mechanism of action is thought to be to block reuptake of dopamine into the cell, thereby producing an enhanced dopamine effect, a number of dopamine antagonists have been evaluated in experimental paradigms. Although it seems clear that drugs that block the D2 subset of dopamine receptors can reverse or protect against more of cocaine's effects than drugs that block the D1 subset of dopamine receptors, the agonist–antagonist interaction is not nearly as clear as that shown by opioid agonists and antagonists. Dopamine antagonists have more disruptive effects on normal behavior, even when they are given alone, than do opioid antagonists, suggesting that the dopamine system has considerably more ongoing activity under normal circumstances than does the opioidergic system. Dopamine antagonists can produce profound and permanent changes in motor behavior when they are given on a chronic basis (tardive dyskinesias). The currently available dopamine antagonists are therefore unsuitable for use in the treatment of cocaine abuse.

Drugs that have cocainelike effects have also been evaluated, using a methadonelike approach to dealing with cocaine abuse. Methylphenidate was evaluated briefly as a potential blocker of cocaine self-administration in humans but was found not to produce satisfactory results (Gawin and Ellinwood, 1988). The toxic effects of cocaine and drugs like cocaine are much more severe than are those of opioids, suggesting that the methadone analogy to developing treatments for cocaine abuse may be far more dangerous with this class of compounds.

Cocaine is self-administered in a cyclic pattern, with each "run" followed by a period of sleeping, eating, depression, and a gradually increasing craving for cocaine. Some have attempted to disrupt the cycle during the withdrawal phase by administering the antidepressant desipramine. Some evidence suggests that this drug may be effective in reducing cocaine abuse under certain conditions, and it is important that other antidepressants be evaluated for their ability to accomplish this goal as well (Gawin and Ellinwood, 1988). Whether these effects of desipramine will be maintained for long periods of time and in a large number of cocaine users has not yet been clearly demonstrated.

Nicotine

By and large, the toxic effects of smoking cigarettes are due to the particulate and aerosol contents of the smoke, particularly the "tar" and carbon monoxide, and not the nicotine. Since it is primarily nicotine that is responsible for the maintenance of smoking behavior, making nicotine available in a delivery system that avoids the more toxic consequences of cigarette smoke seems a reasonable approach to assist people who want to stop smoking. This has been accomplished in several formulations, one of which, a resin complex in chewing gum, has been approved by the FDA and is currently available by prescription. Nicotine polacrilex gum, or nicotine gum, allows nicotine that is contained in an ion exchange resin base to be released in the saliva during chewing. The nicotine is buffered so that it can be absorbed through the mucous membranes of the mouth. The currently available form of nicotine gum contains 2 mg nicotine per piece, which is insufficient to produce blood nicotine levels as high as those produced after smoking a single cigarette. Nicotine blood levels rise more slowly after chewing nicotine gum than they do when a cigarette is smoked. Nevertheless, nicotine gum appears helpful in reducing cigarette smoking for a fairly large number of people.

Studies indicate that some of the putative nicotine withdrawal signs are reduced by chewing nicotine gum. The more blood nicotine levels were increased by chewing the gum, the more symptoms were relieved (Surgeon General's Report, 1988). Unfortunately, the urge to smoke cigarettes was one nicotine withdrawal sign that was not consistently relieved by chewing nicotine gum (Surgeon General's Report, 1988). Weight gain, however, does seem reduced in smokers who switch to chewing nicotine-containing gum (Surgeon General's Report, 1988). Data obtained thus far indicate that those who use nicotine-containing chewing gum may be more successful in stopping smoking than those who do not. The more gum they use and the more effectively they use it (i.e., the higher their blood nicotine levels), the more likely they may be not to resume smoking. The gum itself is not pleasant to chew, however. Its taste is not particularly good, specific chewing procedures are required for the nicotine to be released effectively, and the user is encouraged not to swallow the accumulating saliva, since the nicotine is not well absorbed through the stomach. Thus, a high degree of motivation is necessary for an individual not to simply stop chewing the gum and resume smoking cigarettes.

The fact that nicotine replacement can effectively reduce smoking behavior encourages the search for a better formulation. Transdermal nicotine patches are newly available, and intranasal nicotine gel, and nicotine aerosols have been developed and may be approved for use in the future. One or more of these formulations may prove more successful than chewing gum in reducing cigarette smoking and the cancer and heart disease that result from it. Whether these other mechanisms of providing nicotine prove to have abuse liability themselves remains to be carefully determined.

REFERENCES

Azrin, N. H., R. W. Sisson, R. Meyers, and M. Godley. Alcoholism treatment by disulfiram and community reinforcement therapy. *J Behav Ther Exp Psychiat* 13:105, 1982

Conner, T., and E. Kremen. Methadone maintenance. Is it enough? *Brit J Addict* 66:53, 1971

Dole, V. P., and M. Nyswander. A medical treatment for diacetylmorphine (heroin) addiction. *J Amer Med Assoc* 193:646, 1965

Dole, V. P., M. Nyswander, and M. J. Kreek. Narcotic blockade. *Arch Int Med* 120:19, 1966

Finnegan, L. P. Influence of maternal drug dependence on the newborn. In: Kacew, S., and S. Lock, eds., *Toxicologic and Pharmacologic Principles in Pediatrics.* New York: Hemisphere, 1988, p. 183

Gawin, F. H., and E. H. Ellinwood. Cocaine and other stimulants: Actions, abuse, and treatment. *N Engl J Med* 318:1173, 1988

Gerstein, D. R., and H. J. Harwood, eds. *Treating Drug Problems,* Vol. 1. Washington, D.C.: National Academy Press, 1990

The Health Consequences of Smoking: Nicotine Addiction. A Report of the Surgeon General. U.S. Department of Health and Human Services, Washington, D.C.: U.S. Government Printing Office, 1988

Jaffe, J. H. Drug addiction and drug abuse. In: Gilman, A. G., L. S. Goodman, and A. Goodman, eds., *Goodman and Gilman's Pharmacology and Experimental Therapeutics,* 6th ed. New York: Macmillan, 1980, p. 535

Jaffe, J. H. Drug addiction and drug abuse. In: Gilman, A. G., T. W. Rall, A. S. Nies, and P. Taylor, eds., *Goodman and Gilman's Pharmacology and Experimental Therapeutics,* 8th ed. Elmsford, NY: Pergamon, 1990, p. 522

Kranzler, H. R., and B. Orrok. The pharmacotherapy of alcoholism. *Rev Psychiat* 8:397, 1989

Louria, D. B., T. Hensle, and J. Rose. The major complication of heroin addiction. *Ann Int Med* 67:1, 1967

Rall, T. W. Hypnotics and sedatives; ethanol. In: Gilman, A. G., T. W. Rall, A. S. Nies, and P. Taylor, eds., *Goodman and Gilman's Pharmacology and Experimental Therapeutics,* 8th ed. New York: Pergamon, 1990, p. 345

Steinberg, A. D., and J. Karliner. The clinical spectrum of heroin pulmonary edema. *Arch Int Med* 122:122, 1968

Streissguth, A. P., S. Landesman-Dwyer, J. C. Martin, and D. W. Smith. Teratogeneic effects of alcohol in humans and laboratory animals. *Science* 209:353, 1980

CHAPTER 12

Drug Abuse and the Law

DRUG ABUSE AND THE AMERICAN FEDERAL LAW

Although the federal government has long been interested in regulating the public's access to drugs, it has had to develop gradually its powers to do so. The laws that would ordinarily be related to drug use and abuse, laws that define moral behavior, define, restrict, and punish criminal acts, and laws that regulate the medical profession are all limited by the Constitution to the states. Federal legislation restricting drug use has had to approach the problem obliquely, using the constitutionally defined powers of the U.S. government to generate tax revenue, to regulate interstate commerce, or to enforce international treaties in order to enact laws that limit drug availability. The federal government has had one important ally in its attempts to legislate access to drugs and that has been the consistently strong antidrug sentiment of the large majority of Americans since before the turn of the century.

A history of the development of federal, state, and local laws concerning access of the American public to drugs of abuse has been presented in fascinating detail by David Musto in his book *The American Disease: Origins of Narcotic Control* (1987). The following section summarizes aspects of the federal approach to drug control as described by Dr. Musto.

The first federal law that pertained to narcotic drugs (narcotic in this case also referred to cocaine and cannabis) was the Pure Food and Drug Act of 1906. Prior to the enactment of this law, there was no restriction on the use of any drugs, nor any requirement that medications' labels indicate the drugs that they contained. Opiates and cocaine were quite common in everyday American life, appearing, often unrecognized, in products such as Coca-Cola, hay fever treatments, and various patent medicines. The primary condition of the Pure Food and Drug Act was that all patent medicines that were shipped across state lines had to have their active ingredients listed on their labels. Because the American public was beginning to be concerned about the consequences of drug taking, this simple requirement resulted in a sharp decrease in the sale of such medicines.

Of greater significance was the Harrison Narcotic Act of 1915. This legislation attempted to control drug use through the federal powers of taxation and through federal powers to enforce treaty agreements. The treaty in this case was the Hague Opium Convention of 1912 that restricted preparation and international distribution of medicinal opiates and cocaine. As a signatory, the United States was obliged to develop and enforce its own restrictions on opiates and cocaine. The Harrison Narcotic Act required those who dealt with drugs, physicians and pharmacists, to be federally registered and to pay a tax of one dollar per year. Records of drug transactions were to be made in most cases. Patent medicines containing small amounts of opium, heroin, cocaine, or morphine were exempt from this legislation, as were chloral hydrate and cannabis.

The goal of the Harrison Narcotic Act was to restrict the use of narcotic drugs to medical purposes. Enforcement was to be by the Bureau of Internal Revenue within the Treasury Department. The Harrison Narcotic Act raised several questions. One was whether it prohibited or permitted supply of opioids by physicians to those who needed these drugs to maintain an opioid habit. This question was to be raised again and again during the early history of drug abuse regulation in the United States. Another question was whether the government could use police powers to regulate the availability of narcotics, as would be the case if it were carrying out the mandates of a treaty, or whether it would be limited to record keeping and gathering of information about drug use that could be made available to local authorities. The government's position was that habitual users of narcotics or cocaine were not to be supplied with their accustomed drugs. It also assumed police powers and began to arrest, but more often to warn, physicians and druggists who were deemed to be providing addicts with drugs. The typical procedure was for the physician, the pharmacist, and the addict they were supplying to receive a combined charge of not prescribing "in good faith" (a troublesomely worded part of the law), of conspiring to give drugs unlawfully to an addict, or of aiding and abetting the user to possess illegal drugs. The user himself, who could not legally register to possess narcotic drugs, was charged with possession of narcotics that were not prescribed "in good faith." Good faith, in this case, clearly did not include prescriptions intended solely to maintain an opioid habit.

The initial judgments concerning the Harrison Narcotic Act were setbacks to the government's position. In May, 1915, a district judge in Pennsylvania ruled that since addicts were not allowed to register to possess narcotics, they could not be guilty of possessing narcotics without proper registration. Other judges rendered similar verdicts on the basis that the law did not specify or limit the amount of narcotic physicians could prescribe. The Supreme Court had an opportunity to interpret the Harrison Act in 1916 when it heard the case of Jin Fuey Moy. Dr. Jin Fuey Moy was a Pittsburgh physician charged with conspiracy to supply an addict with opium. A lower court, interpreting the Harrison Narcotic

Act strictly as a revenue act, ruled that the Act was unconstitutional when it attempted to regulate the practice of medicine within a state. By a majority of seven to two, the Supreme Court upheld the decision of the lower court, and the police powers of the federal government in regulating narcotic use were suspended. Judge Oliver Wendell Holmes, Jr., writing the majority opinion, stated that the wording of the Act did not indicate that the law was necessary to fulfill a treaty obligation, and that, even if it had, the section requiring prescriptions to be written in good faith was not required by treaty.

The government quickly went to work to shore up the Harrison Act by increasing the stipulated tax on narcotics and by requiring that all taxed drugs carry a stamp. This strengthened the notion of the law as a revenue act rather than an act in support of a treaty. It also made it illegal to possess unstamped drugs, making it easier to prosecute addicts who might have such drugs. Concern for the addict, who was to be precipitously deprived of his physician-prescribed drugs, was demonstrated by a plea that Congress provide for the treatment of addicts, and cooperation of the Public Health Service was requested to care for the treatment of drug-deprived addicts. The Public Health Service was anxious to avoid such a commitment and was able to do so because of specific restrictions against its providing services to the civilian population.

Although these changes were quite modest, the next Supreme Court decision with respect to the Harrison Narcotic Act returned to the government the powers that had been removed by the previous decision. The relevant case, heard in 1919, again concerned a physician who had supplied a known addict with morphine tablets. The lower court had ruled that the law that proscribed this prescription was irrelevant to the collection of revenue and therefore exceeded the constitutional powers of the federal government. The Supreme Court reversed this decision by a vote of five to four. On the same day, in a similar case involving a druggist and a physician accused of conspiracy to supply a known addict with maintenance doses of morphine, the Court ruled that such behavior was a "perversion of the meaning" of the law.

The dramatic change in the tone and consequences of the decisions of the Supreme Court between 1915 and 1919 can be understood in the context of the changes in the public view of narcotic use during this time and the events that produced this change. World War I had been fought in the interim, and the nation, rather than rejoicing in victory, was suffering from a lack of self-confidence. The public was deeply frightened by the prospect of anarchy and a Bolshevik revolution in this country, like the one that had just occurred in Russia. It was a period of intolerance of anything foreign and anything that suggested that the American system should be questioned. Dissent was suppressed at every level. Habitual narcotic use was thought to lead to degeneracy and antisocial behavior, and the public strongly supported laws that restricted such use. It was during this time that the constitutional amendment prohibiting the production and sale of alcoholic beverages was passed; the country was to be cleansed not only of immoral users of opiates and cocaine, but also of degenerate alcoholics.

Throughout most of this period, the position of the American medical profession did not differ substantially from that of law enforcement officials. The typical physician knew little about drug users. Issues relating to medical management of drug abuse were not dealt with in medical school, and most education on the issue came later from older colleagues, who taught that drug users were moral degenerates, virtually incapable of telling the truth, and usually criminals. Young physicians were warned, not inappropriately in many cases, that addicts were uncooperative, unreliable patients whom they would be well advised to avoid, for the outcome of any attempt toward rehabilitation was likely to be a failure and, moreover, by dealing with drug users, a physician might well end up involved with the police or federal agents. Though the record of this period is studded with many valiant individual attempts to portray drug abuse as a disease and to help drug users, most practitioners were content to ignore the problem and they commonly refused to accept the user as a patient. Exceptions were made only in the case of alcoholism, the most socially acceptable form of drug abuse, though even alcoholics were often grudgingly accepted as patients.

With the assertion of the constitutional authority of the federal government to enforce the Harrison Narcotic Act came governmental restrictions on maintenance clinics. Several state-supported clinics existed to "treat" addicts by gradually reducing their dose of opioids and to offer hospitalization if withdrawal appeared sufficiently uncomfortable to warrant it. One of the results of this attempt at "treatment" was the discovery that most addicts were not interested in stopping their drug use; after they had utilized the clinic's facilities and were discharged, they turned to the street dealer to continue their habit. The inability to cure drug addiction through the clinic approach led some prominent physicians to develop the opinion that addicts suffered from a character disorder that preceded the development of addiction.

During the 1920s, Congress continued to express concern about the use of illicit drugs in this country. Of primary concern was the apparent increase in export of processed opium to China and other countries, and in 1922 the Narcotic Drug Import and Export Act was approved. This Act was intended to limit international trade in narcotics with nations that had signed the Hague Convention. American attempts to require international control of opium production through The League of Nations Geneva Conference of 1924–1925 were not successful. Countries that produced opium for export were unwilling to agree to a limitation on this source of income.

At home, enforcement of the Harrison Narcotic Act was resulting in severe overcrowding in federal prisons as hundreds of addicts were incarcerated. Prison wardens found the addicts difficult to deal with and also found that their imprisonment did little or nothing to effect a "cure." Legislation to establish "narcotic farms" that would serve as separate prisons for addicts was easily passed by the Congress in 1928. The hope was that not only would the existing federal prison system be relieved of overcrowding but these farms would provide a place where the disease of addiction could be treated. The two institutions, set up under auspices of the Treasury Department and operated by the Public Health Service, were located in rural areas of Lexington, Kentucky, and Fort Worth, Texas. These combined prisons and farms were intended, by involving addicts in the hard but productive labor required by agricultural pursuits, in the context of clean, healthy rural life, to establish moral character, the lack of which had caused these unfortunate people to become addicted. The narcotic farms were no more successful at treating addicts than other medical or legal programs had been; their usefulness was primarily in training clinical researchers and in providing addict subjects for many research projects that have greatly enhanced our understanding of the effects of narcotics.

In the late 1920s, the Federal Bureau of Narcotics (FBN), as a separate entity from the liquor law enforcement branch of government, was established to enforce the Harrison Narcotic Act and to represent the nation's drug control goals at foreign conferences. The first head of this bureau was Harry J. Anslinger, who brought excellent leadership and a strong law enforcement approach to narcotics control. It was during Anslinger's 32-year tenure as head of the FBN that a law enforcement approach to drug abuse had its heyday, starting with legislation to prohibit use of marihuana. In the 1930s public concern about the dangers of cannabis rose dramatically and legislators felt pressure to regulate its use. This drug had been ignored by the Harrison Narcotic Act, with most congressional testimony asserting that it was not habit forming or dangerous. At the time legislation providing for the narcotic farms was written, however, habitual cannabis users were designated as eligible for treatment. Use of this drug was associated particularly with Mexican immigrants, and demand for control was greatest in areas where the population of these immigrants was highest. The Depression and the unemployment it produced made the once-welcome Mexican farm workers undesirable aliens, and habits attributed to them, particularly drug use habits, were loudly decried. Although the FBN attempted to encourage states to enact antimarihuana legislation, since federal control would be very difficult to implement, pressure for the federal government to move on this problem proved overwhelming. Attempts by American representatives to the Geneva Conference for the Suppression of the Illicit Traffic in Dangerous Drugs to include cannabis among the drugs to be controlled met with failure. It was therefore not possible for the federal government to control cannabis by applying its power to enforce treaties, and it instead had to rely on its power to tax to enact antimarihuana legislation. The Marijuana Tax Act of 1937 was modeled after the National Firearms Act, which had attempted to limit the use of machine guns by gangsters by requiring that anyone transferring firearms had to pay a transfer tax. Such a tax was peculiar, even when applied to machine guns, and was termed "ridiculous" when the suggestion was made to apply it to marihuana. However, after Congress had elicited testimony as to the horrors of marihuana, including the possibility that its use could lead to insanity, it passed the Marijuana Tax Act in 1937. The Act mandated virtually total prohibition of marihuana; the only form permitted was seeds in canary food, and this had to be sterilized before it could be sold.

During World War II, drug abuse problems were minimal since opportunities for importing raw and processed opium were markedly reduced. Following the war there was concern that reinitiation of trade, as well as the return of a large number of young men who might have been exposed to drugs of abuse while overseas, would result in an upturn in drug abuse. The FBN supported stiff mandatory sentences for first convictions; these were incorporated into federal law in the Boggs Act of 1951 and were made even harsher in 1956. Public sentiment against drug abuse at this time was much as it had been during the Red Scare of 1919. Fear of internal subversion as seen during 1919–1920 was mirrored in the McCarthy era of the early 1950s; paranoid concern about communism and other "un-American" activities seemed, in both time periods, to carry over to public sentiment about the evil of drug abuse and the immorality and subversive nature of those who abused drugs. The American Medical Association and the American Bar Association stood virtually alone in urging maintenance clinics and less severe penalties for offenders. A joint report by these two organizations contained a description of and praise for the British "system" of opioid maintenance. The FBN response to this measured report was a vituperative condemnation of such suggestions.

The "drug scare" attitude of congress and the American public was not long-lived. The postwar period was a time of greatly increased government spending for medical research and mental health research in particular. As Congress provided financial support for mental health centers, it began to pay more attention to mental health professionals whose attitudes towards drug abuse were markedly different from those of the FBN. Many influential psychiatrists had been trained at the "narcotic farms," where they had, in effect, been caretakers, not physicians. They could see that incarceration had little effect on the process of addiction. Perhaps opioid maintenance, resembling medical treatment for addiction, would have better success.

Even in the face of dramatic increases in abuse of illegal drugs during the 1960s, social attitudes toward addicts and addiction were changing. It was perhaps because drug abuse was becoming so severe that the public determined that the law enforcement and interdiction approach of the FBN was not adequate to solve the problem, and might be inappropriate as well. Under the impact of almost daily reports in the 1960s from the communications media about the growing incidence of drug abuse, particularly among adolescents and young adults, the attitude of many members of the general public changed in the direction of conceding that perhaps rehabilitation had a place in the fight against drug abuse. The addict was coming to be seen less as a criminal or a person of immoral character and more as an unfortunate victim of circumstance. A Supreme Court decision in 1962 made clear its position that addiction was a disease, not a crime, and although courts treated drug dealers harshly, their sentences were tempered if the dealer was also addicted. In 1966, the shift in public opinion toward addicted persons was reflected by the passage of the Narcotic Addict Rehabilitation Act by Congress, the first federal legislation to designate opioid abuse a disease rather than a crime.

Still, the problem of drug abuse grew. Attempts to deal with the rising number of users of illegal drugs included, in 1965, the Drug Abuse Control Amendments of the Harrison Narcotic Act. These amendments established the Bureau of Drug Abuse Control (BDAC) within the Department of Health, Education, and Welfare and added stimulants and depressants such as amphetamine and barbiturates to the drugs that were to be controlled. The constitutional basis of drug control was moved from the government's tax authorization to its interstate commerce authorization. In 1968 Congress coped with the disarray existing among the various federal agencies responsible for enforcement of drug abuse laws. Up to this time, the Bureau of Narcotics dealt with offenses involving narcotics and marihuana; its agents could not, however, impound LSD, barbiturates, or amphetamines. Offenses involving these drugs fell under the provisions of the new Drug Abuse Control Amendments of 1965; the responsible unit within the Federal Drug Administration (FDA) was the BDAC. As patterns of mixed drug abuse became more prevalent—a given seller might, for example, have both LSD and marihuana in his possession—the problems of law enforcement grew more complex. To resolve the problem, Congress merged the Bureau of Narcotics and the BDAC into the Bureau of Narcotics and Dangerous Drugs (BNDD), which for a variety of reasons, was lodged within the Department of Justice (Walsh, 1968). This agency was given considerable resources with the aim of reducing the importation of illicit drugs and enforcing federal regulations concerning drug abuse.

In 1970, the most important legislation since the Harrison Narcotic Act was passed by Congress. This was the Comprehensive Drug Abuse and Control Act or the Controlled Substances Act of 1970; it incorporated into one statute the many changes in drug abuse legislation that had evolved since the Harrison Narcotic Act had originally been passed. One goal was to limit the importation, manufacture, prescription, and distribution of drugs that had abuse potential. All individuals or companies that wished to use drugs in research, to prescribe them to patients, to manufacture and sell them, or to import them, had to register with the BNDD and keep careful records of amounts of drugs manufactured and sold, obtained, dispensed, or used in research. The drugs that were to be restricted were indicated individually and assigned to one of four categories or schedules. Drugs in Schedule I were deemed to have no medical use in the United States and to have a great risk of abuse. These included heroin, marihuana, and LSD and related compounds. Use of these drugs was restricted to research purposes only. Drugs in Schedule II were those with high abuse potential, but with some medical indication; prescriptions for these compounds could not be refilled. Opioid analgesics such as morphine and methadone were included in this schedule, as were amphetamines, cocaine, and barbiturates. In Schedule III were drugs with medical indications and a lower risk of abuse potential. Drugs such as the sedatives glutethimide and methyprylon, as well as the stimulants chlorphentermine and phendimetrazine, were included in Schedule III. Drugs considered to have even less risk of abuse were placed in Schedule IV. These were primarily central nervous system depressants including various benzodiazepines, long-acting barbiturates, meprobamate, and chloral hydrate. Prescriptions for drugs in this category could be refilled indefinitely. The law encouraged frequent review of the variously scheduled drugs and a compound that was found to show increasing or decreasing patterns of abuse could be moved from one schedule to another. This Act did not establish any minimum sentence for violators; it did recommend probation for a first offense of possessing a small amount of marihuana. One harsh enforcement aspect of the law permitted "no-knock" searches of private homes.

During the early 1970s, in response to the continuing increase in drug abuse, Nixon's war on drugs was getting into high gear. This broad approach to dealing with drugs involved a greatly increased emphasis on law enforcement, increased support for drug abuse treatment, and, as described in Chapter 3, increased funding for research on causes of and treatments for the disease of drug abuse. Law enforcement took the course of discouraging Turkey from growing opium poppies, of breaking up the traffic of raw opium from Turkey to France where it was converted to heroin before being shipped to the United States, and of increasing border surveillance and drug interdiction. The number of methadone maintenance clinics was increased in the hopes of decreasing demand for opioids, but as opium from Turkey disappeared, that from Mexico, Pakistan, Afghanistan, and other countries increased, suggesting that demand was still high. The Office of Drug Abuse Law Enforcement was established in early 1972 to deal with enforcement issues at home. The "no-knock" provision of federal law allowed this organization to enter private homes unannounced in its search for illegal drugs. This unpopular policy contributed to the merging of this group with the BNDD; the resulting enforcement agency is the current Drug Enforcement Administration (DEA).

The research aspects of Nixon's policy resulted in the establishment of the National Institute on Drug Abuse (NIDA) in 1973. This was a sister institute to the National Institute on Alcohol Abuse and Alcoholism, both within the National Institutes on Mental Health. NIDA was initially given the mandate to provide treatment as well as to conduct and support research on the drugs themselves and to coordinate prevention programs.

Under the Ford and Carter administrations, attitudes toward drug use, particularly marihuana use, were considerably more relaxed. Admission that it was impossible to eliminate all illicit drug use allowed policy to emphasize the more dangerous drugs, at this time heroin and other opiates. The request for decriminalization of private marihuana use by President Carter early in his administration was tempered later after his Special Assistant for Health Issues was involved in a drug scandal. A grassroots parents movement against use of drugs, particularly use of the increasingly popular marihuana by young people, also blocked administration and congressional attempts to decriminalize this drug.

The election of Ronald Reagan brought back to the administration the strong antidrug attitude of President Nixon. This attitude was backed by increased funding for law enforcement efforts to combat drug abuse but no substantial increase in research or treatment funding. The additional law enforcement monies had no apparent effect on the amount or quality of drugs available on the street. One of these drugs was "crack" cocaine, which was abundant and cheap. The resulting epidemic use of a drug that had been considered fairly innocuous prior to this time produced a massive increase in spending to combat drug abuse. The Anti-Drug Abuse Act of 1986 authorized nearly $4 billion to fight drug abuse. Despite earlier experiences of the difficulty of reducing drug abuse by reducing drug supply, this money was designated primarily to enhance federal law enforcement and drug interdiction capability. One of the more interesting aspects of interdiction was the provision related to "controlled substance analogues" or what are usually termed "designer drugs." Earlier legislation enumerated each drug and assigned it to a specific schedule. If a clandestine chemist synthesized a novel compound that had properties like that of an abused substance, there was no restriction on the sale of this chemical. The 1986 legislation placed all such drugs (identified as drugs with chemical structures similar to those of scheduled substances, drugs with pharmacologic properties similar to those of scheduled substances, or drugs that were represented by a seller as having properties similar to those of scheduled drugs) into Schedule I, the most restrictive schedule. The Act also established the Alcohol, Drug Abuse and Mental Health Administration, which would consist of the three National Institutes of Drug Abuse, of Mental Health, and of Alcohol, Alcohol Abuse and Alcoholism. This agency was charged with continuing research on drug abuse and alcoholism and with establishing prevention programs that included dissemination of information about the health hazards of drug use.

More recently, the Crime Control Act of 1990 contained several sections of relevance to drug abuse. Interestingly, given the title of the Act, it elaborated and expanded some of the educational provisions of the 1986 law, particularly those related to "drug-free school zones." These programs were aimed at young children and attempted to provide them with educational programs that would help them to recognize and resist opportunities to experiment with drugs. Funds were set aside for states to use to train teachers and counselors to better educate elementary and secondary schoolchildren about the risks involved in drug abuse. In the 1990 legislation, attention was paid for the first time to the risks of anabolic steroid abuse, and this drug class was added to Schedule III.

The overall pattern of drug abuse in this country is a cyclic one, as has been mentioned in earlier chapters. Use of illicit drugs was common at the turn of the century. After World War I, the use of opioids and cocaine decreased gradually; just before World War II, and even more so during this war, there was simply very little drug abuse in this country. Following World War II, drug abuse began to increase again, rising to epidemic proportions during the 1980s. It appears that use of illicit drugs in this country has begun to wane again as we enter the 1990s.

The reasons for this cyclic nature of illicit drug use are not clear; history suggests that they may be complicated. Common sense suggests that the rise, fall, and rise again of drug abuse reflects the concerns, knowledge, and experience of the American public with respect to drug abuse and drug addiction rather than the rigor of law enforcement programs. Those who live during a period of high drug abuse prevalence are able to pass on to their children their knowledge of the risks and dangers of such use. But as social memory fades, drug-taking experiments increase and the number of individuals who become heavily involved in drug abuse increase. Generally, even young people do not engage in behaviors they believe to be quite dangerous. Their understanding of what may be dangerous comes from their own experiences, those of their parents and teachers, and what they see on television, in advertising, and in other media. As drug abuse increases, information from each of these sources combines to convince the public, particularly the young, that drug taking is a dangerous activity; consequently, drug abuse begins to decline.

The role of laws, law enforcement, and interdiction in the cyclic pattern of drug abuse is not clear. Public demand for strong antidrug laws has changed over the years. Attitudes toward minority groups and the drugs they are reported to use has intensified the views of the majority about drug abuse and drug abusers and influenced the types of laws enacted to restrict and punish such use. Times of national paranoia about foreign influences appear to result in harsh laws and penalties for those apprehended for drug abuse. When use of illicit drugs became prevalent among the children of the majority, the reaction was less draconian and tended to deal with drug abuse as an illness. Lessons of the past suggest, however, that significant downturns in drug abuse prevalence have not come by pouring millions of dollars into drug enforcement and interdiction programs.

Thus, attempts to limit the supply of drugs to any significant extent seem nearly futile. Neither, however, have increased treatment programs produced any clear changes in demand for drugs. There are as yet few clearly effective programs that treat abuse of any particular drug. Research efforts have proven exceptionally useful in increasing our understanding of drug mechanisms but have not yet produced better treatment strategies. Decreasing demand for drugs seems to come most profitably and inexpensively from educational programs designed to prevent the onset of drug abuse. This seems to be the road taken most recently by Congress in the 1990 Crime Control Act. Whether the recommendations of this Act can be implemented successfully in the face of drastically reduced dollars for education remains to be seen. Fortunately, much drug abuse education is carried on outside the classroom, particularly by television, where the dangers of drug abuse are brought home dramatically on a frequent basis. It is to be hoped that real-life experiences of many of our most vulnerable youth will dissuade them from starting to use illicit drugs.

THE ENGLISH "SYSTEM"

During the 1950s, the contrast between the incidence of opioid abuse in America and in Great Britain was truly striking; we had a population of abusers that numbered in the tens of thousands, and it seemed to be growing daily, whereas Britain had a relative handful of opioid abusers and their numbers were stable. It seemed as if the British had an almost magical technique for coping with opioid abuse. American physicians and politicians spoke glowingly of the English "system" and advocated its adoption by this country.

No one was more surprised than the British to hear that they had a "system" for coping with opioid dependence. In truth, the British "system" consisted of nothing more than the right of physicians to supply opioids legally to dependent individuals for the purpose of maintaining their dependence, providing certain stipulations were met. In the words of the Rolleston Report of 1926, dependent individuals for whom morphine or heroin could be prescribed included "Persons for whom, after every effort has been made for the cure of addiction, the drug cannot be completely withdrawn, either because: (1) complete withdrawal produces serious symptoms which cannot be satisfactorily treated under the ordinary condition of private (general) practice; or (2) the patient, while capable of leading a useful and fairly normal life so long as he takes a certain non-progressive quantity, usually small, of the drug of addiction, ceases to be able to do so when the regular allowance is withdrawn." The report also recommended that opioid maintenance should not be undertaken by a physician without the concurring opinion of a colleague. No physician was required to inform any governmental agency of the existence of opioid-dependent people in his practice, but it was a legal offense for the patient to obtain opioid from more than one physician. The opioid-dependent population was identified and counted, however, by means of routine governmental examination of pharmacists' records.

From the 1920s until well into the 1950s, Britain never had at any one time more than a few hundred addicts; many were middle-aged, a large fraction was from the medical and paramedical professions, and most were classified as "therapeutic" addicts, that is, they had been exposed to opioid first in the course of medical treatment (Glatt, 1965). Few English physicians accepted opioid-dependent individuals as patients and they typically did little for their patients but provide the necessary prescriptions. Most British physicians who accepted these patients exhibited no more interest in or concern about the welfare of opioid abusers than did American physicians. Some urged hospitalization on their dependent patients with a "cure" as the goal, but one, when an "addict" had returned to him after months of hospitalization for rehabilitative purposes, unhesitatingly gave that patient his usual opioid prescription (Glatt, 1965). Another physician prescribed 9000 mg of heroin for an opioid user; three days later, to replace pills "lost in an accident," he prescribed an additional 600 mg of heroin for the same patient (Louria, 1968, p. 66). Though the English newspapers wrote often of dependent patients being "under treatment," it is evident that British physicians, by and large, accorded their addicted patients little "treatment"; they were inert conduits through which the user received his supply of opioids.

The "dam broke" on opioid dependence in England in the mid-1960s, as the number of new users identified rose from 56 in 1961 to 259 in 1965. And in 1966, 522 new users became known, a number greater than the total of all new users identified throughout the period 1945 to 1964. More alarming still were the findings that the new users were quite young, many in their twenties and some in their teens, and that a high percentage of the newcomers had become dependent through illicit channels (Bewley, 1965). Some English physicians held that the British "system," at least as manifested by the activities of some practitioners, contributed both to the spread and the persistence of heroin abuse. Physicians who laxly prescribed greater quantities of opioids than required by users gave heroin abuse, according to these critics, the character of an infectious disease. Glatt observed, "Of the many youngsters taking hemp or amphetamines, the more adventurous begin to experiment with heroin obtained from 'registered' addicts. They become addicted and introduce a fresh circle of acquaintance to the habit" (p. 172). And Bewley concluded, "The chief source of illicit heroin and cocaine in this country is the sale of these drugs by addicts who have more than they need prescribed for them . . ." (Bewley, 1965, p. 1286). The easy availability of opioids from the few physicians known as "easy marks" to the users also impeded rehabilitation; Glatt noted, "Relapse is the more probable because of the ease with which recognized addicts can lawfully obtain drugs from their doctor" (Glatt, 1965, p. 172).

In their advocacy of the British "system" some Americans have maintained that our problems of death from overdoses and the various infectious diseases that typically plague American heroin users would essentially disappear if our users were granted legal access to pure heroin and professional equipment for injection. This argument was refuted when Bewley and his colleagues published the results of a survey of mortality and morbidity among British heroin users in 1968. They found that although users were supplied with sterile, disposable needle-and-syringe units designed to be used only once, many used the same syringe repeatedly, until it no longer functioned. Many carried the syringes loosely in coat pockets and, although there would appear to be no need to do so, many shared their syringes with fellow users. The survey noted that there had been a minor epidemic of hepatitis among users in London in 1966. Most disturbing were the mortality figures. Bewley et al. (1968) calculated the mortality rate among British heroin users as 27 to 28 deaths per 1000 users per year; though no reliable rate can be computed for American users, Bewley's estimate is nearly twice as high as the highest estimate we have encountered for opioid abuse mortality in this country. An English observer concluded, "It is certain that the British practice of prescribing maintenance doses for addicts, so that the patient knows how much he is taking (and that it is pure), has not made heroin taking safer" (Gilder, 1968, p. 1018).

The findings of Bewley's group cast doubt on the validity of two common assertions about drug abuse. When opioid users are asked about their preference for heroin, many reply that heroin fulfills their needs in a way that no other drug does. When an American opioid user adopts a pattern of multiple drug abuse, supporters of "legalized heroin" often explain that such a pattern would not be necessary if American users could obtain reasonably potent heroin at a nominal price and in reliable supply. The typical user in Bewley's study, however, took 260 mg of heroin and 110 mg of cocaine daily; for 63 percent of the users, use of cocaine began *after* use of heroin had been established. Moreover, in addition to being heavy smokers, 88 percent of Bewley's subjects used two or more additional drugs regularly; in addition to the cocaine already mentioned, cannabis preparations, amphetamine (by mouth), and barbiturates were popular drugs of abuse.

The original British "system," which was terminated in 1968, seems to have suffered from flaws both in theory and practice. The "enabling act" of the British "system," the previously described Rolleston Report of 1926, stipulated that maintenance be conducted with a "nonprogressive quantity" of opioid. If strictly adhered to, such a prescribing pattern would mean that, within weeks or several months at most, the users would experience only weak and transient drug effects because tolerance to heroin had developed. It is doubtful that many users would remain content for long under these conditions; young users, in particular, would supplement the legal heroin with illegal opioids, supplement the legal heroin with other drugs, or adopt both practices. Many British users, as Bewley's group discovered, did resort to a combination of legal and illegal drugs.

In practice, the British "system" failed in part because British physicians, by and large, had no greater concern about drug users than their American counterparts had. As in America, many physicians in Great Britain declined to accept drug users as patients; and those who did accept them often treated their dependent patients in what appears to have been a negligent fashion. It seems that many did not even describe the technique of sterile injection to their patients (Bewley et al., 1968). Most seemed to regard drug abuse as an essentially incurable condition and confined their "therapeutic" efforts to the issuing of prescriptions for opioids. A few (probably less than 10) became widely known among London drug users for the liberality of their opioid prescriptions; by providing the excess opioids that would be sold by users to susceptible nondependent individuals, these physicians most probably contributed significantly to the spread of heroin abuse in England.

In 1968 the original British "system" was revised so that only physicians attached to abuse treatment centers or clinics could prescribe opioids for the maintenance of dependence. Physicians who saw opioid abusers for maintenance were required to have a special governmental license, according to The Dangerous Drug Acts of 1967, which established the regulations of the revised "system," and the identity of each user under treatment was to be reported to the Home Office. In this revised "system" a greater attempt is being made to rehabilitate the patient, though the usual difficulty of motivating a user to cooperate in rehabilitative measures remains an important impediment. Some heroin addicts have been switched to maintenance on methadone and, thus, the revised British "system" is not unlike the methadone maintenance programs currently in effect in the United States.

REFERENCES

Bewley, T. Heroin addiction in the United Kingdom (1954–1964). *Brit Med J* 2:1284, 1965

Bewley, T. H., O. Ben-Arie, and I. P. James. Morbidity and mortality from heroin dependence. *Brit Med J* 1:725, 1968

Gilder, S. S. B. The London letter: Heroin morbidity and mortality. *Canad Med Assoc J* 98:1018, 1968

Glatt, M. M. Reflections on heroin and cocaine addiction. *Lancet* ii:171, 1965

Louria, D. B. *The Drug Scene*. New York: McGraw-Hill, 1968

Musto, D. F. The American Disease: Origins of Narcotic Control. New York: Oxford University Press, 1987

Walsh, J. Narcotics and drug abuse: The federal response. *Science* 162:1254, 1968

Index

Abdomen, 46, 170, 174; and alcohol withdrawal, 65; examination, 174–75; pain, 36
Abscess, 12, 13, 15, 54, 140, 169, 170, 173
Abstinence. *See* Withdrawal
Acetaldehyde, 24, 57, 67, 190
Acetate, 67, 87, 94
Acetone, 87, 90, 94
Acid-base balance, 49
Acquired Immune Deficiency Syndrome. *See* AIDS
Acute brain syndrome. *See* Marihuana: acute brain syndrome
Addiction. *See* Dependence
Adenosine, 143
Adrenal cortex, 30
Adulterants, 175; diluents, 13, 15; lactose, 45, 153, 169; mannitol, 45; oil of mustard, 86; quinine, 13, 45, 169; talc, 13, 169, 173
Aerosol, 85–97; absorption, 86; content of smoke, 191–92; effects of, 90–91; patterns of use, 88–90; physiologic dependence, 91; preparations used, 87; psychologic dependence, 91–92; tolerance, 91; toxic effects of, 92–95; use by youth, 85–87. *See also* Inhalants
Afghanistan, opium from, 201
Africa: and caffeine use, 142; and khat chewing, 141; and marihuana use, 118, 127
African Americans: and AIDS, 13; and PCP use, 99
AIDS (HIV): and amphetamine users, 140; and crack users, 154; in diagnosis of drug abuse, 164; and i.v. drug users, 13–14, 45, 53–54; and nitrite users 95; and *pneumocystis carinii*, 173

Alcohol, 56–73; absorption and fate, 57, 66–68; anxiolytic effects, 69; beneficial effects of, 69; blood levels, 62; butyl, 94; central nervous system effects of, 61, 71–73, 167; cross-dependence, 57; dependence, 57, 64–66, 156, 184; depressants compared with, 56, 57, 75, 76; digestive system effects of, 68, 70–71; epidemiology of use, 3–4, 10, 56, 58–59, 122; ethyl (ethanol), 94; ethylene glycol, 57; and GABA, 63; as heroin substitute, 42; inhalation of, 87, 94; *in utero* effects (FAS), 68–69, 186–187; lethal effects, 73; marijuana compared with, 124–25; mechanism, 63; methyl (methanol, wood alcohol), 57, 94; overdose, 181; partition coefficient, 67; patterns of use, 60–61; social attitudes towards, 58; tolerance, 62, 63–64; use with cocaine, 12; use with other sedative-hypnotics, 74, 79, 80, 81; water-lipid coefficient, 67
Alcohol dehydrogenase, 57
Alcohol, Drug Abuse and Mental Health Administration (ADAMHA), 202
Alcoholic hallucinosis, *see* Alcoholism, withdrawal syndrome
Alcoholism: blackouts and amnesia in, 62; and chronic organic brain syndrome, 72; diagnosis of, 58, 166–67, 171, 176; and the endocrine system, 175–76; genetics of, 60; and liver disease, 70–71, 175; malnutrition in, 71–73, 166, 186; management of, 189–90; neuropathy in, 71; and pancreatitis, 70; and physical examination, 166–67; treatment of withdrawal, 184; withdrawal syndrome, 64–66

Alphaprodine, 44
Amblyopia. *See* Ophthalmic effects
Amenorrhea: in medical diagnosis, 176;
    in methadone maintenance, 188
American Bar Association, 199
American Medical Association, 199
Amnesia: and alcohol, 62; and
    benzodiazepines, 80; and PCP, 98,
    100. *See also* Memory
Amphetamines, 132–149; absorption
    and fate of, 139–40; Benzedrine, 135;
    and bruxism, 140; cocaine compared
    with, 150, 154–59; "crystal," 134;
    diagnosis of abuse of, 166–68, 171–
    72, 174, 176–77; effects of, 136–37;
    "ice," 135, 137; legal aspects of, 200,
    201, 205, 206; mechanism of action,
    139; and memory impairment, 140; as
    nasal decongestant, 134; in obesity
    treatment, 134; overdose treatment,
    182; physiologic dependence on, 138;
    and sensitivity to haloperidol and
    apomorphine 140; tolerance, 138; in
    treatment of attention deficit
    disorder, 134; and treatment of
    narcolepsy, 134; withdrawal
    ("crash"), adult, 136, 138, 184–85;
    withdrawal, infant, 186. *See also*
    Methamphetamine; Propylhexedrine
Amotivational syndrome, 128
Amyl acetate, 94
Amyl nitrate, 87
Analgesics: antagonism of, 50; codeine,
    52; and cigarette burns, 171;
    endogenous, 51; ketamine, 99–100;
    methadone, 183; phencyclidine, 98;
    semisynthetic, 42; synthetic, 42–44
Anesthetics, dissociative. *See*
    Phencyclidine
Anhedonia, 156
Anslinger, Harry J., 198
Antabuse. *See* Disulfiram
Antidrug Abuse Act of 1986, 202
Antisocial personality disorder, 8
Apomorphine, 140
Arteriosclerosis, 33, 34
Asia: opium culture, 40; tobacco
    culture, 23; use of caffeine, 142; use
    of volatile solvents, 87
Attention deficit disorder, 134, 147
Australia, use of volatile solvents, 86,
    87

Barbiturates, 73–78; absorption,
    distribution, metabolism, 76–77;
    cross-tolerance, 19; dependence, 17,

19, 78; effects of, 56–57, 75–76; and
    hallucinogens, 110, 124; legal aspects
    of, 200, 201; mechanism of action,
    63; medical diagnosis of abuse, 167–
    69, 171–72, 177; overdose treatment,
    76, 181–82; patterns of use, 74–75; in
    polydrug abuse, 56, 74, 80, 206;
    stimulants compared with, 138, 156;
    tolerance, 77–78; treatment of
    alcohol withdrawal, 66; volatile
    solvents compared with, 90–92;
    water-lipid coefficient, 77;
    withdrawal, 184
Benzene: in cigarette smoke, 35; in
    cocaine extraction, 151; in glue, 86;
    toxicity, 92; in volatile solvents, 87
Benzedrine abuse. *See* Amphetamines
Benzodiazepines, 78–81; and alcohol,
    79, 190; barbiturates compared with,
    56–57, 73; dependence, 80–81, 145,
    184; effects of, 56, 79, 80; and
    GABA, 63, 76; legal restrictions, 201;
    and methadone, 80, 189; overdose
    treatment, 181; patterns of use, 79;
    safety, 75; tolerance, 80; volatile
    solvents compared with, 90, 92. *See
    also names of drugs and compounds*
Beta-endorphin: as endogenous opioid,
    51; and nicotine, 30
Beta-lipotropin, and nicotine, 30
Bewley, T. H., 205, 206
Blood: alcohol levels in, 62, 64, 67–69,
    190; barbiturate levels in, 76–77; and
    cigarette smoke, 24; cocaine levels
    in, 152, 153, 155, 157; drug levels in,
    169; glucose levels with stimulants
    in, 136; leukocytosis and LSD, 105;
    methemoglobinemia and nitrite use,
    95; and nicotine, 36; nicotine levels
    in, 25, 28–29, 37, 192; normocytic
    normochromic anemia, 94; and
    stimulants, 136; THC levels in, 125;
    volatile solvents and anemia, 92, 95
Blood pressure: amphetamines and,
    134, 136; caffeine and, 143; cathinone
    and, 141; classical conditioning and,
    5; cocaine and, 155, 157, 158; DOM
    and, 112; hallucinogens and, 100,
    102, 105, 112, 113; marihuana and,
    122; MDMA and, 147; neonates and,
    187, nicotine and smoking and, 30,
    33, 36–37; opioids and, 46, 49; use in
    medical diagnosis, 167, 168
Boggs Act of 1951, 199
Bolivia, and cocaine production, 151
British "system," 204–7
Buprenorphine, 48, 189

Bureau of Drug Abuse Control, 200
Bureau of Internal Revenue, 195
Bureau of Narcotics and Dangerous
  Drugs, 200
Buspirone, 81
Butyl acetate, 94
Butyl alcohol, 94
Butyl nitrite, 87

Caffeine, 142–45; British use of, 143; in
  Coca-Cola, 150; effects of, 143–45;
  Japanese use of, 143; patterns of use,
  142–43; physiologic dependence,
  144–45; use, 135; use in Africa, 142;
  use in China, 142
Calcium channel blockers, 182
Cannabinoids, 118–21, 123; acute
  adverse effects, 127; laboratory
  detection, 177; receptors, 126;
  tolerance, 126
Cannabis sativa, 117, 118
Carbon dioxide, 180
Carbon monoxide and smoking, 35, 37,
  191
Carbon tetrachloride, toxicity, 86, 94
Cardiac arrhythmias: and cocaine, 158;
  in neonates, 187; in stimulant
  overdose, 182; with volatile solvents,
  93, 94
Carter, J., 202
Catecholamines: and amphetamine,
  139; and nicotine, 30, 32
Cathinone, 132, 141–42
Cell membranes: alcohol and fluidity
  and, 63; and Cl⁻ ion channels, 63;
  and THC, 125–26
Central nervous system depressants,
  56–97; and blood pressure, 168; and
  nystagmus, 172; overdose, 76. *See
  also* Alcohol; Barbiturates;
  Benzodiazepines; Volatile Solvents;
  names of drugs and compounds
China: and opium control, 197; and use
  of caffeine, 142
China White (alphamethylfentanyl), 43,
  54
Chloral hydrate, 73, 195, 201
Chlordiazepoxide, 79
Chloroform, 87, 94
Chronic organic brain syndrome, 72–73
Cirrhosis, and alcohol consumption,
  71, 175
Classical conditioning, 56
Cl⁻ ion channels. *See* Cell membranes
Cleaning solutions, abuse of, 86, 87,
  89; toxicity, 93

Cocaine, 150–63; absorption and fate,
  160; compared with amphetamines,
  132–35, 137–39, 148; compared with
  caffeine, 143; compared with khat/
  cathinone, 141; "crack," 4, 10, 135,
  150–52, 154, 158, 202; diagnosis of
  use, 165, 166, 171, 172, 175, 177;
  effects of, 155–56; *in utero* effects,
  158–59; and legal restrictions, 160–
  62, 194–95, 197, 201, 203, 205–6;
  local anesthetic effects, 159–60;
  mechanism of action, 191; overdose,
  182–85; patterns of use, 11–12, 154–
  55; physiologic dependence, 156;
  polydrug use, 12, 74, 80;
  sensitization, 157; tolerance, 157;
  toxicity, 158; treatment, adults, 190–
  91; treatment, neonates, 186; use
  with alcohol, 56, 58; use with
  nicotine, 29
Codeine: as opium derivative, 40, 42;
  oral availability, 52; and receptor
  binding, 51; use with glutethimide,
  12, 74
Coffea arabica, 142
Cola acuminata, 142
Columbia, and cocaine production,
  151–52, 154
Comprehensive Drug Abuse and
  Control Act, 200
Conocybe mushroom, 113
Constitution, The, 194
Controlled Substances Act of 1970, 200
Convulsions: and alcohol withdrawal,
  57, 65–66; and barbiturate
  withdrawal, 57, 78; and
  benzodiazepine withdrawal, 81; and
  cocaine overdose, 158, 161, 182; as a
  disulfiram-alcohol reaction, 190; in
  neonates, 186; and nicotine, 36; and
  opioid withdrawal, 180; and PCP
  overdose, 102; and sensitization with
  stimulants, 157; and stimulant
  overdose, 132
"Crack." *See* Cocaine
Crime Control Act of 1990, 202
Cross-dependence, among central
  nervous system depressants, 57;
  between methadone and heroin, 183
Cross-tolerance: among cannabinoids,
  126–27; between cathinone and
  amphetamine, 141; among central
  nervous systems depressants, 64, 91;
  definition of, 19; among
  hallucinogens, 108, 111, 114, 115;
  between methadone and other
  opioids, 183, 187

Cryofluorane, 93
Cyclohexone, 94

Delirium tremens. *See* Alcoholism,
    withdrawal syndrome
Dementia: and alcoholism, 72; and
    aromatic hydrocarbons, 93
Department of Health, Education and
    Welfare, 200
Department of Justice, 200
Dependence, definition of, 16–19. *See
    also names of drugs and compounds*
Depressants, central nervous system.
    See Central nervous system
    depressants; *individual drugs*
Depression, the Great, 198
Designer drugs: and legislation, 202;
    MDMA, 132, 145, 146; and toxicity,
    54
Desipramine, 191
DET (N,N-diethyltryptamine), 114
Dextrorphan, 98
Diagnostic Interview Schedule, 59
Diazepam: with methadone, 74, 80; in
    PCP overdose, 102; treatment of
    overdose, 181; use of, 79–80;
    withdrawal, 184
Dichlorodifluoromethane, 93
Dihydromorphinone, 42
Dilaudid, 42
Diluents. *See* Adulterants
2,5-dimethoxy-4-ethylamphetamine.
    See DOET
2,5-dimethoxy-4-methylamphetamine.
    See DOM
Dimethyltryptamine. *See* DMT
Diplopia. *See* Ophthalmic effects
Discriminative stimulus properties: of
    amphetamine and cathinone, 141; of
    caffeine, 143
Disease concept of alcoholism, 4
Disulfiram, 190
Divided attention task, 61
DMT (N,N,-dimethyltryptamine), 98,
    114–15
DOET (2,5-dimethoxy-4-ethyl-
    amphetamine), 112
Dole, V., 187
DOM (2,5-dimethoxy-4-methyl-
    amphetamine, STP), 98, 106, 111–13
Dominican Republic, 152
Dopamine, and amphetamine, 139, 140,
    182; and cocaine, 159–60, 191; levels,
    reinforcing effects, 31; and opioids,
    52; and PCP, 103; release, 32; theory
    of reward, 8
Doriden™. *See* Glutethimide

Driving, and alcohol, 62; and
    marihuana, 125
Drug abuse, diagnosis of, 59, 164–78;
    measurements of, 17, 59, 61;
    treatment of, 179–93
Drug Enforcement Administration
    (DEA), 146
Drug habituation, definition, 16–17
DSM III-R (Diagnostic and Statistical
    Manual Revised), 17–18, 58–59, 138
Dynorphin, 51

"Ecstasy." *See* MDMA
Edema: central nervous system, 73, 94;
    kidney, 175; pulmonary, 37, 94, 173,
    179–80; tongue and buccal
    membranes, 68
Endogenous opioid peptides, 30, 51
Enkephalins, 40, 51
Endocarditis: in i.v. drug abusers, 15,
    54, 140; in medical diagnosis, 169,
    173–74
Endocrine system, 175
Endorphin: discovery, 51; as
    endogenous peptide, 40; release by
    nicotine, 30
England: and caffeine use, 143; and
    opioid dependence, 205, 207; and
    tobacco use, 22
"English system." *See* British
    "system"
Enterohepatic circulation (THC), 121
Enzyme-multiplied immunoassay
    technique (EMIT), 177
Ergot alkaloids, 103, 107
Erythroxylon coca, 151
Esters, ethyl, 87
Ethanol. *See* Alcohol
Ethchlorvynol, 73
Ether, 86–87, 151–53
Ethinamate, 73
Ethyl acetate, 94
Ethyl alcohol. *See* Alcohol
Ethylene dichloride, 94
Ethylene glycol. *See* Alcohol
Etonitazene, 52
Etorphine, 40, 52
Europe: and aerosol abuse, 86–87; and
    anxiolytic drug availability, 81; and
    caffeine use, 142; and cocaine
    import, 152; and tobacco cultivation,
    22–23. *See also individual countries*

FAS. *See* Alcohol, *in utero* effects
Federal Bureau of Narcotics, 198
Federal Drug Administration, 200

Fentanyl, 41, 43–44, 53–54. *See also* China White
Fetal alcohol syndrome. *See* Alcohol, *in utero* effects
"Flashback," 102, 110, 129
Flurazepam, 79
Ford, G., 202
Formaldehyde, 57
Formate, 57
France, and tobacco, 22; heroin from, 42, 201
"Free basing," 152
Freud, Sigmund, 155

GABA, and sedative-hypnotic action, 63, 76
Gamma-amino butyric acid. *See* GABA
Gasoline, abuse of volatile solvents, 85–87, 90; toxic effects, 92
Gastritis, and alcohol consumption, 68, 70
Genetics: and alcoholism, 60, 71; and initiation of sedative-hypnotic abuse, 75; and theories of drug abuse, 4–5, 7–8, 10
Geneva Conference for the Suppression of the Illicit Traffic in Dangerous Drugs, 198
Glucuronide. *See* Heroin or Morphine, absorption and fate
Glue sniffing, 85–91; and reactive rhinitis, 172
Glutamate, and PCP mechanism, 102–3
Glutethimide (Doriden): absorption, 76; abuse, 73; and neuropathy, 176; scheduling, 201; use with codeine ("loads"), 12, 74
Glycolaldehyde, 57
Glycols, abuse of, 94
Glycolate, 57
Grain alcohol. *See* Alcohol
Greece: and tobacco drying, 23; and tolerance to marihuana, 127
Growth hormone, and cocaine, 175; and nicotine, 30

Hague Opium Convention of 1912, 195, 197
Hallucinogens, 98–116. *See also names of drugs and compounds*
Hallucinosis: and alcohol withdrawal, 65; and barbiturate withdrawal, 78; and LSD, 109
Halogenated hydrocarbons, 93
Haloperidol: sensitivity to after amphetamine, 140; in treatment of

PCP overdose, 102; in treatment of stimulant overdose, 182
Harrison Narcotic Act of 1914, 40, 150, 195–198, 200
Hashish. *See* Marihuana
Hazard rate, 10
Headache, and alcohol withdrawal, 64–65; and caffeine withdrawal, 144–45; and disulfiram reaction, 190; and THC, 127–28; and volatile solvents, 91, 93
Heart rate, and amphetamine, 134, 168; and caffeine, 143; and classical conditioning, 5; and cocaine, 155; and disulfiram reaction, 190; and DOM, 112; and LSD, 105; and marihuana, 122–23; and MDMA, 147; and nicotine, 20, 30, 36, 37; and opioids, 49; and PCP, 100. *See also* Tachycardia
Hemorrhage, and alcoholism, 70; and cocaine, 182; and volatile solvents, 92, 94
Hemp, 117–18, 205
Hepatitis, and alcoholism, 71; London epidemic, 206; in medical diagnosis, 164, 169, 172, 174–75; types in drug abusers, 14
Heroin, 39–49; absorption and fate, 52; analgesia, 171; blood-brain barrier to, 52; complications of use, 13, 15–16; legal aspects, 195, 201–2, 205–7; medical diagnosis of abuse, 165, 168–69, 171–73, 175–76; and methadone, 187–90; overdose, 180–81; patterns of use, 13, 44–46; physiologic dependence, 48–49; source, 40–44; subjective effects, 46–47; substitutes for, 74; toxicity, 53–54; trade routes, 42; withdrawal, 182–83
Hexane, 92, 94
Hexamethonium, 32
Histamine, 46
HIV. *See* AIDS
Hofmann, A., 113
Holmes, Judge O. W. Jr., 196
Homosexuals, and aerosol use, 90, 95; and AIDS, 13
Hydromorphine, 42

"Ice." *See* Amphetamines
India, and marihuana use, 118, 120
Infectious disease, 13–16; among amphetamine users, 140; management of, 179; among nitrite users, 95
Inhalants, absorption, 86; and blood

Inhalants (*Continued*)
changes, 95; "huffers," 88;
"poppers," 87. *See also* Volatile
Solvents and Aerosols *and individual
compounds*
Intravenous administration, 9, 13–15;
of amphetamines, 135, 137–38; of
barbiturates, 76; of cocaine, 152–55,
157–58, 161; of heroin, 42, 44–46, 52–
54; of LSD, 107; medical diagnosis,
169–70, 173, 174, 184, 188; of
nicotine, 27; of stimulants, 147–48; of
THC, 121
In utero effects of, alcohol, 68–69;
cocaine, 158–59
Isbell, H., 64, 113, 114
Isobutyl nitrite, 87
Isopropanol, 87, 94
Isoquinoline alkaloid, 111

Jamaica and marijuana use, 118, 127–28
Japan, and amphetamine use, 134; and
caffeine use, 143; and methaqualone
use, 74; and solvent use, 87

Ketamine, 98–100
Ketanserin, 106
Ketones, 77, 87, 94
Khat, 132, 141–42
Korsakoff's psychosis, 72–73, 76, 167

Lacquer thinners, 86
League of Nations, Geneva Conference
of 1924–1925, 197
Leary, Dr. T., 103
Lighter fluid sniffing, 86, 87
Lisuride, 106
Liver, alcohol effects on, 67, 70–71,
184; and amphetamine deamination,
139; and barbiturate inactivation, 77;
and cocaine metabolism, 160; and
hepatitis, 14–15; and medical
diagnosis, 171, 174–76; and nicotine,
27–28; and opioid metabolism, 52;
and solvent toxicity, 92–95; and i.v.
drug use, 54, 140
"Loads." *See* Glutethimide
LSD, 44, 98, 103–10; absorption, fate,
and excretion, 107–8; acute adverse
reactions; 108–9; antagonists, 106;
"bad trips," 108; "bummer," 108;
cardiovascular effects, 168;
catatonia, 109; compared with DMT,
114–15; compared with psilocybin,
113; conjunctival injection, 105;

cross-tolerance with mescaline, 111;
cross-tolerance to psilocybin, 114;
effects of, 105–6; ergot alkaloids,
107; "flashback," 102, 110;
homicidal behavior, 108; legal
aspects, 200–201; mechanism of
action, 106–7; morbidity and
mortality, 108–10; patterns of use,
104–5; persistent adverse reactions,
109–10; physiologic dependence, 107;
tolerance, 107
"Ludes." *See* Methaqualone
Lysergic acid diethylamide. *See* LSD

"Mainlining." *See* Intravenous
administration
Malnutrition, and alcohol use, 70, 71,
72, 184, 190; and amphetamine use,
140; and cocaine use, 158; and
sedative-hypnotics, 75; and toluene
abusers, 89
Marihuana, 117–31; absorption,
biotransformation, and excretion,
120–21; acute adverse effects, 127–
28; acute brain syndrome, 127;
amotivational syndrome, 128; *bhang*,
118; binding, 121, 126; blood-brain
barrier, 121; *charas*, 119; chemistry,
118–20; conjunctiva, 122; culture and
processing, 117–18; *dagga*, 118;
driving, 125; epidemiology of use,
10–12; example of drug abuse, 18;
and "flashbacks," 110; *ganga*, 118;
as an hallucinogen, 98; hashish, 118;
heart rate, 122–23; hemp, 117; and
hepatitis, 14; *kif*, 118; legal aspects,
198–202; *macohona*, 118; mechanism
of action, 125–26; medical diagnosis,
164–65, 167, 168, 171–72, 175, 177;
mental processes, 124; oligospermia,
129; partition coefficient, 121;
patterns of use, 122; persistent
adverse effects, 128–30; physiologic
dependence, 126; physiologic effects,
122–23; prevalence of use, 4;
psychologic effects, 123–24;
psychomotor effects, 123; pupil size,
122; teratogenic effects, 129;
therapeutic uses, 130; tolerance, 126;
as vehicle for DMT, 115
Marijuana Tax Act of 1937, 198
Mayan Indians and tobacco, 22
MDA (methylenedioxyamphetamine),
147
MDMA
(methylenedioxymethamphetamine—
"ecstasy"), 132, 145–47

Mecamylamine, 32
Mechoulam, R., 119
Memory, and alcohol, 62; and
  amphetamine abuse, 140; and
  benzodiazepine use, 62–63; and
  chronic organic brain syndrome, 73;
  and Korsakoff's psychosis, 72; and
  THC, 124–25
Men, and AIDS, 53; and alcohol use, 7,
  59, 175; and development of drug
  abuse, 10; and marihuana, 129; and
  nicotine, 26; and opioids, 49
Meperidine, as precursor of MPPP, 44;
  stimulant effects, 53; as a synthetic
  opioid, 40–42
Meprobamate, 78; scheduling, 201
Mescaline, 110–11, compared with
  LSD, 98, 106, 108, 114
Mesolimbic system, and dopamine, 8;
  and nicotine, 32
Methadone, and diazepam, 74, 80;
  discovery, 42; legal aspects, 201, 207;
  in neonates, 185–86; oral availability,
  52; and physiologic dependence, 49,
  180–81, 183; toxicity, 53; in treatment
  of opioid abuse, 183, 187–89
Methamphetamine ("speed,"
  "crystal," "ice"; Methedrine), 133,
  134–35, 137, abuse cycles with
  cocaine, 150; and organic brain
  damage, 140; sniffing, 172
Methanol. *See* Alcohol, methyl
Methaqualone, 73–74, 177
Methedrine. *See* Methamphetamine
Methyl alcohol. *See* Alcohol, methyl
Methylated benzenes, 92
Methylated xanthines, 142–45
Methyl butyl ketone, 87
Methyl cellosolve acetate, 95
Methyldihydromorphine, 42
Methylene chloride, 87
Methylenedioxyamphetamine. *See*
  MDA
Methylenedioxymethamphetamine. *See*
  MDMA
Methylethyl ketone, 94
Methyl isobutyl ketone, 94
Methyl n-butyl ketone, 94
Methylphenidate (Ritalin™), 132–33,
  147–48; compared with caffeine, 143;
  treatment of cocaine abuse, 191
Methylphenylpiperidine. *See* MPP+
Metopon, 42
Mexican Indians, use of peyote, 110;
  use of psilocybin, 113
Mexico, as heroin importer, 39, 201;
  and inhalant abuse, 87; and peyote
  use, 110

Mianserin, 106
Mimosa, 114
Minor tranquilizers, 78–81
Model cements, abuse of, 86
Morocco, and marihuana use, 128
Morphine, absorption and fate, 52; and
  analgesia, 47; cross tolerance and
  cross dependence with methadone,
  183; and drug dependence, 17, 19;
  half-life, i.v., 53; legal aspects, 196,
  201, 204; mechanism of action, 50–
  51; in patent medicines, 195; pattern
  of use, 44; relative potency, 20, 43;
  and respiration, 48; source, 40–41;
  subjective effects of, 47; substrate
  for heroin synthesis, 42; toxicity, 53
Moy, Jin Fuey, 195
MPP+ (methylphenylpyridine), 44
MPPP (4-propyl-4-phenyl-N-
  methylpiperidine), 44, 54
MPTP (1-methyl-4-phenyl-1,2,3,6-
  tetrahydropyridine), 44, 54
Mucous membrane, and alcohol, 68;
  and bacteria, 16; and cocaine, 172;
  and drug absorption, 9; and nicotine
  absorption, 23, 192; and volatile
  solvents, 94
Musto, D., 194
Myocardial infarction, and cocaine,
  158, 161, 182; and smoking, 33

Nalbuphine, 48
Nalorphine, 50
Naloxone, morphine antagonist, 50; in
  treatment of opioid overdose, 53,
  180; synthetic opioid, 40, 41
Naltrexone, in treatment of opioid
  abuse, 189; in treatment of opioid
  overdose, 53
Naphthalene, 87
Narcotic Addict Rehabilitation Act, 200
Narcotic Drug Import and Export Act
  of 1922, 197
National Institute on Alcohol Abuse
  and Alcoholism (NIAAA), 201
National Institute on Drug Abuse
  (NIDA), 201
National Institute on Mental Health
  (NIMH), 201–2
Native American Church, and peyote
  use, 110
Native Americans, and gasoline
  sniffing, 86; and volatile solvent
  abuse, 88
Near East, and opium culture, 40
Neonates, and exposure to alcohol, 69;
  and exposure to cocaine, 159; and

Neonates (*Continued*)
   exposure to methadone, 188; and
   exposure to nicotine, 34–36;
   treatment of drug exposure, 185–87
Nicotiana tabacum, 22
Nicotine, 22–38; absorption, 27;
   antagonists, 32; and heart rate, 20,
   30, 36, 37; hypotension, 36;
   mechanism of action, 31–32;
   neuroendocrine effects, 30; onset of
   action, 9; physiologic dependence,
   29–30; physiologic dependence, 29–
   30; physiologic effects, 30–31;
   receptors, 31; subjective effects, 28;
   tobacco culture, 22; tolerance, 29–30;
   withdrawal, 191
Nicotine polacrilex gum, 31, 192
NIDA. *See* National Institute on Drug
   Abuse
N-nitrosamines, in sidestream cigarette
   smoke, 35
Nitrous oxide, abuse of, 86–87; as an
   analgesic, 47; with fentanyl as
   anesthetic, 43
Nixon, Richard, 39, 201–2
N-methyl-D-aspartate. *See* NMDA
NMDA, 102–103
N,N-dimethyltryptamine. *See* DMT
Norephinephrine, and amphetamine,
   139; and mescaline, 111; and
   nicotine, 30, 32
Numorphan, 42
Nystagmus. *See* Ophthalmic effects
Nyswander, M., 187

Oil of Mustard. *See* Adulterants
Oligospermia, 129
1-Δ-3,4-trans tetrahydrocannabinol.
   See THC
Ophthalmic effects, of alcohol, 62, 64,
   65, 71; amblyopia, 71; and classical
   conditioning, 5; diplopia, 91; of
   DOM, 112; of heroin, 46; of LSD,
   105; in medical diagnosis, 166, 171–
   72; of methanol, 94; of MDMA, 147;
   nystagmus, 100, 172; of opioid
   overdose, 180; of opioid withdrawal,
   49; of PCP, 100; photophobia, 91,
   105, 126, 171; of psilocybin, 113; of
   THC, 122, 126; tolerance to, 50; of
   volatile solvents, 91
Opioids, 5, 39–55; absorption and fate,
   52; alcohol abuse compared with, 61,
   64; analgesia, 47–48; antagonists, 40,
   41, 50; barbiturates compared with,
   74, 78; benzodiazepines compared

with, 80; and dopamine levels, 8; and
   gastrointestinal effects, 48; and
   laboratory detection, 177; legal
   aspects, 195, 197, 199, 201, 203–7;
   mechanism of action, 50–52; in
   neonates, 185–86; overdose, 179–81;
   patterns of use, 44–46; PCP
   compared with, 98; and physical
   examination, 166–69, 171–72, 174–75;
   physiologic dependence, 48; in
   polydrug abuse, 12; and pulmonary
   complications, 16; and respiratory
   effects, 48; sources of, 40–44;
   stimulants compared with, 138, 156;
   subjective effects of, 46–47;
   tolerance to, 49–50; toxicity of, 52–
   53; treatment of abuse of, 185, 187;
   treatment of withdrawal, 182–83;
   withdrawal and abuse; 19. *See also
   names of drugs and compounds*
Ototoxicity, and toluene, 93
Oxycodone, 40
Overdose, with alcohol, 73; with
   barbiturates, 76; with
   benzodiazepines, 56, 79; with
   cocaine, 151, 182; with opioids, 43–
   44, 53–54, 179–81; with sedative-
   hypnotics, 169, 181–82; with
   stimulants, 182; treatment of 179–82

Paint thinner, abuse of, 87
Pakistan, as source of opium, 201
Panic, and cocaine, 155; and DMT,
   115; and DOM, 113; and LSD, 108;
   and THC, 124, 127–28
Papaver somniferum, 40
Paraldehyde, 73, 167
Paranoia, and LSD, 109; and
   stimulants, 155; and THC, 124, 127
Parkinson's disease, amphetamine in
   treatment of, 134; produced by
   MPTP, 44, 54
Partition coefficient, of alcohol, 67; of
   barbiturates, 77; of marihuana, 121
Paullinia, 142
PCP (phencyclidine), 44, 98–103;
   absorption, 101, 102; atropine-like
   actions, 102; and dopamine levels, 8;
   effects of, 100–101; "flashback,"
   102; laboratory detection, 177;
   mechanism of action, 102–3; as a
   model of schizophrenia, 112;
   overdose, 101–2; patterns of use,
   100; physiologic dependence, 101;
   Sernyl, 98; and teeth grinding, 101;
   and tolerance, 101; toxicity, 101–2

Penile erection, in PCP withdrawal in monkeys, 101; in THC withdrawal in monkeys, 126
Pentazocine, in polydrug abuse, 12, 46, 54, 74
Personality, changes with chronic organic brain syndrome, 72; changes with LSD use, 110; changes with marihuana use, 128, 129; contribution to drug abuse, 4–5, 8, 10
Peru, in cocaine culture, 151
Petroleum distallates, 92
Petroleum naphtha, 92
Peyote, 110–11
Phencyclidine. *See* PCP
Phenmetrazine, abuse of, 132, 147–48; as compared to caffeine, 144
Phenobarbital, 76; as treatment for drug withdrawal in neonates, 185–86
Phenothiazines, 102
Photophobia. *See* Ophthalmic effects
Picrotoxin, 76
Piloerection, 101, 126
Piptadenia, 114
Pirenperone, 106
Pituitary, effects of alcohol on, 176; effects of nicotine on, 30
Placenta, crossing by barbiturates, 77; crossing by cocaine, 158
Placidyl.™ *See* Ethchlorvynol
Plasma protein, binding by barbiturates, 76–77; binding by nicotine, 27
Pneumonia, bacterial in drug abuse, 15, 16; in cocaine smokers, 158; in medical diagnosis, 173; in opioid overdose, 180–81; from passive smoke, 36; in smokers, 34
Pneumocystis carinii, 173
Polydrug abuse, 12, 99
Polyneuropathy, and alcoholism, 71
"Poppers." *See* Amyl nitrite
Preludin.™ *See* Phenmetrazine
Prevalence: of alcohol-related disorders, 59; of chronic respiratory problems in children of smokers, 36; of cigarette smoking, 26–27; of drug abuse, 3–4, 203; of heroin users, 39–40; of NANB hepatitis, 14; of poly drug abuse, 12; of solvent abuse, 86, 90
Procaine, 160
Prolactin, and cocaine, 175; and nicotine, 30
Propyl acetate, 87
Propylhexedrine, 135
Psilocin, 113

Psilocybe mexicana, 113
Psilocybin, 98, 113–14
Public Health Service, 196
Puerto Rico, and alcohol abuse, 59
Pulmonary, deficits, opioid induced, 15–16, 179–81; disease, nicotine-induced, 37; hemorrhage, 92; infection as a sign of drug abuse, 173; talc granulomatosis, 13, 148; septic infarcts, 174; ventilation, 24, 102, 168
Pure Food and Drug Act of 1906, 194

Quaaludes.™ *See* Methaqualone
Quinine. *See* Adulterants

Reagan, Ronald, 202
Receptor binding, alcohol, 63; barbiturates, 63, 76, 77; benzodiazepines, 63, 76; GABA, 63, 76; nicotine, 31; opioids, 50–51; stereoselectivity, 51; THC, 126
Receptors, chemoreceptors, 30; CNS, 9; dopamine, 159, 191; GABA, 63, 76; glutamate, 102; marihuana, 126; nicotinic, 31; NMDA, 102–3; opioid, 20, 40, 48, 50–51, 189; serotonin, 106–7
REM (Rapid Eye Movement), 74, 124
Resin, cannabis, 117–18; nicotine, 191–92
Respiratory system, in medical diagnosis, 167, 168, 173; opioid effects on, 48; in opioid overdose, 179; and smoking, 32, 34, 36; and THC, 122
Rhinorrhea, in opioid withdrawal, 49
Rhinitis, as solvent use side effect, 91, 172
Ritalin.™ *See* Methylphenidate
Rolleston Act of 1926, 204
"Rum fits." *See* Alcohol, withdrawal

Schizophrenic reactions, produced by amphetamine, 137; produced by LSD, 109; produced by PCP, 102. *See also* Paranoia
Secobarbital, 76–77
Sedation, and benzodiazepines, 79–80; benzodiazepines and memory, 63; and neonates, 185; and opioids, 46, 188; and sedative–hypnotics, 56, 76; and THC, 119, 124

Sedative-hypnotics. *See* Central
  nervous system depressants; *names
  of drugs and compounds*
Seevers, M.H., 16
Seizures. *See* Convulsions
Septicemia, 169, 174
Sernyl.™ *See* PCP
Serotonin, and amphetamine, 139; and
  LSD, 106–7; and MDMA, 147; and
  nicotine, 30, 32; and psilocybin, 113
Sexual behavior, and AIDS, 13; alcohol
  effects on, 62; and amphetamine use,
  136; and cocaine use, 155; and
  classical conditioning, 5; and
  methaqualone, 74; THC effects on,
  124, 130; and toluene abuse, 89; and
  toxic effects of MDMA, 147
Sidestream smoke, 35
Sinusitis, 34
"Skin popping," 169
Sleep, during alcohol withdrawal, 66;
  and amphetamine use, 135, 136, 137;
  and benzodiazepines, 79, 81;
  barbiturates and rebound insomnia,
  78; and caffeine, 143; and cocaine,
  155, 156; and cocaine withdrawal,
  156; and marijuana, 123, 124, 126,
  127; and medical diagnosis, 165; and
  methaqualone, 74; and nicotine
  withdrawal, 29; opioids, 46; and
  opioid withdrawal, 49; and PCP use,
  100; and peyote use, 111; REM, 74
Small intestine, and alcohol absorption,
  66–67; and barbiturate absorption, 76
Smoking, amphetamine, 135, 136;
  cocaine, 10, 152, 154, 158; heroin,
  45; marihuana, 120, 129, 172;
  passive, 35; PCP, 100; tobacco, 10–
  12, 22–37, 191–92
Sniffing, "huffers," 88; and medical
  diagnosis, 172; solvents, 85–94
Snorting, cocaine, 10, 150, 152–55, 158,
  160; heroin, 44–45; PCP, 99, 100
"Speed," 134
"Speed freaks," 135, 136, 140
South America, and caffeine, 142; and
  cocaine, 151–52; and leaf chewing,
  141; and THC, 118. *See also
  individual countries*
Speech, and solvents, 90, 93; effects of
  alcohol on, 61–62; effects of
  marihuana on, 125; effects of PCP
  on, 100; in medical diagnosis, 166–67
Staphylococcus aureus, 15
Stereoselectivity. *See* Receptor binding
Stereotyped behavior, and cocaine,
  157; and PCP, 101

Steroids, and alcohol, 176; as
  hallucinogens, 98
Stimulants, Central Nervous System,
  132–163; cardiovascular effects, 132;
  comparison to hallucinogens, 98,
  100; use with sedatives, 74. *See also
  names of drugs and compounds;*
  Amphetamine; Cocaine; Khat;
  Caffeine; MDMA; Methylphenidate
STP. *See* DOM
Stropharia mushroom, 113
Suicide, and barbiturates, 181; and
  benzodiazepines, 79; and LSD, 109;
  and sedative–hypnotics, 75
Supreme Court, 195–96, 200
Synesthesia, 105, 111
Synthetic opiates. *See names of drugs
  and compounds*

Tachycardia, and alcohol withdrawal,
  66; and marihuana, 123, 127; in
  physical exam, 167, 168. *See also*
  Heart rate
Taiwan, and alcohol-related disorders,
  59
"Tango and Cash," 44
Tatum, A.L., 16
Teenagers. *See* Youth
Teeth grinding, and amphetamine, 140;
  and PCP withdrawal, 101
Teonanacatl, 113
Teratogenic effects, of alcohol, 69; of
  marihuana, 129
Testosterone, effects of marihuana on,
  129
THC. *See* Marihuana
Thea sinensisa, 142
Thebaine, 40
Theobromine, 142
Theobroma cacao, 142
Theophylline, 142
Theories of drug use, 4–9
Thiamine, deficiency in alcoholism, 71–
  72, 184
Tinnitus, and volatile solvents, 91, 93
Tobacco smoking, 22–38; and
  bronchitis, 32, 34; and cancer, 32,
  33–34; carbon monoxide, 35; chronic
  disease, 36; coronary artery disease,
  32, 33–34; epidemiology, 24–27; fetal
  development, 34; morbidity and
  mortality, 32–37; mortality ratios, 32;
  myocardial infarction, 33; nausea, 30,
  36; N-nitrosamines, 35; passive
  smoking, 35–36; patterns of use, 24–
  27; peptic ulcers, 34; sidestream

smoke, 35; toxicity, 36–37; weight loss, 31

Tolerance, and barbiturates, 77–78; and benzodiazepines, 80; and classical conditioning, 5; and cocaine; and LSD, 107–108; and marihuana, 126–27; and opioids, 49–50; and sedative-hypnotics, 63–64; and stimulants, 138; and volatile solvents, 91

Toluene, abuse of, 85, 87–94; in cigarette smoke, 35

Toxic psychosis, and khat use, 141 and LSD, 108–9; and marihuana, 127–28

Transdermal nicotine patch, 192

Treasury Department, 195

Triazolam, 79, 184

Trichloroethylene, 87, 93

Trichlorofluoromethane, 93

Triglycerides, 70

Tripelennamine, abuse in combination with pentazocine, 12, 46, 54, 74

"T's and Blues," 54, 74. *See also* Pentazocine; Tripelennamine

Turkey, and heroin import, 39, 201; and opium culture, 40; and tobacco culture, 23

Urine, alcohol levels in, 67; amphetamine levels in, 139; barbiturate levels in, 77; DOM levels in, 112; laboratory detection of drug in, 164, 176, 177, 182; LSD levels in 107; opioid glucuronides in, 52; PCP levels in, 101, 102; screen in drug treatment, 188–89; THC levels in, 121

Valium™. *See* Diazepam

Valmid™. *See* Ethinamate

Vasoconstriction, classical conditioning and, 5; and cocaine, 158, 159–60, 172; tolerance to amphetamine, 138

Vasopressin, 30

Virola, 114

Volatile solvents, 85–97; absorption, 86; effects of, 90–91; gasoline sniffing, 86; glue sniffing, 85; "huffers," 88; model cements, 86; morbidity, 92; mortality, 92; patterns of use, 90; physiologic dependence, 91; preparations used, 87–88;

tolerance, 91; toxicity, 89, 91–95; use among Hispanics, 86; use among homosexuals, 90; use among Native Americans, 87; use in Australia, 87; use in Europe, 87; use in Japan, 87; use in Mexico, 87. *See also names of drugs and compounds*

Weight loss, and alcohol, 166; and nicotine, 31; and stimulants, 140, 147, 166

Wernicke's encephalopathy, 72–73, 76, 167

Withdrawal, alcohol, 61, 64–66, 167; barbiturate, 78; benzodiazepine, 81; caffeine, 144–45; cocaine, 150, 156–57, 162, 191; and classical conditioning, 6; definition of, 16, 18–19; desipramine in, 191; general CNS depressants, 57, 184; management of, 179–87; methadone in, 183; neonates and, 185–87; nicotine, 25, 29; opioids, 48–49, 167, 168, 171, 172, 182–83; PCP, 101; stimulants, 136, 138, 184–85; THC, 126

Women, and AIDS, 13–14, 53; and alcoholism, 59, 176; amenorrhea associated with opioids, 176, 188; and development of drug abuse, 10–11; and smoking, 26

Wood alcohol. *See* Alcohol, methyl

World War I, 196, 203

World War II, 42, 134, 199, 203

Xylene, 87

Youth, and aerosol use, 85; and alcohol use, 7, 56, 58, 59; deaths related to cocaine in, 151, 158; detection of drug abuse in, 164, 167, 170, 172, 174, 176; and development of drug abuse, 8, 10–12, 75; in the English "system," 205, 206; and heroin use, 39; and illicit drug use, 3; and the law, 203; and marihuana use, 122, 128, 129, 202; and MPTP, 44, 54; and opioid disposition, 52; and passive smoking, 35; and PCP, 99; and smoking, 27, 28; and volatile solvent use, 85–86, 88–90, 93